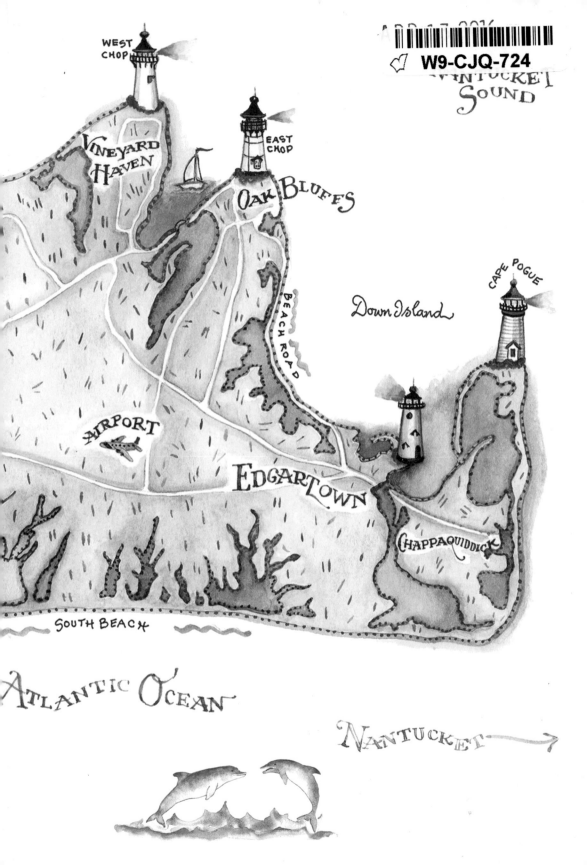

There is no season such delight can bring,
As Summer, Winter, Autumn, & Spring...

William Browne
1630

The cure for anything is salt~

Sweat, tears, or the sea.
♥ Isak Dinesen

My Book  ----------------------------

Give us the sun and the sea,
The waves on the sand,
The wind in our faces,
We walk hand in hand.
Though Summer must end,
We dance on the shore,
To the song of the sea,
In our hearts evermore.

♥ Nancy Walker

MARTHA'S VINEYARD

Isle of Dreams

Susan Branch

SPRING STREET *Publishing*

MARTHA'S VINEYARD · MASSACHUSETTS

Spring Street Publishing
P O BOX 2463
VINEYARD HAVEN, MA
0 2 5 6 8
sales@springstreetpublishing.com

FIRST EDITION
ISBN 978-0-9960440-2-8
Library of Congress Control Number
2016900171

10 9 8 7 6 5 4 3 2 1

RRD-IN
PRINTED IN THE
UNITED STATES OF AMERICA

Preface

To live is to be slowly born.
Antoine de Saint-Exupéry

When *The Fairy Tale Girl* ended, I was despondent, broken up and broken hearted, leaving California and everyone I knew and loved, flying, which I really hated to do, by myself, across country, running away from home, with no idea what I would do next, since the life I'd known was suddenly gone and there was no plan B.

I'd always wanted to see what it was like to live where there were seasons, so I'd decided to escape the pain of my break up with a big change of subject (for the previous six months I'd done nothing but think about it, talk about it, hear about it, and cry about it, ad nauseam to the inth degree, and I have to add, in the spirit of full disclosure, I wasn't quite done yet) and go stay on the East Coast, on the island of Martha's Vineyard (a place so small that back in the early 80s when you mentioned it, most people would say "where's that?") for three months, "just to try it." I'd go from winter, to spring, to summer before I went back to California. As this book begins, I'm clinging to the last shreds of being 34 years old, and about to land in Boston for a much needed change of scenery. It's early March, so the scenery, just like me, is a little bit raw and winter worn.

Preserve your memories, keep them well, what you forget you can never retell.
♥ Louisa May Alcott

Once upon a time. . .

MARTHA'S VINEYARD

Isle of Dreams

I want to have
a little house
with sunlight
on the floor,
A chimney with
a rosy hearth
and lilac by the door.
♥ Nancy Bird Turner

March 5, 1982

What wind blows you here, Pip?
Charles Dickens

LADIES and GENTLEMEN, AS WE BEGIN OUR DECENT
INTO LOGAN, PLEASE EXTINGUISH YOUR CIGARETTES
AND MAKE SURE YOUR SEAT BACKS AND TRAY TABLES
ARE IN THEIR FULL UPRIGHT POSITION. THE TEMPERATURE
IN BOSTON THIS MORNING IS A DELIGHTFUL 34 DEGREES.

Phew, I thought, that's cold. I peeked through the plane window to see what was out there. A cluster of Boston skyscrapers were vaguely silhouetted black against the sky, city lights diffused in the frigid air. In the distance, a pink horizon line slashed through the smoky-blue dawn at the edge of the dark and menacing sea. Soon, fingers crossed, and assuming ice hadn't formed on the wings, we'd be landing and I'd be on a bus heading down to Cape Cod to catch the ferry to the island of Martha's Vineyard.

I popped a mint into my mouth, and stuffed my diary and my books into my carry-on. The ground was coming up fast. On went the headphones. I closed my eyes, held my breath, wiped my hands on my jeans, gripped the armrests, and let Gloria Gaynor block out the plane-landing noises by screaming my new theme song into my ears . . .

♪ At first I was afraid, I was petrified... ♫
Kept thinkin' I could never live without you by my side...

If I went deaf in later life, I thought, that would be his fault too.

7

've always been one of those who applauded when the wheels of the plane skidded onto the ground. I wanted to kiss the pilot for not cartwheeling us across the tarmac. I was slaphappy for two hours after I got off a plane. The sky was bluer, the air was fresher; I would almost skip through the terminal to the baggage claim from the sheer joy of being alive. And the really great thing about getting off the plane this time was knowing I would not be going back home to California for three whole months ~ I wouldn't have to start worrying about that plane ride for a long time.

picked up my bags and wrestled them onto a cart. After a stop at the information desk and a moment to button my pea coat and pull on mittens and a hat, I dragged the cart out the door into cold air so sharp it made my eyes tear up. Through clouds of my own frosty breath I quickly loaded my bags into the luggage compartment and found a seat on the almost empty bus for the two-hour ride to Woods Hole where I hoped to catch the 10:45 a.m. ferry to the Island.

put my headphones back on, fit a cassette into my Walkman, and Johnny Cash began singing, "Mmmmmmmmm, I keep a close watch on this heart of mine, I keep my eyes wide open all the time . . ."

leaned my head against the cold window and watched as we made a wide left turn onto the freeway. We traveled south out of the city, and soon we were in the countryside, where hazy towns, leafless woods, inlets, and marshes flew by, as colorless as an old black and white movie. Now and then a church spire topped the tree line, gleaming white against the pale charcoal sky.

8

It was definitely not springtime in California, which is what I'd just left behind, but that was exactly the point. I'd always wanted to see what it was like to have a change of seasons. The view was dark and foreboding, but it was also mysterious and foreign. Despite my broken heart, or rather, because of it, I was grateful to be where no one knew me. I was totally invisible here. I didn't have to pretend to be happy or nice or that everything was okay. I breathed on the window, made a foggy spot, and drew a heart in it with my finger and listened to the music.

"Because you're mine, I walk the line . . ."

An hour and a half later, the bus pulled in next to the ferry terminal. Seagulls swooped above the three-story white boat moored at the dock. A line of cars and trucks thumped through big metal doors across the threshold into the black hole of the *Uncatena*. I went inside the terminal, bought a ticket, put my bags on the luggage cart, and picked my way carefully through the slushy muck into the same opening the cars were using to get on the boat.

Burly guys in heavy work jackets with knitted hats pulled low waved me toward the stairs and shouted to each other ~ echoing across the cavernous freight deck, over the noise of wind and waves. They were pointing and gesturing to buses, trucks, and cars and yelling, "Hey, buddy, ovah heah!" ~ telling drivers (in Massachusetts-speak) whea to pawk the cahs.

9

I clattered up a flight of metal stairs to the heated passenger deck, passing rows of seats and windows, and sat down in a booth near the snack bar. Hardly anyone was there ~ just a handful of guys reading newspapers. When the vehicle loading finished, heavy chains clanked, the ferry doors slammed shut, the boat blew its whistle and shuddered as we cut ties to the Mainland and backed away from the dock into the choppy grey waves. I got a cup of hot chocolate at the snack bar and listened to an announcement about where to find life jackets, thinking that under no circumstances would I want to put on a life jacket.

Watching our progress out the window across the dark, churning, white-capped swells, I wondered how I managed to pick such a perfect day. Then I thought, maybe it's always like this in the winter, which it technically still was. A frozen gray mist hung over the sea and blurred everything. I could barely tell where the water ended and the sky began. Gusts of icy wind whipped across the deck as the boat bobbed and swayed deep into a wave, then up, cresting the swell, then down, shuddering, and again ~ taking me away from shore, away from everything.

hen all collapsed, and the great Shroud of the sea rolled on as it rolled five thousand years ago. Herman Melville

I sat there for a while, but the snack bar was hot and stuffy and the motion was making me queasy so I decided to take myself out on deck for some fresh air. I pulled my scarf higher around my face, buttoned all the buttons on my coat, pulled on my gloves, braced myself and pushed hard against the heavy door. I whirled in the wind to slam the door shut behind me, struck by the gale, the salt smell of the sea, and shearing cold across my eyes.

I steadied myself at the rail and stared back at a seagull eyeing me from his perch farther down. Little white feathers on the top of his head ruffled up in the wind. Slowly he unfurled his wings and caught the breeze, his feet barely lifted from the rail. He hovered there for a moment, suspended, then fell backward toward the sea, away from the boat with a long sad cry, taken up by the gusts, and airborne. I wiped tears away, wondering, If I left them on my face would they freeze?

And then, slowly coming into view, materializing through the frost like an icy mirage was the Island. I leaned on the rail as we pitched through the water past the lighthouse. The rough elemental nature of it ∼ the sound of the sea pouring onto itself and washing the sides of the boat, the wind and the cold air ∼ was refreshingly uncomplicated.

As we drew closer, I saw the same picturesque scene I remembered from seven years before, when I'd come to the Island with my husband, Cliff, to celebrate Thanksgiving with his grandmother and her sisters. It still felt like another world from another time.

The 100-foot, square-rigged schooner I remembered from last time (because it looked like the pirate ship in Peter Pan) was rocking at anchor next to where the ferry was about to dock. Hugging the whitewashed shore, in a kind of hilly, up-and-down pattern, were dozens of two-story, wood-framed white houses with black shutters and dark windows and porches that looked out to sea. Gray smoke curled from redbrick chimneys; church steeples broke through bare treetops and gleamed white against the sky.

"... There's a land that I heard of ∼ once in a lullaby..."
♥ Somewhere Over the Rainbow

The ferry's engines roared into reverse. We slowed, water rushed, buoys clanged, chains were wound, and there was a small impact as the boat bumped the dock. I followed a straggling group of fellow passengers through the doors and stepped onto the Island.

No one was waiting for me. Cliff's grandmother and his two great aunts were very old when we'de met before and had all passed away by this time. I didn't know a soul on the Island. In fact, because this was 1982 and there were no cell phones, for all practical purposes, no one in the whole world knew exactly where I was. I didn't mind a bit. I didn't want to be found. The last six months had been awful, the split with my husband and the way it had happened had all our friends, and even people we didn't know, talking. I'd kept trying to pretend I was okay when I wasn't ~ I was relieved to be away from it. If I was going to be miserable I wanted to be miserable in private.

I headed across the parking lot to the taxi stand. The "cab" was a beat-up station wagon. The driver was tall and pale with dark circles under his eyes and long sideburns, wearing a work jacket and a knit cap pulled tight over a scraggly blond pony-tail that snaked down his back.

"Where ya going?" he asked, taking my bags off the luggage cart and putting them into the back of his car.

THE SHENANDOAH, *The Pirate Ship in Vineyard Haven Harbor.*

I didn't really know. I hadn't made a reservation. I thought I'd just find something when I arrived. I asked him for a recommendation. While he thought about it, we climbed into the front seat where I shivered gratefully in the blast of heat coming from the floor.

"Most everything is still closed for the winter," he said, taking the car out of park and looking behind for traffic, "but the Kelley House in Edgartown is open. It's a good place."

WEST CHOP LIGHT

"Okay, let's go there. Things close in the winter?" I hadn't thought of that.

"Yeah, we get lots of tourists in the summer, but in the winter, nobody comes. In fact, I think you might be the only person here that doesn't live on the island." He took a left at the stop sign.

I smiled. "What is the population here?"

"About 7,000 people year-round, but it goes up to maybe 50,000 or 60,000 in the summer."

"Wow. Where do they all stay when they come?" When I was here before it had seemed so small.

He said there were lots of "summer houses" ~ places people used for a few weeks when the weather was nice ~ and then rented out the rest of the year.

Oh, good, I thought, that should make it easy to find a place for my three-month stay.

The driver followed a windswept two-lane road that hugged the shore, past a pond, over a bridge, into a small town with a little main street and a bandstand in a park that overlooked the sea.

THE BANDSTAND IN OCEAN PARK ON A MUCH WARMER DAY.

The driver leaned over to turn up the volume on the radio and James Taylor sang, ". . . the first of December was covered with snow, and so was the turnpike from Stockbridge to Boston . . ." ♪

What do you do here all winter? I mean, for fun," I asked, remembering Cliff's tirade the last time we were here and his take on the excitement chronicled in the local paper: "Four pages of 'Billy saw a blackbird.'"

"Well, there's not much to do. It's wicked dead here. Mostly we drink."

I laughed, even though it occurred to me he wasn't kidding. I thought maybe I'd fit right in here. I felt a little wicked dead myself.

15

"What are you doing here?" he asked.

"It's a long boring story," I said. "you don't really want to hear it." Oh dear, I thought, here we are again, the reason I left home, in a nutshell. This story. No reason to let my first Island acquaintance know how crazy I am and why. I didn't want to talk about it.

One-lane Main Street in Edgartown was about four blocks long and it ended at the water's edge. It was lined with 19th century two-story shops and inns, with porches and dormers and several churches with tall white steeples. Most of the buildings were painted white with black shutters and doors. It was as quiet as could be, a New England ghost town. The only things missing were tumbleweeds and the theme song from *The Good, the Bad, and the Ugly*. I couldn't see any lights in the stores and no cars on the street but there were lots of hand painted signs on doors that said, "Closed for the Season."

A block up from the harbor, the driver stopped in front of a long, two-story, white clapboard building with an American flag blowing over the front door.

KELLEY HOUSE, EDGARTOWN, MASS.

THE KELLEY HOUSE A LONG TIME AGO

16

The floor creaked as I walked to the front desk of the Kelley House. The only other noise, besides my bags hitting the floor, was the metallic sound of a grandfather clock ticking the minutes away. It was so quiet I hated to speak and almost whispered to the man who came from the door behind the counter "I'd like to check in, please."

TICK - TOCK!

I was given a key and directed to a freezing-cold room with windows covered in flowered draperies. The slipcovers, bedspread, and wallpaper were all in the same Laura Ashley flowery pink pattern.

I found the thermostat, turned up the heat, and un-packed my suitcases with my coat on. When it warmed up, I took a shower and put on flannel jammies, socks, slippers and two sweaters. I gazed out the window at the unfamiliar landscape, the bare trees, and splotches of dirty snow. It was drizzling again. I had nowhere to go, and no reason to leave. It was only just noon, but it had already been a long day. I ordered room service, got out my diary, turned on the TV, pulled a throw off the bed, wrapped it around me, and collapsed into an armchair.

My pen was poised. I was trying to figure out what day it was when I heard someone on the TV say John Belushi's name. I thought I heard him say John was dead. I turned up the sound. ABC was reporting that John Belushi had been found dead at a hotel in Los Angeles at the age of 33.

EXCUSE ME, WERE YOU SPEAKING TO ME?

I slapped the arms of the chair and deflated into a slump. It was so depressing, another one gone ~ only 33, almost the same age as me. After a moment of sitting there and thinking about it, I got mad, actually angry. Not because I was such a huge fan of John Belushi's ~ it was just that two years earlier John Lennon had been murdered. Before that we'd lost John F. Kennedy and his brother Robert, plus Martin Luther King, the massacre at Kent State, not to mention tens of thousands of young lives in Vietnam. Then the total disappointment of everything Nixon, and, just the year before, President Reagan was shot. Each of these events was a total shock and I was sick of it. No wonder so many people around my age had been turning to (and dying from) drugs. We were in group trauma. Post-traumatic stress. Self-medicating depression for a generation brought up believing in fairy tales. How did we get from flowers in our hair to THIS?

... We've only just begun
to live...
white lace & promises,
a kiss for luck & we're on our way...
The Carpenters

My eyes filled with tears as my problems and the world's woes mixed together in my mind. I took it almost personally. People shooting people, drugs, lies, war, and man's inhumanity to man were not what I thought life was going to be like. It was so discouraging. What was wrong with everyone?

The Pandora's box in my head, where I kept all the bad stuff, was getting crowded with world-class disappointments too upsetting to allow to run loose. My parents' divorce and the split with Cliff were two more to add to the pile of wrongness. Since hitting my thirties, it had been more and more difficult to tell myself that these incidents were aberrations.

Separating them in my mind, closing the door on that not-so-airtight room, was the only way I could manage. Otherwise I would have been constantly sad.

Above all else, guard your heart.
Proverbs 4:23

I watched the screen as the news cut to clips of John Belushi, his eyebrow cocked, sucking down a plate of green Jell-O in *Animal House* and chopping sausage with his Samurai sword on *Saturday Night Live*. He made such a good Joe Cocker! So sad. Such a waste. I couldn't help thinking about his mother.

I stayed in the room the rest of the day. All I did was sleep. I felt heavy, a dead weight, like the lead blanket they put on you in the dentist's office. I would jerk awake with a scary, empty feeling, not knowing where I was. When I got my bearings, I reached for my latest self-help book, *The Cinderella Complex* ∼ which was not a book of fairy tales ∼ in fact, just the opposite.

The author was saying that women "feared independence" and that we'd been raised with an expectation that we would be rescued from running our own lives. Once we'd found our Prince Charming, we tended to stop believing in ourselves. I was finding myself in this book. Why had I never noticed any of this on my own? Don't answer that.

Room service brought tea and bacon sandwiches on soft white bread with mayonnaise and iceberg lettuce. I phoned my mom and then my dad and told them where I was and what I was doing in a way I hoped would keep their worrying at bay ~ lightly and cheerfully saying, "Just a getaway, only for three months." I was supposedly a grownup, almost 35, I could do this if I wanted. I called my girlfriends and my sisters to let them know I was alive; Shelly put the phone up to my kitty's ear so that I could talk to her. "Pooh-Bear," I cooed with tears in my eyes, along with more cat baby-talk that I will spare you.

DID YOU KNOW MY MOMMY IS INSANE?

The second day I put on my hat, coat, gloves, and scarf and faced the great outdoors ~ walking over to the corner drugstore to get the paper so that I could look at car ads. It was my dad's idea that I should buy a cheap used car rather than rent one. After my three-month stay, I could sell it and it would end up costing a lot less than a rental.

I called a couple of numbers from the paper and the next day a guy brought over a 1976 faded blue Honda Accord for me to look at. I drove it around the block. It seemed okay, the two most important things, the radio and the heater, both worked, no smoke came out from anywhere, the brakes felt good. I thought it would last three months, so I bought it.

20

The fourth morning on the Island, I was having breakfast in the dimly lit dining room of the hotel, just me and the newspaper in a sea of wooden tables and spindly, high-backed Windsor chairs. It was pin-drop quiet except for the creaking floor when the waiter brought my tea. The wind beat against the long row of windows on the front wall of this hotel that had been here since the days of muskets and tricorner hats. I read on the menu that the oldest part of the hotel had opened its doors in 1732, and I could feel every bit of it in the low ceilings, dark beams, thick plaster walls and worn wood floors. I pulled my shawl tighter and tried to get the newspaper into a manageable size, folding it next to my plate, so I could put butter and jam on my toast and read at the same time.

Suddenly, there was a lot of commotion outside the windows. I couldn't even begin to tell you how out of character noise of any kind was in this hotel. So far I'd seen maybe six people total, counting the waiter, the lady at the drug store and the guy with the car.

I sat up in my chair and looked across the room through the blurry little panes of glass, and saw that two large, black motorcycles had rumbled up (motorcycles in the snow didn't make sense, but what did I know?).

Guys in black leather jackets and helmets straddled the bikes. At the same time, two stretch limousines arrived, double parking and pretty much blocking off the street. What could this be? Chauffeurs were opening doors, people were spilling out into the street, slinging bags over their shoulders, pulling suitcases from the trunks of the cars, everyone bundled up in full-length over-coats, hats and leather jackets.

DESPITE THE OVERCAST  THEY WERE ALL WEARING SUNGLASSES.

The door opened, a blast of icy air blew across the room, and maybe 15 people began to crowd in and mill about. At my faraway table in the shadows, I put the paper down and watched them, sipping my tea, curious about this abrupt change in the action.

I slowly began to make out faces and features and realized with huge confusion that I recognized some of these people ～ which was simply not possible. In fact, I knew some of them really well, like family or best friends. I was very startled.

No way!
But I do!
You can't!
But look at them! I do!

I thought maybe I went to high school with them, I thought I should get ready to say hello. I shook my head to get the cobwebs out. A moment later I realized I was looking at Dan Aykroyd, Lorraine

Newman, Bill Murray, and Lorne Michaels. It was *Saturday Night Live!* But for real. Out here in the middle of nowhere. I did not know them, and even more importantly, they did not know me. It felt like it was in the nick of time that I didn't say hello.

I closed my mouth, shrank back in my chair, and raised the paper in front of my face, carefully observing, gathering intelligence to tell Diana later. It's hard to put into words just how out of context this was. Why are they here?

Then I remembered a movie-star detail I'd read or heard somewhere: John Belushi had a house or had lived on the Island at one time. *Ohhhhh*, it came to me, they must be having the funeral here.

Everyone looked tired and bleary-eyed, and their shoulders sagged. It was a room full of broken hearts in mourning for lost innocence (including me ~ and not just us, probably our entire generation). I wished we could all wake up and go back to the way it was such a short time ago, when we were young, and the world was our oyster.

Most of them slowly melted away through the door to check in, in the reception room with the ticking grandfather clock that, I think everyone would agree, had made one tick too many. Lorne Michaels and Bill Murray pulled out chairs and sat down heavily at a table across from me, ordered coffee, and didn't talk at all.

I looked back at my paper shaking my head at the strange-ness of life in general: For Rent, Houses and Apartments.

Later, over the phone, I told Diana the whole thing. "Wow, that's surreal," she said. "How about Chevy Chase, was he there?

Diana had a crush on Chevy Chase (among others).

"I didn't see him . . . but there were a lot of people."

"Did any of them talk to you?"

"No way. I don't think they even knew I was there. They had their own problems. I stayed behind the newspaper."

Deep breath. "I can't believe it. You lead such an exciting life."

"Yeah, well," I said, "that's one way to look at it."

"Did you find a place to live yet?"

"No, but I bought a car! And I saw a couple of interesting-looking houses for rent in the paper. I'm calling the realtor after I get off with you."

I told her I'd call her back after I looked at the houses. Despite the distance, as always, we were in it together.

"I have lost my dew drop," cried the flower to the morning sky that lost all its stars.
♥ Rabindranath Tagore

Chapter Two

Hello? Is it me you're looking for?

Suddenly, the fairy stood before her.
"Take heart," she said, "all will go now well."
♥ French Folktales

The next day dawned cold and gloomy and stayed that way. After the rest of the hotel guests left for Abel's Hill to bury someone who had very likely been the light of their lives, I received a call from Lucy Rogers from Cronig's Real Estate. She was the agent for two of the houses I'd seen advertised in the paper, both of them in Vineyard Haven, the town where Cliff's grandmother had lived.

Lucy picked me up, and we drove across the Island for the 20-minute trip, out deserted Edgartown-Vineyard Haven Road, a straight, no-nonsense, two-lane road carved out of the woods, with a few houses sprinkled here and there on either side.

Lucy thought she had found the perfect rental house for me, but she asked if I minded if we made a quick stop to check on another house first.

"No, I don't mind. Is it for rent?" I wondered if it was something for me.

"No, actually it's going up for sale." she said. "It's a cottage that's been closed up for a while, ever since the owner went into a nursing home. I just have to poke my head in, make sure the furnace is okay and take a couple of pictures. You can come with me and look around if you want."

"OK, I will." I liked looking at houses, especially houses called "cottages," and after four days of hardly speaking to anyone, it was nice to be doing something ~ almost like going out with a friend.

We got to Vineyard Haven and Lucy made a left turn, away from the downtown. The landscape became more rural again, more countrified. We curved around past a stone wall with an old wooden gate and at the end of the wall she made a another left.

There was a stretch of deep woods, with a tall white farmhouse and a barn set back and barely visible. She slowed down and turned onto a dirt driveway that curved around into a stand of young oak trees. We parked at the doorstep of a cottage nestled in a clearing in the woods, a tiny house with white-trimmed windows

 and shingles darkened by age. The house was so small and plain it looked like a child's drawing: Door. Windows. Roof. A hand-painted sign, green with white letters, was nailed to one of the trees. It said, "Holly Oak." A house with a name. Where I came from houses didn't have names.

Tattered brown leaves still clung to the mostly bare oaks sur-
rounding the house, 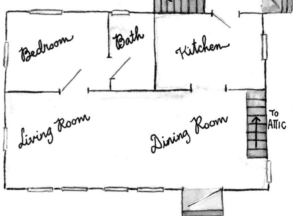 with splotches of snow clumped here and
there on the ground below them. Our frosty breath clouded
around us as we climbed a couple of steps onto an unadorned,
postage-stamp sized, cement porch. Lucy pulled back an
aluminum and glass outer door, unlocked the front door, and
pushed it open. We stepped into a small rectangular dining-
living area that smelled like mothballs and mice. It was freezing
inside, we could still see our breath.

Without taking a step I
could look into every room,
all three of them, not
counting the bathroom.
Behind us was a set of
narrow wooden stairs that
led to the attic. To our right
was a small kitchen. It
would have been better if
the house were empty because the few furnishings
left behind were sad and broken with not a speck of comfort or
color. Yellowed shades were pulled down unevenly on the four
double-hung windows that went across the front of the house,
and a gloomy underwater feeling came from the dim gray window
light and the drab, hospital-green walls.

"Agnes Brooks was her name," said Lucy, by way of
explanation for the condition of the place. "She passed
away about six months ago. She was a cousin of the Brooks
family who owns the farmhouse next door. She was ill for quite a
while; no one has lived here for a long time. The property has
been in probate, and we're just about to put it on the market."

It wasn't my business, but I still felt bad. This is the end of a whole life? This house of unwanted things? The only chair, a ratty brown Naugahyde Barcalounger, ripped and repaired with a large T of frayed silver duct tape, sat on a raw homemade wood base pushed against the wall. The chair faced an old TV that sat on a chipped, gold-colored metal stand on wheels. Above the TV, a pencil sharpener with a crank, like the ones we had in grammar school, was screwed to the trim between the windows. Also on wheels was a TV tray and a small homemade footstool. Old books were stacked and falling over on the plywood shelves under the windows and all the way up the stairs that led to the attic. The wood floor was covered with a dingy area rug. It was like being on the inside of a dirty gray ice cube. I couldn't help but wonder and worry about this woman whose house I was in. Where was her family, her husband, her children? My hope was that they'd already come and taken away the good stuff. . . because if this was it, this was very sad.

28

"She was alone, never married, no close family," Lucy said, confirming my worst fears. "She was a nurse at the hospital for years, before she got sick. And then she died."

Perfect, I thought. This is what happens.

I turned around to look outside. So quiet, this gray island, where people seemed to be dying a lot. I wonder if the sun ever comes out?

"I'm going downstairs to the cellar to check the furnace," said Lucy. "Want to come?"

"No, thanks, I'll wait here if you don't mind."

Where I was from in California, there were no attics or basements. I'd never been in a basement and the only attic I'd ever seen was my great-grandmother's in Iowa when I was five, and there was a great big baby doll up there that had belonged to my mother, so I really didn't notice my surroundings. Other than that, all I knew was that attics and basements had terrible reputations from horror movies.

My dad always made us kids scream with his campfire-story about a lunatic who lived in a basement who was very slowly, but steadily, never-endingly, one stair-step at a time, coming up to GET us, we just never knew exactly when, then sending us all into shrieks when his hand leaped out to squeeze someone's knee, usually mine, as he growled, GOTCHA, scaring the liver out of everyone.

This neglected cottage of death could easily have a maniac living in the basement.

While Lucy was downstairs, I peeked into the kitchen. Small saucepans hung on hooks; frying pans, Pyrex baking dishes, and canning jars were stacked under a kind of homemade kitchen counter. Plywood planks on metal brackets served as shelves.

Over the sink, a double-hung window with dirty glass panes looked out to the woods. A knife rack on the wall next to the window held an assortment of mismatched plastic-handled knives. There was a dish drainer on the counter, cracked and rutted soap in a saucer, and a spindly dead plant on the windowsill. The only bright spot was an old-fashioned 1950s white enamel gas stove with six burners, two ovens and two broilers, a lot like the one my mom had when I was growing up.

As Lucy came clattering back up the stairs ～ still in one piece, I was happy to see, no claw marks on her face ～ I said, "Look at this wonderful old stove. My mom had one just like it!" I had an image of my little brothers and sisters in their pajamas, huddled over the open door of our oven on cold mornings, keeping warm, and the smell of pancake batter bubbling in an iron frying pan.

She looked at me curiously "Yes, that's a beauty. They don't make them like they used to. Come outside. I'll show you around while I take some more pictures."

Our boots crunched over a football field-sized stretch of frozen grass, between clumps of snow and fallen tree branches to a narrow path that went through the woods behind the house and disappeared around a bend. Tiny snowflakes began to fall, whirling lightly around us, like magic is what I thought. I'd seen snow before, but only when we'd gone to a ski resort where you'd expect it, never in real life. I thought of John Belushi's friends, all in black, huddling in a raw cold graveyard with this snow coming down and mixing with their tears.

We stopped so that Lucy could push aside the frozen leaves with her foot to find the granite boundary marker, fit a square flashbulb into her Instamatic and take her pictures.

"How big is this place? How much property?" I asked.

"A little over an acre," she said. "The main floor of the house is 600 square feet. There's not much I can add since you just saw it. One bedroom, one bath, basement and attic. No frills. What you see is what you get."

"An acre. Wow." I looked back at the cottage with the sloping roof through flecks of falling snow. *Little thing, I thought.*

Magic in the air . . .

We followed the path a little farther stopping under the trees next to a white farm fence. "That's the way to Pilot Hill Farm and Long Pond," she said, pointing with her green-mittened hand. Turning around, she continued, "If you follow the path around that way, you get to Brook Farm."

On the other side of the fence was a large open meadow that stretched down as far as I could see to the shore of the pond; several white horses were grazing near the woods bordering the other side. Closer to us was a flock of Canada geese nibbling their way across the weather-beaten grass;

one of them kept his head up and an eye on us. The trees were bare, there was no color anywhere, the air smelled clean, of salt and sea and there were faint cries from a seagull.

We shuffled through dead leaves back toward the house where Lucy gave a nod to the thigh-high brambles sticking out of the patchy snow under the trees. She waved her arm across the landscape and said, "These are all wild blueberry bushes."

My eyes swept across the desolate yard. Wild blueberries? I'd never seen a wild blueberry. Or even a tame blueberry, except in the frozen food section. But I could see them now, at least in my imagination, and they were impressive. I could even see how good they would taste, fresh-picked in a little bowl, with cream poured over the top.

HOLLY OAK

Close to the back of the cottage, we skirted a large holly tree, thick with shiny green spiked leaves and red berries, now speckled in snow. Ah, I thought to myself, that explains the name on the sign out front. I thought it was funny some- one had gone to the trouble of naming this nondescript little place and had even painted a sign for it. The only houses I'd heard of that had names were in fairy tale books.

At the side of the house was a large fenced garden with an iron gate falling off its hinges. A wooden bird feeder was hanging from a tree branch by one chain, on end and useless. It had a rickety little lichen-covered roof over a feeding tray. I felt myself wanting to rescue it, but I couldn't ask Lucy for it. It went with the house. It's plainness and purpose embodied New England charm and history (as I saw it) no matter how sad, old and broken it was.

33

eyond the garden, Lucy pointed out the dark shingled house and barn of the nearest neighbor, barely visible through the trees, an acre of oak trees and blueberries away. A person could cry and scream her heart out here and no one could hear her, I thought.

We went back inside. Lucy locked the back door while I took a quick look at the tiny nine-by-nine-foot bedroom with windows on each outside wall that looked out to the holly tree, over the blueberries, and into the woods. There was a thin, lumpy, black- striped-ticking twin mattress hanging half-off a matching box spring on a metal frame in the corner of the room. I looked into the bathroom that opened off the bedroom. It had a chipped black-and-white checkerboard linoleum floor, a porcelain sink with chrome legs, one tiny window, white plastic tiles around the tub, and another rusted chrome grab bar screwed to the wall.

s I stepped back into the living room, thoughts ran through my mind: This place is so small, it would cost practically nothing to fix it up: a couple of rolls of wallpaper and a gallon of paint would change everything. Someone could make curtains for those little windows. They could pick blueberries in the summer and make pies in that old oven. If the tub was clean, it would be perfect for bubble baths. Someone could grow roses on that garden fence, fix that bird feeder and feed the birds. A whole acre. What more could someone want? This little place shouldn't be left out in the woods all by itself.

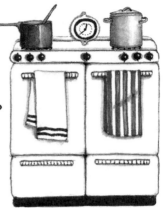

Lucy was in the kitchen. I glanced at the stove, distinctly smelled my grandma's pie-crust baking in the oven, and heard myself say, "How much are they asking for this place?"

Her answer was almost shocking, ridiculously low for an acre of land and a little house like this, less than what Cliff paid for his car. It would have been six times that amount in California. I glanced around the room one more time, imagined old-fashioned tile counters and cupboards with open shelves, turned back to Lucy, and said, "I'll take it." Exactly as if I were buying a dress.

"Really?" asked Lucy, surprised. Her eyes flickered over me looking for other signs of insanity. "Seriously?" I nodded, Yes, and that was it. No thought involved at all. Even today I can't tell you for sure how it happened or why, but it did.

I had no experience in house buying. I didn't try to negotiate the price. I didn't get a home inspection or do "due diligence" (whatever that meant). I didn't go down to the basement until later, when I had to, when I found out that's where they kept the washer and dryer. My purchasing experience was in dresses. All I really needed to know was, Do I look good in this and I thought, Yes, it's just my size.

I'd only been on the Island a few days but apparently my "three-months-just-to-try-it" experiment had taken a turn. Because of a broken heart, 🖤 an old stove, 🔲 some wild blueberries 🫐 and a 🏠 rickety bird feeder, 🔲 I'd accidentally bought a one- 🔲 bedroom cottage in 🔲 the woods on an island in the Atlantic, thousands of miles from home.

In the next days, I vacillated between thinking it was the greatest thing I ever did or that I'd lost my mind. But somehow I stayed stuck to it and was never sure if I rescued the house or it rescued me.

I bought a house in the snow!

Old wives say that blueberry plants are protective and associated with treachery and deception. They will not return treachery, but they will protect it from reaching you. This was what I needed.

Because we were legally separated, I had to call Cliff and tell him what I'd done. A part of me (the never give up part) hoped he would say, "Don't be ridiculous. Get home right now." But he didn't, and I'm sure I wouldn't have done it anyway. It would have taken more than a crook of his finger at that point. He was full of judgment, this guy who didn't want me anymore.

"I know you're upset," he said, "but do you think this makes sense?"

I took a deep breath and looked out my hotel room window at the light snow falling outside. I hated it when he talked about sense. He had never seen me as a logical person. "Why do you say that?"

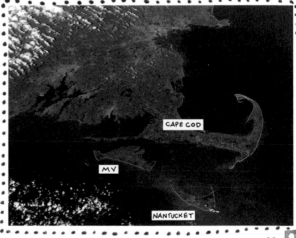

"I don't know, moving to a freezing-cold island, so far from home, where you don't know anyone, where you have to get on a boat to go anywhere and everything is a thousand years old. I don't get it. What are you trying to prove?"

"I'm not trying to prove anything. Why do you care? I'm pretty sure I'm free to go."

"I'm just worried about you. You should think this over carefully before you commit."

"I thought it over, I'm already committed," I said, not meaning it, but not telling him, "and don't bother worrying about me. Even if I change my mind, with a little paint I could probably sell this house for more than they're asking for it."

I changed the subject. He was really much more interested in the
John Belushi story.

After he finished making me feel like I had just made the
biggest mistake of my life, it turns out he wasn't really
upset about the house, especially when he found out how cheap it
was. Then came the question I knew he would ask: "I hope you
had someone look at it. Check for termites? Look at the wiring?"

I was ready. "Of course I did."

I was always much better at lying when I had a
chance to plan for it.

LOGIC? GOOD GRACIOUS! WHAT RUBBISH!
E.M. Forster

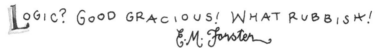

"Well, that's good. You realize you're running away from home,
right? You've bought a house. You're not coming back? You're
leaving everything? What do you think you'll find there that you
can't get here?"

I hated his questions. For one thing, I won't have to watch you
cavorting under my nose with your 20-year-old girlfriend(s).
I'll have peace of mind, and you won't be able to tell me what to
do for a change.

Seeking something sensible and less controversial for a
reply I said, "Nothing is set in stone, and you know
I've always wanted to see what it's like to have seasons. Now
seems like a pretty good time. I can always change my mind. And
you know what?" I said proudly, taking complete ownership as if
I'd made it happen myself, "It's snowing outside right this minute!
You should see it ～ it's beautiful."

"Uh, I don't think so. Anyway, whatever you want. I just want you to be happy. Are you still coming back in June?"

Pffff, I thought. Happy. Ha! I told him, Yes, I had to come home and get Pooh, pack everything and hire a moving van to bring my furniture to the Island.

Better to be without logic than without feeling.
Charlotte Bronte

Telling Diana was much harder.
    She literally screamed at me over the phone:

"YOU BOUGHT A HOUSE? You haven't even been there a week! What happened to 'Three months just to try it?'"

"It's all your fault," I said.

"How is this my fault?"

"You always say, 'Follow your heart, listen to your inner voice.' My inner voice said 'You should buy that house.' So, I did."

"You never listened to me before, why start now? This is the worst. You're leaving me. It's the end of an era. Have you told Cliff? Are you guys getting divorced?"

I answered that I didn't know if we were getting divorced. I wasn't sure about anything, only that I'd be back in California in June. But it wasn't like I wanted to get married again. In fact, heaven forbid. Diana said Paul told her Cliff said I needed to be taught a lesson ∼ because I was spoiled. That's what this was all about, she said. Punishment. I begged her never to tell me anything Paul said that Cliff said ever again.

"I thought you'd think it was good, like maybe it's not over," Diana said." Maybe when he gets done teaching you a lesson he might want to get back together."

"Get back together? Kimmi is a lesson? Oh, Diana, I hope this thing is old news before I get home in June. I am so tired of talking about it ∼ tired of thinking about it. And don't worry, no matter how far I go, I'll never leave you. You know too much."

You can't be spoiled if you do your own ironing.
♥ Meryl Streep

It was going to a take at least two months to close on the house, but Lucy arranged for me to rent it from Agnes's estate so that I could move in right away. She had the utilities turned on and gave me a set of keys and for a couple of weeks I was back and forth between the hotel and the house, checking at the post office to see if the boxes I sent out from California had arrived ∼ I planned to move in when they came. I spent hours at the house every day working to make it livable.

Spring Cleaning

I went to sleep in my hotel bed, making lists in my head. It was a refreshing change from thinking about Cliff and about a thousand times more productive.

Despite the word "spring" on the calendar, it was freezing outside, which fit me fine, fit my heart; little snow flurries popped up, which made the drive from the hotel to the house rather festive.

I kept my hat and jacket on and went to work. I opened the front and back doors and let freezing air blow the lifelessness out of the house. I rolled up the dirty rug and dragged it out to the yard and swept the whole house counterclockwise (for luck ~ I read somewhere you should do that with a new house). I filled Agnes's galvanized bucket with hot soapy water and scrubbed the floors with her big sloppy cotton mop, stood on a step stool to wash the walls, got rid of cobwebs, vacuumed up the mouse poo with Agnes's old Hoover from 1904 (it seemed), cleaned the stove, scrubbed out the fridge, wiped down the shelves and cupboards, washed every dish in the house in the hottest water I could stand, scoured the tub and the toilet, mopped the bathroom floor, and washed the windows inside and out.

I sat on a pillow on the cement stoop in the cold thin sunshine and drank tea, watching a brown rabbit nibbling along the edge of the woods and began to feel what I had done. Against the odds, and for whatever reason, this little house was mine. I could close the door and no one would ever find me.

While washing Agnes's pots and pans and looking out toward the woods through her now sparkling-clean kitchen window, something caught my eye and made me stop. On a tree limb was the reddest bird I'd ever seen. I was surprised because I knew what it was. It had to be a cardinal ~ I'd seen them on Christmas cards but never in real life. He had a crest on his head like a little shark fin, a bright orange bill, a black mask around his eyes, and a long red tail. He took off through the washed-out, dead gray woods like a bright red, flying Valentine.

Lucy sent over a guy with a truck who took away the rug and the Barcalounger and all the rest of the unsalvageable stuff, the metal handrails screwed to the floors and walls, and that awful bed. I decided that once I got moved in I'd have a yard sale for the rest of it ~ some of it could still be useable, just not by me.

Lucy also lent me some furniture from her other rentals that would work until (and if, because I still had no idea what I was doing) I moved my belongings out from California, or found furniture for it myself. There was a small wooden table, two kitchen chairs, a clean bed, and a red-plaid upholstered, overstuffed armchair. The house still echoed with my footsteps, but I had the basics. I decided to keep the old TV until mine came; it was a black-and-white, but it would be company. I opened a bank account, ordered a phone and rented a post office box. Every day I marked things off my list: check, done. Slowly it was coming together. As soon as my boxes came with all my stuff from home, I would move in.

Tom Hodgson

Welcome, Spring

Today is the first day of spring. Last Saturday, Tom Hodgson of West Tisbury reports, he pulled back some leaf litter at the base of a white oak in his yard to find these mayflower blooms awaiting the light of day.

From the Vineyard Gazette

I went to Cronig's Market and bought milk, eggs, butter, tea, honey, extra crunchy peanut butter, cheese, bread, bacon, and potatoes so that I could make potato pancakes, plus chocolate and flour and walnuts so I could make brownies.   I wanted my new house to smell lived in, and not just by mice. I figured that cooking was the fastest route to a normal-smelling house.

At the market I asked the lady at the cash register if they had a potato peeler. She shook her head no. "Is there a hardware store near here?" I asked. She nodded her head yes. I was hoping she'd follow up by telling me where it was, but she handed me my change and went to the next person.

She wasn't very friendly. I thought her personality might still be hibernating for the winter. Or, more likely, coming here from the land of rejection, she probably got an uncomfortable whiff of my eau de heartbreak ~ a perfume that didn't wear off. I probably scared her.

There was also this thing about Californians being flaky and New Englanders being distant. Already I could see both sides of the argument. I tried not to be flaky, but it was probably ingrained in my psyche, coming from a rambunctious, Arf-and-Arfy speaking family and overly enthusiastic by nature. Later I found out that for them it was more of a privacy thing. They weren't unfriendly, they were polite; they didn't want to intrude. Where I was from, intrusion was a way of life. Perfect strangers spoke to each other in the grocery store all the time. Whole standup comedy routines took place between strangers in line at California supermarkets; not intruding felt like rejection. After I was there for a while, I thought about painting a big yellow happy face on my house just to see what everyone would do.

Spring Peepers

The first songs of spring peepers, known also as pinkletinks in these parts, was reported to the Gazette Monday. Mac Young of Lambert's Cove Road in Tisbury heard them in a nearby marsh on Sunday night, just a day after celebrating his eighth birthday.

Spring Peepers are tree frogs that sing in the spring on Martha's Vineyard. (And p. s. Billy saw a blackbird.)

43

I got lost a lot while trying to find my way around. I was fine driving the straight road between my house in Vineyard Haven and the hotel in Edgartown, but anytime I went off the main road, I got lost. Luckily the Island was small, less than a hundred square miles, and fairly flat, the highest point was only 300 feet above sea level. What's the worst that could happen? It was an island; there were edges. Anywhere else and I might still be driving. Added bonus is that if you go around in circles long enough, pretty soon everything starts to look familiar!

I recognized the small graveyard that I stopped to walk through when I was here with Cliff.

In California I knew all the shortcuts and back roads, but not here. There were very few street signs, and many of the side streets weren't even paved, they were bumpy dirt roads. I thought it was funny that one of the few paved streets with a sign was "Dirt Road." I never realized how much I took things like shortcuts and knowing where they keep the peanut butter at the supermarket for granted.

But it was beautiful, there were peeks of ocean around every curve; long flat stretches of beach, charming old houses with low eaves and steep roofs and picket fences; thick tumbledown rock walls; ancient graveyards, and the woods . . . I'd never seen dense woods like these. Redwood forests, yes, on camping trips with my parents ~ were majestic and

awe-inspiring. But these woods on the Island were dark, earthy-smelling with composting leaves, and trees heavily laced together with vines and tangled thickets. In the mist, the woods around Holly Oak looked haunted. There were rabbit warrens, squirrel holes, owls' nests, and small, scurrying woodland creatures. It occurred to me that elves could easily be living in these woods. It was their kind of place.

One freezing cold, darkly Romantic (as in Edgar Allen Poe Romantic) blustery day with nothing special to do, I foolishly indulged my loneliness and feelings of loss when I put on suicide-inducing classical music and drove past the tumbledown dry-stone walls bordering farmlands and pasture, up to Menemsha, on the western end of the Island, perhaps the loneliest place in the world in March, to explore a little. The movie Jaws was filmed

in several locations on Martha's Vineyard including Menemsha ~ if you saw the movie, you know what a picture postcard this tiny fishing village is (at least when it isn't being pressed into the sea by a thick roiling shroud of black thunder clouds).

Menemsha Fishing Boats

45

MENEMSHA BY-THE-SEA, MARTHA'S VINEYARD, MASS.   123565

A Picture Postcard

I sat in the Honda next to the harbor and listened to music and the thumping windshield wipers while being rocked by wind gusts and blasted with sea spray and felt myself a million miles from home. I looked out over the choppy gray-green water and watched gray gulls swarm gray fishing boats looking for gray fish guts, and cried. Even on a good day when everything was going right this would not have been the most uplifting thing to do.

CHAPTER THREE

Stranger in a Strange Land

Three elves came & conducted her to a hollow mountain where the little folks lived. Everything was small but more elegant & beautiful than can be described. ♡ *Brothers Grimm*

March was almost over and the weather became milder everyday. I was beginning to worry because my boxes hadn't arrived. I was still living at the Kelley House, and there were already little signs of spring. The snow had almost completely melted.

Snowdrops

On the 28th, I wrote in my diary: "There are clumps of tiny white flowers in the lawn at Holly Oak! Not another flower in sight, not even leaves on the trees and now these! I checked Agnes's wildflower book. They're called snowdrops and apparently they are the first to come up in the spring."

As for my mental state, allow me to quote Kierkegaard: *Anxiety is the dizziness of freedom.* Although that sounds kind of good because the word freedom is in there, anxiety attacks don't feel like freedom. Since that first one I had while I still lived with Cliff, they hadn't stopped, and they showed up without warning. Weeks could go by without one, and then bam, for no apparent reason, I would experience a terrifying half-hour of shaking and breathing into a brown paper bag thinking I was going to die. I could be anywhere, at the market, in my car, reading, brushing my teeth, when suddenly the bottom would drop out from under me.

47

My dad suggested I try cranberry juice, but it didn't work. I always had to just wait them out. I never knew what triggered them. Years later, an acupuncturist friend told me to visualize myself as a tree with roots from my feet going deep into the earth and anchoring me there. I did that, and for whatever reason, the "dizziness of freedom" finally stopped.

I finished reading The Cinderella Complex and saw where I went wrong. Look at Cliff. I left, and his life went on. Insert new girl and nothing changed. He had a house with yellow tile in the kitchen and towels in the closet, a career with a paycheck, and even his version of love, pathetic as it was, but because I voluntarily chose to support his life with mine, I now had no life at all. Let this be a lesson to me.

Security is a superstition. It does not exist in nature. Life is either a daring adventure or nothing at all.
♥ Helen Keller

I know it's rude to say, "Oh shut up" to Helen Keller, but I couldn't help it.

It felt like Christmas when my boxes finally came ~ the ones I'd sent out from California for the rental ~ with all my homey good stuff in them. I took them over to the house and unpacked. Each thing now had about 500 times more meaning than it ever had before. I cleaned each piece first, then carried it around the house deciding where it would look the best, then stood back and admired it, noting how it practically shined in the dark with beauty, before going to the next.

IT'S THE LITTLE THINGS THAT MEAN THE MOST

I felt so much better with my own sheets and towels and the nap blanket my grandma knit, seeing my watercolors and brushes, the Beatrix Potter people, my recipe box, and a couple of cookbooks I'd sent out for my three-month stay. Not to mention the pile of self-help books I was determined to read to see if I could figure out how I got myself into this mess. I still couldn't believe I had done what I had. But, I reminded myself, this situation didn't have to be permanent. I could go if I wanted to. No one was holding me there.

I hung my clothes in the closet, plumped my pillows with the embroidered pillowcases, and put pictures of Pooh, among others, on the fridge. In that mostly empty, rugless, clattering house, even a bottle of shampoo and a box of yellow Kleenex were relatively festive. At Vineyard Dry Goods downtown, I bought dishtowels, a mattress cover, extra blankets, and throw rugs for the bathroom and kitchen and one for next to my bed.

49

I put all my new purchases around the house and hung the dishtowels over the oven-door handles. It was a start. Even with the ugly wall color, the lack of curtains (which, considering my location, wasn't as much a problem as you might think, especially since I was only there during the day), and the stained floors, the house was clean. And probably no worse than any other rental I would have found. And, despite everything, a voice inside kept saying I was doing the right thing. That voice and I often argued the pros and cons of the situation, but I was just taking it one day at a time.

BUT YOUR SOLITUDE WILL BE A SUPPORT & A HOME FOR YOU, EVEN IN THE MIDST OF VERY UNFAMILIAR CIRCUMSTANCES, AND FROM IT YOU WILL find ALL YOUR PATHS. ♥ RANIER MARIA RILKE

APRIL

On the morning of my 35th birthday, I checked out of the Kelley House and moved into Holly Oak. Diana called to say Happy Birthday and we lamented about how far away from each other we were. I told her the only way I could stay here was if I made long-distance phone calls part of the cost of living, like food and water.

It is very odd to have your birthday all alone in a strange place with no friends around. I hadn't thought about how strange it would feel until I was doing it. I got the new Country Living at the bookstore and took it and my diary along with letters from Shelly and my grandma to lunch in town at the Black Dog Tavern.

ME!

Susan Branch
General Delivery
Vineyard Haven, Mass.
02568

The restaurant was built right on the sand, just up the beach from where the ferry docked. The dining room was dark; it felt like the inside of a ship captain's library, a little bit briny in a good way, and smelled like woodsmoke and grilled hamburger. On the far wall was a huge open fireplace with a log fire flickering across the wide-plank wooden floor. The nautical décor included antique half-hull boat models, several hand-carved name boards from old schooners, navigational charts, and oil paintings with ships in full sail in wild seas were pinpointed with little spotlights, and hung on thick plaster walls and from heavy beams in the low ceilings. There were oil lamps with glass chimneys burning on every table and an old schoolhouse clock ticked away the hours. Natural gray ocean light filtered through a long bank of windows on a kind of porch on the right side of the dining room where I went to sit.

Hand-carved name boards

The tinny sound of a radio played Bob Dylan, *It Ain't Me Babe* in the kitchen that ran down one side of the half-filled restaurant. The kitchen was open to the room, with black gas stoves and pots steaming and griddles sizzling and two fast-moving cooks, brandishing spatulas, wearing black berets and long white aprons over sweaters. No one in California wore berets, it was always too hot, but it was normal headgear on the Island. I added it to the growing list of the many differences between the two places. It was more like a foreign country, that's how different it was. The day was cold and overcast; the water crashed on shore about eight feet from the windows. I read my mail and watched the waves roll in and go out.

Since it was my birthday, I ordered my first real lobster. Back home, all we had were frozen lobster tails from Australia, but here they were fresh, local, steamed bright red, and served whole with head and feelers and claws all still attached. The waitress told me that Islanders called them "bugs." She gave me a plastic bib and showed me how to twist the tail off the body, how to squeeze it until the shell cracked, which of the other parts were edible, and how to get the meat out of the claws with a pair of walnut crackers. It was a sloppy, buttery, wonderful mess to eat, and SO delicious. And after it was all over, I was given a steaming-hot towel wrung out in hot lemon water to wash my hands. I liked the hot towel almost as much as I liked the lobster. From my table, while I was eating, I could read while watching the ferry boat come and go. Such a strange sight to my eyes, and so beautiful. I felt lucky to be in a place where there was such a thing.

A breath of fresh air...

On the way home from lunch I found a flower shop called Tellurian. It was packed with buckets of daffodils, and every color of tulip. I took a deep breath of the fragrance of hyacinths and lilies of the valley that filled the room. It didn't look much like spring outside, but it sure was in there. I bought a big bunch of daffodils and a potted pink hyacinth. I took them back to the house and arranged the daffodils in one of Agnes's canning jars on the kitchen windowsill, and put the hyacinth on top of the television.

My first night at Holly Oak was just as strange as you might imagine. Somehow there is a lot more camaraderie in a hotel room even if you're by yourself than there is out in the middle of nowhere, especially after dark.

I was happy to have the TV for company. I lit a candle and made it as cozy as possible, but with no curtains it wasn't easy. I locked all the windows and doors, pulled down the shades tucking them in around the edges as best I could so that no one could peek in ~ if I ever saw a face in the window, it would be the end of me. I talked to my dad, who said if that ever happened I should just grab something and throw it right AT the face. I glanced around looking for something to throw. But I knew if I saw a face, I would probably just hit the ceiling and wet my pants.

Her imagination was by habit ridiculously active; when the door was not open it jumped out the window.
Henry James

I turned up the TV loud so I could hear it in the kitchen while I roasted a chicken with onions and carrots in Agnes's speckled roasting pan. I made gravy from the giblets and poured the whole thing over torn-up buttered sour dough bread and ate it out of one of Agnes's glass mixing bowls on the little table while watching Dynasty in black-and-white and reading Country Living magazine. It was quiet and strange, but the house itself was good, I felt no evil afoot.

I wrote in my diary, watched TV, and drank wine out of a jelly jar all evening ~ alert as a cat for all the little creaks the house was making. It was about midnight when I figured I was tired enough to pass out and turned off the TV.

It was Very Quiet out there in the Dark in the Middle of Nowhere...

The April wind whistled through the trees, branches brushed and clunked against the house. I took my grandma's nap blanket into the bedroom and stood at the window looking at the ring around the moon through a maze of crooked tree limbs silhouetted against the sky and thought about where I was and wished that Pooh was there.

I heard a car pass by out front and tried to put certain things out of my mind ~ like, for instance, what lives in the woods, I had no idea. Hopefully not wolves. I reached to shut the closet door. My gaze went to the ceiling thinking of the closed door at the top of the stairs that opened to the dark attic over my head where I still hadn't been. Too many fairy tales were imprinted on my imagination. Talking trees with branches like tentacles that could break windows and open doors and things like that. I went and got the hyacinth and brought it into the bedroom for purity and strength.

AS GOD IS MY WITNESS, AS GOD IS MY WITNESS, THEY'RE NOT GOING TO LICK ME. I'M GOING TO LIVE THROUGH THIS & WHEN IT'S ALL OVER, I'LL NEVER BE HUNGRY AGAIN. Scarlett O'Hara

If I have to, I can do anything... ♥ HELEN REDDY

Actually, I was lucky because I was never really alone. I had guardian angels. My great-grandma Alice Carpenter was one of them, but I felt there were at least two others. I wasn't sure who they were, but was sure I was related to them and I knew they took care of me. If someone I loved was sick or sad, I'd mentally send my angels to climb in bed with that person, take their pillows, and pile them all the way down both sides of my loved one, and then sort of moosh the pillows together so that my person was encased in them; protected, insulated and safe. I had my guardian angels for a long time before I knew they were there. When I finally became aware of them, I knew they had always been there. But no one else knew about them, not even Cliff.

This night I needed them for me.

I got between the cold sheets and put pillows under the covers next to me so that when I was asleep I wouldn't know I was alone. I wished again for Pooh, she would have made all the difference. I read until my eyelids got heavy, which, because of the wine, took about three seconds. I turned off the lamp next to the bed, and pulled the covers around my ears. Swirling into a sleep filled with echoes, I saw Cliff bounding toward me that day in the warehouse basement. I felt his arms, his joy, and that amazing kiss. Tears leaked from the corners of my eyes, and that's the last I remembered before I fell asleep.

The next morning, when I pulled up the shade, the woods were enveloped in dense white fog. I could hardly see the holly tree. I crawled back into my warm bed, and lay there in the silver light, listening to the sound of the foghorn. I was 23 years past 12 and one day old, on an Island in the Atlantic, in the woods,

in the fog, in this little green underwater bedroom with no kitty . . . it didn't seem real.

. . . all that she had had, and all that she missed, were lost together, and were twice lost in this landslide of remembered losses.   Katherine Anne Porter

The thermometer screwed to the outside of the bedroom window said it was 43°. I put on my jacket, hat, and gloves, the whole winter uniform, and went in search of a good place to take a walk. I wanted something like my golf course at home, where I could go every day for exercise.

I walked out behind the house to the farm fence, where the white horses grazing in the meadow looked like a painting. The path took me to a rutted dirt road that meandered for a mile and a half through the woods, curving around, and offering glimpses of a large pond through the trees. At the end, the woods stopped, and I walked

out from the canopy of tree branches and held my breath at the view. The sandy strip of road was narrow and fragile and barely there, with the pond on one side and the ocean on the other and me in the middle. It came to an end at the shore of a small sandy beach where the pond flowed through a narrow channel to the sound. I was alone in a wide-open space of blue sky and fast-moving white clouds, with the smell of the sea, and the low dark horizon of the woods behind me.

There were several lonely looking, gray-shingled fishing shacks sunk into the beach-grass-covered dunes next to the water and boarded up for the winter. Several far-away houses dotted the shore of the pond. A heron grazed

along a sandbar; seagulls cried and swooped, the waves rolled in and rolled out. It was so magical, I thought I might even find a bottle with a message in it from somewhere faraway. I wandered

along the shore gazing at the millions of colorful pebbles rolling in the surf and slipped some tiny yellow shells into my pocket. Across the sound, Cape Cod was wrapped in a violet haze; the only boat was the ferry, far away and white against the water, making its way back to the Island.

Reward at the end of the dirt road.

Heading home under the skeletal oak trees, I could feel pockets of chilled air coming up from the thawing earth with the smell the mulching leaves. It didn't look like spring, but the woods were full of birdsong; brown bunnies scattered in front of me and dove into thickets. There were three or four small cottages like mine, acres apart and back from the road, and the smell of spicy wood-smoke drifted in the cold air. The wild nature of it all was wonderful. SO much better than the golf course

They're known as "jingle shells."

where I used to walk in California! That was almost like a movie set compared to this wildness. I made up my mind to go there everyday.

For the rest of my life . . .

Martha's Vineyard, Mass.

An old postcard view of the pond in another season.

When I called home later that day, Shelly answered the phone— her voice sounded so good. I'd written her about Holly Oak and she was worried about whether I was still coming home in June. I told her definitely, I'd be there.

"What's going to happen?" she asked, "Are you guys getting divorced?"

"I don't know. I don't seem to be in charge. I don't think so, not yet anyway, he hasn't mentioned it to me. Maybe he's keeping it as a surprise."

She laughed and said, "I think you'll get back together. You always do."

"I know, but this time feels different. I don't know if I even want to."

"I hope you do. I want you to come home."

"I'll be there before you know it, then we'll see. I miss you too, Belle." She was Belle, as in Mee-shell ma belle, soam-blay mon kee bon tray bien on sombl. (French phonetics? Oui!) Shelly was born when I was in the eighth grade and my mom let me name her. I named her Michelle after the most popular girl in my school, whose name was Shelly Stewart.

Shelly put the phone to Pooh's ear and I told my kitty how sorry I was about leaving her and that I would never do it again. As you might guess, this was more for me than for her.

Mary & Shelly

My other sister Mary had moved in with Shelly along with one of her girlfriends, Nancy. So now there were three 20-year-old girls living in the house I had rented. My clothes and my car, still there, now living with them, were in serious jeopardy. I asked Shelly to send my sewing machine and reminded her that Pooh had no hands and to make sure she was fed, petted and loved, and in at night.

Topper, with Cary Grant and Constance Bennett, was on TV and kept me company while I worked around the house, setting up my art things. I put the paints and water dish, rulers, pads of paper and brushes along with my little office of scissors, tape, stamps and stationery on the table in front of the living room windows. For letter writing, or in case

I could find something to paint, I was ready. Maybe I would paint some pinecones, or maybe the daffodils in the jar in the kitchen. It seemed like forever since I'd drawn anything ~ not since I put that bunny on the wall of my house, a lifetime ago. I just hadn't felt like it.

Because of the aloof cashier at Cronig's Market and my fear of being perceived as flaky, I tried to be extra nice at the hardware store, which I think actually made it worse. "Brrr," I said, chattily to the girl behind the counter, "cold outside! When do you think we'll start seeing some spring around here?"

I, like, probably reeked "Valley girl" and didn't know it.

She just looked at me, so I asked for a potato peeler and she harrumphed jerkily down the aisle to get it for me. You would have thought I was asking her to come home and peel the potatoes.

As if!

Then I asked her if she could please cut me a piece of chain for the bird feeder, which I told her a little about, how it was hanging there by one chain and wanting to save it and all, which I can see now was probably too much information, but on top of that, unfortunately, I also needed a toaster, which meant she had to climb a stepladder. Horrors!

She answered my questions either not at all or by raising or lowering her eyebrows. She didn't laugh when I tried to be funny, didn't respond when I apologized for being too much trouble.

Did I, like, talk too much? Was I, like, a California flake? I couldn't tell, but my morale wasn't great, I felt pretty much like nothing, like a person in the way no matter where I went, so I was sure it was me, the stranger in a strange land.

I couldn't believe there was no toaster at Holly Oak. I'd looked everywhere. How did Agnes survive without toast? Toast is the remedy for almost everything. Or at least it makes good padding for the harshness. No toaster? Why? Living in Agnes's house with reminders of her all around made me curious as to what kind of life she'd lived here.

It didn't look good. Everything she left behind was strictly utilitarian. Except for the piles of books, there was not one thing in that house to nurture or inspire. Besides no toaster, which was ridiculous in and of itself, there were no flowers or ruffles on her sad, limp pillowcases. No rickrack on her potholders, her dishtowels were faded and stained, her umbrella was black ~ you have to have an umbrella, why not one with flowers on it? Not even dog bowls or leashes in the house, and not one single vase. No indication of any life softeners like pets or bubble bath or feather pillows. Her pillows were hard, yellow, unforgiving, non-mooshable foam. It was very sad. The only pretty thing I'd found was a row of beach glass on the lintel over the front door. I washed the blue and green glass pieces and put them back, and from then on, whenever I went for a walk on the beach, I hunted for more of them to add to Agnes's collection.

I was making piles of things to throw out and things to sell in the yard sale. When I finally ventured to the attic (which I knew I'd have to do sooner or later because apparently this was my house) I stood on the top step of the wooden stairs, turned the knob, pushed the door open and waited. No bats came flying out so I peeked in. There were windows at either end. In the dim light I could see stacks of cardboard boxes. It wasn't so bad. Just dusty. I started picking through a jumble of old denim, mittens, and wool blankets; disregarding the piles of town reports, nursing journals, and Reader's Digests. In one box, I found a couple of old books that turned out to be Agnes's baby book and her photo album. I sat down on a wooden box under one of the windows to look at them.

The baby book was covered in gold cloth with "Baby's Record" scrolled in gold leaf on the cover. It was a shared book. The first entries began in 1886 with the birth of Agnes's mother, Margaret. The other half was for Agnes, born in 1916. Tucked between the thick pages covered with spidery hand-writing were relics of another time, engraved calling cards, poems, child's drawings ∼ and, most touching, a tiny envelope, with two folded bits of tissue, each holding a blond curl of baby hair, labeled and dated, one for Agnes and one for her mother. Agnes's dolls' names were listed, old-fashioned

AGNES

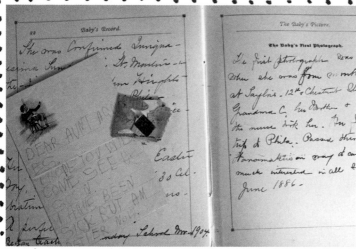

Written in childish hand, "MY SIX DOLLS ARE VERY SICK."

names: Bessie, Aunt Fannie, Polly, Izzy and Sailor Boy. Her photo album contained her baby pictures including a dark photo of Agnes with her dolls. There was also a pair of very old, leather, button-up baby shoes in the box.

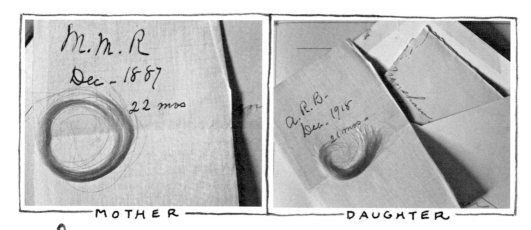

MOTHER ———————— DAUGHTER ————————

These personal treasures had been left behind, just like the house, unloved, uncared for, unwanted. That's when I mentally adopted Agnes and made her my own. The house still echoed with her, like the tune you hear even after the music stops. She'd lived an independent life, but it looked lonely too. I hoped loneliness wasn't the price exacted for independence. It made me cry for Agnes and whatever it was that kept her from buying sheets with flowers on them. I would just have to do it for her. Each moment I felt more invested in Holly Oak.

I took the baby book, the photo album, and the shoes downstairs and put them in display mode with my own things.

I cleaned out the basement too, sweeping up dead moths and centipede carcasses. I decided to keep the snow shovel, the push lawn mower, and all of Agnes's garden tools.

I knew I wouldn't use Agnes's old waders or the fishing poles, although I was glad she went fishing, and was out there in nature. She seemed very hardy, fishing and nursing and making jam and presumably taking care of that big garden out there.

The fishing things would go into the yard sale along with the limp old pairs of men's overalls that were folded on the closet shelf, the big brown corduroy jacket with the fake fur collar, the tattered and frayed towels and sheets, the wool blankets, and those ugly metal tables on wheels.

I kept the large speckled stock pot and the roaster that were in the basement and left the jars of homemade blueberry jam lined up on the shelf down there where I found them. I wasn't going to eat the jam ~ who knew how long those jars had been there. But they looked industrious, and they had labels with Agnes's handwriting on them. They would make perfect basement décor.

A man should choose
with a careful eye
the things to be
remembered by.
Robert P. T. Coffin

✳   ✳   ✳

One early spring day I was waiting for the furnace man
to come because the heat had gone off and I didn't
know what else to do since I'd already gone to the basement
and kicked it ∼ the extent of my furnace-fixing knowledge.
The house was cold; it wasn't even 40 degrees outside. I was
wearing Agnes's old wool sweater and boiling water for tea
in one of her little saucepans; I saved the tea-
bag for my eyes, (I still cried) in a little bowl I kept
in the fridge. I had a rhubarb crisp in the oven; both for
sustenance and to warm the house. I snipped the fingertips
off a pair of Agnes's gloves and put them on because my hands
were freezing and turned on the TV for background noise. I
took my cup of tea, dragged a floor lamp over, and sat down
on a wooden box with my grandma's nap blanket over my
shoulders to sort through the piles of Agnes's books.

Rhubarb crisp with ice cream, so easy, so "breakfast" (granola, dairy, and fruit ~ or as my mother would say ~ starch, calcium and ruffage, the basic food groups), so "spring." (The furnace man loved it, and you will to! Known to override smell of mothballs.)

RHUBARB CRISP

TOPPING

375° 8 Servings

½ c. ground almonds
(almond meal or almond flour)
½ c. rolled oats
¾ c. firmly packed brown sugar

¼ tsp. cinnamon
¾ tsp. nutmeg
⅓ c. butter, softened

In a large bowl, mix the chopped rhubarb (See "Filling" below) with the 1 c. sugar & set aside for 1 hour. Preheat oven to 375°. Mix all topping ingredients in med. bowl, use your fingers to make it crumbly. Set aside & continue with filling.

FILLING

5 c. rhubarb, cut into ¾" cubes
1 c. granulated sugar
1½ tbsp. quick-cooking tapioca
½ tsp. cinnamon
1 tsp. minced fresh ginger
zest of one large orange

Pour off all but two Tbsp. of the juice from the rhubarb. Add tapioca, cinnamon, ginger & zest; stir well. Pour into ungreased 8×8 baking dish. Sprinkle topping evenly over rhubarb. Bake 30 min. until bubbly & golden brown. Serve warm with vanilla ice cream or cold with whipped cream—.

here were lots of newer hardcover books, like *The Godfather*, *Rosemary's Baby*, *All the President's Men*, and *Valley of the Dolls*, which went into the yard-sale pile. I kept *All Creatures Great and Small* because I'd never read it, plus an older biography about George Sand and one about Abigail Adams. I also put *To Kill a Mockingbird*, and two John Steinbeck books, *East of Eden* and *Grapes of Wrath*, in the "keep" pile. I'd read them and loved them and thought they'd be good to have around.

here were some really old books that had probably belonged to Agnes's mother ~ leather and linen-bound, some with lovely art on the covers; faded books with tissue-thin pages and pale satin ribbons for bookmarks ~ and two of Kate Greenaway's small "Almanacks" dated 1885 and 1894. There was *Jane Eyre* and *Pride and Prejudice*, an autobiography called *My Life* by Helen Keller, *David Copperfield*, and a tiny blue gold-stamped volume of *Aunt Jo's Scrapbag* by Louisa May Alcott.

ooks about accounting, ice-fishing, and nursing, or with missing covers or broken bindings, went in the to-go pile.

67

Best of all, there were several of my childhood favorites: *Little Women, Peter Pan, Uncle Wiggly, The Bobbsey Twins, Anne of Green Gables, The Secret Garden,* and *Pollyanna,* with painted covers and illustrations showing children playing in gardens and brooks, wearing straw hats and middy dresses. These books were homey and reassuring, treasures of my childhood just lying around in this house in the woods, suggesting that Agnes was a kindred soul.

What one loves in childhood stays in the heart forever.♥

MARY JO PUTNEY

There were several illustrated English garden books from the 1940s, a wildflower guide, a field guide for New England birds, plus a 1946 copy of *Joy of Cooking* with Agnes's signature inside.

Reading is dreaming while wide awake.

Thinking how Cliff would try to talk me out of it, I kept them all; they were definitely not yard-sale material.

It made sense to me that even if I wasn't reading a book, even if I'd finished it and it was just near me, in my breathing area, it might be possible that some of the author's brilliance could transfer to me through osmosis. (Note from the future: right now the finished pages of this book are sandwiched between Ben Franklin's Autobiography and The Quotable Mark Twain, with very high hopes for large transference.) So I kept all the ones I loved. Just in case, because commonsensically speaking, a room full of good books had to be better for your health than a room with no books in it at all.

A fondness for reading, properly directed, must be an education in itself. ♥ Jane Austen

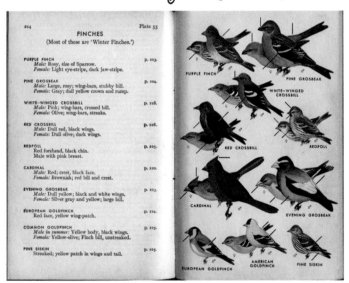

214   Plate 55
                        FINCHES
              (Most of these are 'Winter Finches.')

PURPLE FINCH   p. 223.
    Male: Rosy, size of Sparrow.
    Female: Light eye-stripe, dark jaw-stripe.

PINE GROSBEAK   p. 224.
    Male: Large, rosy; wing-bars, stubby bill.
    Female: Gray; dull yellow crown and rump.

WHITE-WINGED CROSSBILL   p. 228.
    Male: Pink; wing-bars, crossed bill.
    Female: Olive; wing-bars, streaks.

RED CROSSBILL   p. 228.
    Male: Dull red, black wings.
    Female: Dull olive; dark wings.

REDPOLL   p. 225.
    Red forehead, black chin.
    Male with pink breast.

CARDINAL   p. 220.
    Male: Red; crest, black face.
    Female: Brownish; red bill and crest.

EVENING GROSBEAK   p. 223.
    Male: Dull yellow; black and white wings.
    Female: Silver gray and yellow; large bill.

EUROPEAN GOLDFINCH   p. 224.
    Red face, yellow wing-patch.

COMMON GOLDFINCH   p. 225.
    Male in summer: Yellow body, black wings.
    Female: Yellow-olive; Finch bill, unstreaked.

PINE SISKIN   p. 225.
    Streaked; yellow patch in wings and tail.

I put all the books I was keeping back on the shelves; setting aside an interesting-looking one called *The Best of Stillmeadow,* which I thought I might like to read. The bird book went to the kitchen counter so I could figure out what birds were coming to the feeder. I looked up cardinals, and found out that they mark their territories with song (ah, the real world should be like that, countries bordered by birdsong). And I learned that they mated for life; the male courts the female by putting seeds in her mouth, and not just for the first spring when they are young and gay, but forever. He helps her make their nest every year. They do it together. My kind of guy.

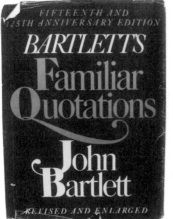

But strangely, as it turned out, the best book Agnes left behind was a big red book called *Bartlett's Familiar Quotations.* I'd never seen a book of quotes before and started thumbing through it. I kept it by my chair and looked at it often. Pretty soon I was laughing out loud and

> 17 It's as large as life and twice as natural.
>   *Ib.* 7
> 18 His answer trickled through my head,
>   Like water through a sieve.   *Ib.* 8
> 19 What's the French for fiddle-de-dee?
>   *Ib.* 9
> 20 It isn't etiquette to cut anyone you've been
>   introduced to. Remove the joint!   *Ib.*
> 21 He would answer to "Hi!" or to any loud cry
>   Such as "Fry me!" or "Fritter my wig!"
>   — Lewis Carroll —

marveling over what I was reading; I began to put stars next to the quotes I liked. Some were funny, such as,

✱Take me or leave me; or, as is the usual order of things, both. ♡ Dorothy Parker

Some used especially beautiful words:

✱And this, our life, exempt from public haunt, finds tongues in trees, books in running brooks, sermons in stones, & good in everything. ♡ William Shakespeare

. . .and some made me think:

✱If you want your children to be intelligent, read them fairy tales. If you want them to be more intelligent, read them more fairy tales. ♡ Albert Einstein

Eureka ～ vindication at last! I thought I should send that last one to Cliff.

'm sure that Agnes, being a nurse and all, made a huge difference in lots of people's lives, but she was my guardian angel. She left me beautiful books, not to mention the perfect house ～ and the stove ～ and those blue-

berries (and the bird feeder). I would never forget her.

There are two ways of spreading light: to be the candle or the mirror that reflects it.
♥ Edith Wharton

here must have been some kind of instinct involved in how I got here, like the magnetic compass sense some animals possess. Like homing pigeons. Otherwise I can't explain how I found my way from the other side of the country to this tiny speck of land surrounded by water and this little house in the woods. Maybe, like the watercolors that had seemed to come from nowhere, it was sanctus espiritus, the breath of God. Because it was as if I'd been moving toward this spot my whole life, maybe even back as far as when I met Diana at Bob's Big Boy and she brought me to San Luis Obispo so I could meet Cliff and he could take me to meet his grandmother on Martha's Vineyard. Or maybe even further back. Could have even been when my dad brought up the subject of pork chops to my 16-year-old mom. I felt like I got here in the nick of time, just before my house would have gone on the market. I was happy I wasn't too late. (Though, in my secret heart, I'm almost positive the house would have waited for me.)

✳   ✳   ✳

WILD VIOLETS IN THE GRASS

The weather was beginning to warm up, I was getting more settled and I decided to paint the living room walls before I had to go back, but first I had to find the paint store. I was told it was in "Chicken Alley" on Lagoon Pond Road across from the post office.

I was out of wine, so after I got the paint, I drove one town over to Oak Bluffs and the liquor store.

April prepares her green traffic light & the World thinks Go.

Christopher Morley

Most of the Island ~ including Vineyard Haven, where I lived ~ had been "dry" for almost 200 years, meaning no alcohol and no bars. I'd never heard of a "dry town," but the bartender at the Kelley House explained it to me. It wasn't against the law to drink alcohol in a dry town; you just couldn't buy it. Only two of the six Island towns ~ Edgartown and Oak Bluffs ~ had bars and liquor stores (euphemistically called "package stores," probably part of the unwritten New England code of privacy). Either you got your "package" there or not at all.

*O*f you were in a restaurant in a dry town and wanted a drink with dinner, it was legal to bring your own. People literally brought ice chests full of packages to restaurants. That took some getting used to. I felt so guilty the first time I walked into a restaurant carrying a bottle of wine. And if you didn't drink it all, you could take the open bottle home in the car with you! SO illegal in California. In addition, all Island package stores were closed on Sundays, period. People had to be organized or they were sure to run out on a Sunday; so they bought their packages in bulk. This was where basements began to make sense.

I found everything I needed and was driving back from Oak Bluffs to Mardell's Hallmark Shop in Vineyard Haven to pick up price tags for the yard sale I was planning, when I noticed that the world was starting to look like an Easter card.

VIEW FROM STEAMER ON ARRIVING 25
AT OAK BLUFFS, MASS

Old Island postcards, other than the clothes, nothing much had changed.

The white ferry, the turquoise sea, the bright blue sky, the yellow forsythia and masses of pink cherry blossoms hanging over white picket fences were a breath of fresh air.

The young leaves unfurling on the trees were the most vivid green I'd ever seen. Blankets and quilts flapped from clotheslines amid crowds of daffodils, their frilly heads bobbing in the breeze. I rolled down the window and turned up Patti Page singing, "If you're fond of sand dunes and sal-tee air, quaint little villages, here and there, oooo-oooo you're gon-na fall in love with old . . . Cape . . . Cod . . ." I passed two women walking on the side of the road, arms folded, heads bent together in conversation and both wearing flowered aprons with sweaters over them. After the barren gray of winter, it was uplifting to see every-thing looking so cheerful.

But listen to me. For one moment quit being sad. Hear blessings dropping their blossoms around you. ❋ R u m i

It just got better and better.

Main Street in Vineyard Haven was bustling with painters on ladders and shop owners with buckets and squeegees, washing store win-dows, sweeping sidewalks and planting window boxes. The hundred-year-old linden tree in the middle of town was still bare of leaves, church bells played "America the Beautiful" while the storeowners did their spring cleaning. I thought that if I had been there in 1935, the same thing would have been going on, since it didn't seem like anything had changed very much since then. Everyone was getting ready for Memorial Day weekend, the official start of the tourist season ~ and also, if I may say so, the perfect time for a yard sale.

Martha's Vineyard Island

Main Street Looking North, Vineyard Haven, Mass.   98610-N

Only the cars had changed.

I had put an ad for my yard sale in the paper, and on the designated Saturday morning it was a breezy 57 degrees, with wispy clouds flying across the sky. I left the door of my house open for the fresh air while I laid Agnes's things on blankets on the lawn ~ happy that her belongings would go to people who had use for them.

ars pulled into the driveway and parked on the side of the road. People wandered around, picking things up, asking questions, and making small talk. Little by little, they carted away boxes of canning jars, Melmac plates, an electric can opener, a food scale, the fishing poles and waders and two broken but mendable lamps. The books, magazines, and town reports were of great interest to an older man in red suspenders who turned out to be my neighbor. He lived in the house I could just barely see through the trees on the other side of the garden.

He introduced himself as Myron Thompson. Myron was about my grandmother's age, with bristly salt-and-pepper hair, deep laugh lines, a strong, stocky build, and those red suspenders that, I found out later, were almost his trademark. We stood visiting under the oaks in the dappled driveway, interrupted every so often so that I could make change for people from my shoebox cash register.

Myron swept his arm across all the paper things: Agnes's books and magazines, the town records, and the sheet music; he wanted it all. He said he could resell it in the used bookstore he operated in his barn next door.

He said he was glad to see lights at the house again and welcomed me to the neighborhood. He told me in a sweet, non-gossipy way that Agnes had been a bit of a recluse in her later years, and since she'd gone to the nursing home, Holly Oak had been dark. He said if I ever needed anything, I was to feel free to call. He was very nice. We talked about the change in the weather; I mentioned I had tried to open my bedroom windows for the first time that morning "But the windows in the house don't open," I said. "There's glass instead of screen."

He glanced at the house with a quizzical look, then back at me, his expression cleared and he laughed, "You must not be from around here," his brown eyes smiled over the gold-rimmed glasses perched halfway down his nose. "They're storm windows, you take them off in the summer and put them on in the winter."

"Ohhhh, storm windows, what will they think of next?" I laughed. We went inside and he showed me how they worked. He told me to look in the basement because the glass in the aluminum door was removable. You replace the glass panels with screens and your storm door becomes a screen door! Brilliant!

When he said goodbye, his hand felt warm and workman-rough, and safe, like my dad's hand. It occurred to me I might like to crawl into it for a long nap. He said, "Come over and meet my wife. Come tomorrow at four for tea."

Tea! In someone's house! Although I spoke to friends and family every single day to stay connected and to keep from being too lonely, it wasn't the same as face-to-face visiting. Plus I loved seeing other people's houses.

So, the next day, excited to be going somewhere, I eagerly knocked on Myron's kitchen door. A dog barked. I heard a woman's voice say, "Shhhhh, no, Peggy, get back." The door opened and a pair of pink cheeks beneath a shock of white hair peeked out. "Susan?" sparkled the blue eyes. "Come in, dear, we're expecting you."

I already loved it that she called me "dear." She spoke with a British accent, introducing herself as Ellie. She nodded to her little Corgi dog. "And this wee beastie is Peggy."

Ha-ha, wee beastie!

Peggy was very excited, wagging her behind, and smiling up at me. Ellie said, "Pay her no mind. She'll settle down as soon as she gets used to you." Pointing to a kitchen chair, she invited me to sit while she made tea.

Peggy was short and wide, like a little hassock, with melting brown eyes. She was apparently *thrilled* to see me and the feeling was mutual. Her dog tags jangled while I rubbed her head with both hands, played with her ears, and scratched under her chin. She went away for a moment, came back and dropped a soft red ball at my feet and stood there bouncing on her two front feet staring at the ball, then up at me. I picked it up and rolled it toward the end of the room.

Ellie twinkled her blue eyes at me and said, "Oh, my, you'll be sorry you did that."

Ellie was little and round and wearing a long brown cable-knit cardigan, a plaid flannel skirt, and yellow wool socks with fleecy leather clogs. She filled a kettle with water and while I played with Peggy, my eyes flitted around her and the kitchen ~ taking everything in, the flickering fire in the woodstove, the birds' nests and shells on the windowsills, the unpolished copper pots stacked on a dresser, the row of old cookbooks with notes sticking from the tops of them, a bouquet of drooping red tulips. She fit three cups into saucers and began spooning loose tea into a blue crock teapot. Of course she would make tea the real way, I thought, because she's English, remembering the afternoon tea I had in London.

I felt a little thrill when my eye was drawn to a black and white cat stretched out over the edge of one of the small stuffed chairs next to the woodstove. The wee beastie had trotted over to give the cat a sniff; it drew back a little and that's when it caught my eye.

"Peggy, leave Gwinnie alone." Myron came into the room carrying a newspaper he tossed on the table and sat down.

Starved for cat fur, I asked if I could pet Gwinnie (full name: Guinevere), and Myron said, "By all means, yes, she loves people" and Ellie added, "She's very fat. She's going to have kittens." (She pronounced it kit-tins.)

While I rubbed my hand through Gwinnie's fur, (and Peggy's too because she started to get anxious) I told them about Pooh, my precious four-year-old yellow gopher-killer. They were very impressed. I explained to them that she was in California, but I was going out to get her in a couple of weeks.

They asked how I liked the Island so far, and I said, "It's soooooo different. Where I'm from in California, there aren't

79

seasons like here." I looked over at Myron, "I like it much better now that I know I can open my windows." He laughed and explained my window predicament to Ellie. I shook my head saying, "Whew! That was a close one."

Ellie poured our tea and gave us dishes of "treacle cake," which I'd never heard of, but it was delicious, like gingerbread. She said it was something from her childhood where she grew up in the north of England.

Myron was born on the Island. He'd been stationed in England during WWII ~ he and Ellie met at a dance, fell in love and were married. When the war was over they came back to the Vineyard to live. Just like my girlfriend Janet's English mom Maisie! She was a war bride too! I told Ellie about Maisie and how she was the one that taught me to love tea. (No, she didn't know her; that would have been asking too much!)

I told them I'd come to the Island alone, but I didn't get into why, and they kindly let that part slide and didn't ask. We talked about birds (my excitement about the cardinals), Peggy, Agnes, cooking, London, the growth of the Island and how much busier it looked to them these days, and I got a little tour of Myron's bookstore. I was thrilled to have a bookstore next to my house!

After I left Ellie and Myron's ~ their darling pets and the comfort of their cozy home ~ I walked back through the blueberry bushes, and opened my own front door, and my empty house with the funky green walls had all the charm of a prison cell. But I was going to change that. The next day I started painting my dishwater-green living room walls with Benjamin Moore's "Snow White." It would be like a clean slate.

"Truly, you should thank the storm fairies," said Father Time, "for had you not been wrecked upon this island, never would you have discovered the lost half hour." ♥ Henry Beston

Chapter Four

You Can't Always Get What You Want

So long as I know what's expected of me, I can manage.
♥ Frances Hodgson Burnett *The Secret Garden*

The days flew, and soon my three months of self-imposed exile were over. I had to go home, wanted to go home, to see how things were, pack, and, most likely, get Pooh ready for the trip back. I wasn't 100 percent sure because I didn't feel firmly attached anywhere at that moment.

Her cat was constantly with her, & ran after her wherever she went, and even sat up proudly by her side when she drove out in her fine glass coach. ♥ The Brown Fairy Book

I felt much better than I did at Christmas, only six months before, when Diana had to come rescue me from possible drowning in tears, but I was still wobbly and struggling to understand how I got to this place, still questioning what I had done wrong and I was VERY homesick. I missed my people.

Going back was both thrilling and scary, a jumble of up and down emotions. I'd get to see my friends, which made my heart leap with excitement, I couldn't wait. But I also assumed I'd be seeing Cliff for the first time in three months, which made my stomach feel hollow and my hands clammy. My mind kept asking the unhealthy and obviously unstable, "What if he wants to get back together?" The future seemed so undetermined (at least to me), so weirdly difficult, like flying blind into an abyss ~ the past was awful, but at least it was known. I'd lived through it. The future was scary. Anything could happen.

Myron said they'd keep an eye on the house and even though I said I could call a cab, he insisted on driving me to the ferry.

Memorial Day had passed, the summer season had officially begun and everything was different. Wisteria dripped from porches and the perfume blew into our windows as we drove by. A car with New York plates came toward us, the wrong way on a one-way street, Myron pulled over to let the guy go by and muttered "chowderhead" under his breath, which made me laugh. No one in California said chowderhead. The harbor was crowded with sailboats. I stood on the top deck of the ferry, leaned on the rail, and

watched as we pulled away from the dock. It was a warm breezy June day, the air smelled like ocean and cut grass. The sea was smooth and flat and spangled like diamonds. I watched the church spires, the little shore houses, and the lighthouse slide by, writing in my diary, "Strange to be leaving, almost sad, I love this place. But I can't wait to get home."

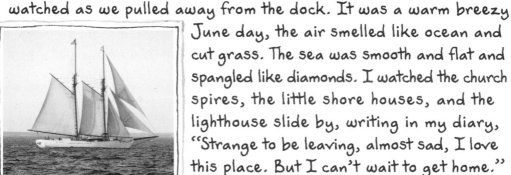

THE SUMMER WIND CAME BLOWING IN FROM ACROSS the SEA...
Frank Sinatra

I took the bus back to Boston and got my lucky seat on the plane ~ always the last in the back because I'd heard the tail was the safest part. I didn't know why they said that; it all went up together. When a wing snapped off in midair, what difference would it make where you were sitting? But still, no one ever heard of a plane _backing_ into a mountain.

With ear-piercing help from Stevie Nicks ("Oooo baby, ooo baby, oo-oo") I once again survived the impossible moment when the jets were screaming and the wheels were barely off the ground ~ jagged, chinky, stabbing metal parts and flammable fuel suspended in midair.

Cliff used to try to explain how planes fly. Trying to control his exasperation with my "unreasonable," "illogical" fear, he lectured me about air pressure, speed, lift, engine thrust, and so on. He said if I was "rational" about the whole thing (which I would never be) I would realize that I was more likely to be killed slipping in the shower. I also heard the excruciatingly boring argument about how driving on the freeway is more dangerous than flying. Cars don't fall out of the sky from 40,000 feet, thank you very much. I rest my case.

83

You can't go home again

The best part about being home again (after seeing my cat!) was the first night at Diana's with just the girls. We all ran into each other's arms, happy and excited to be together. Everyone brought delicious food and we sat in a circle, poured wine, and caught up with each others' lives, admired each others' bracelets, earrings, shoes and haircuts ∼ talked about movies, music, men, money, books, the new vitamin, the new exercise, the new diet. Then we turned up the music and danced.

They brought presents for my new house. Liz made me the most adorable quilted potholders and Janet gave me a bucket filled with tools, nails, and the perfect sized hammer. There were towels, candles, and sexy underwear "For whoever comes next." The cards were funny, with messages like, "Men who don't understand women fall into two groups: married or bachelors" and this one from Lorrie: "I'd tell you to kiss my ass, but I'm pretty sure you'd fall in love and then I'd never get rid of you." Uncontrolled laughter was more evidence of the bad influence we were on each other.

My month-long visit started out fun but went downhill quickly.

Everyone's lives had gone on, only I was available to play day and night, my friends had places to go and people to see; nothing had changed except that I wasn't really a part of it anymore. I tried to be my old self ∼ I didn't want anyone to worry about me.

Shell, Me, Donna, Janet, Marguerite, Kip, Nancy

The first couple of weeks there was lots of partying, wine with lunch, and late nights dancing, but it got old fast, being a happy party girl, there was no future in it, and after a while, nothing, other than my cat, seemed real. I felt like I was pretending to be someone I wasn't. It was exhausting, as living a false life always is and I was falling back into depression. I might have looked normal but what no one could see was that my heart was strung together with duct tape and kite string. And a couple of staples.

Cliff didn't call and I sure wasn't calling him. People commented on the breakup, said they guessed it wasn't meant to be, said I was too good for him anyway, said things always work out for the best. They were trying to be nice, and I was nice back, but I didn't want to hear it. After all, I'd spent almost all my adult years in that relationship.

I could see everyone thought it was over. I felt panicky at the finality of what I had done, buying that house. Perverts began crawling out of the woodwork. The husband of one of my friends, and supposedly my friend too, called and woke me up at 2 a.m. because he was "worried" about me. He sounded drunk. In conversation he mentioned that, "Kimmi must be doing everything right." Sending another arrow to my heart. Then he asked if he could come over. I felt sick. I wished I'd never come home. I wrapped my arms around Pooh and cried myself to sleep.

IF YOU LIKE THE WAY THINGS ARE GOING, JUST KEEP DOING WHAT YOU'RE DOING.

DUDE

I was always aware that Cliff and Kimmi were lurking nearby. Sometimes I'd see his car parked in town, so I was sort of hiding and watchful; I really didn't want to see them together. I did my best when Cliff finally called and dutifully took me to see his mom, but he was remote and had other things on his mind. Nothing had changed. I felt small and awkward. I tried to fill the silences with happy talk, still trying to be what I thought he wanted, and his mom just looked sad.

The broken heart. You think you will die, but you just keep living, day after terrible day. ♥ Charles Dickens

One night I dreamed I was kneading bread in my old kitchen on the hill and Julia Child came in and told me I was doing it wrong. I knew she would never say something like that, but I woke up feeling absolutely lost.

I half-heartedly shopped for things for Holly Oak. At an antique store in Cambria I found cotton cutwork tablecloths I thought I could make into bedroom curtains. In the pet section of Riley's Department Store on Higuera, I bought an airline-approved carrier to take Pooh home. I also went to the vet and got some "kitty Valium" to make it easier for her (I was pretty sure Pooh would feel the same way about flying as I did, she was a very smart kitty).

And I started packing for the movers. I put one foot in front of the other, marching in the direction of I didn't know what, feeling like I didn't belong anywhere anymore.

Calm yourself. The world won't end today— it's already tomorrow in Australia. ♥

About halfway through the visit, two weeks before I was scheduled to go back to the Island, I was lying on the couch with cold teabags on my eyes, thinking this rock and roll life was going to kill me, waiting for Diana to get there because we were going out (again), when the phone rang.

It was Cliff. I sat up and tried to sound awake and happy.

"Hey, I was just thinking," Cliff said. "Do you want our kitchen table? I'm getting a new one."

Another nail in the goodbye coffin, the oak table was dismissed. He was probably getting one made of steel and glass. "Sure, I can use it. How do I get it? Shall I ask my brother to pick it up?" My heart was suddenly doing that thing it did before I had an anxiety attack, as if it were trying to gulp air.

"Don't worry, I'll get the guys to bring it over. The chairs too. We'll put it all in your garage."

"That's perfect, if you can get it here by the fifth," I heard my-self droning, "That's when the movers come." I was rummaging through kitchen drawers looking for a paper bag to breathe into.

"No problem."

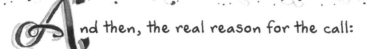

And then, the real reason for the call:

"Also, it's all set," he said. "We sign divorce papers on Thursday. Can you be at David's office at 10 a.m.? Or, better, come at 9:30 so we can talk."

Gulp. Grasp counter. "What?"

The thing squeezing my heart came up and lodged in my throat. OK. Breathe. Suck in stomach, blow out air . . . "You mean, tomorrow?"

I was shaking my head no, no. I didn't expect it and I wasn't ready, but I wasn't going to tell him.

I didn't want to hear him say "Relax" or "Calm down." Or worse, I really didn't what to hear him say, "Because I don't love you." I knew it, but I didn't need to hear it.

I just echoed his words and said, "No problem."

I didn't want him to know how this conversation was affecting me . . . In fact, I didn't want this person to know anything. About me. Ever. Again.

Might as well get a divorce. Why the *hell* not?

To see my future permanently going down in flames with no replacement (that I could think of), that was the problem.

I guess I knew it was coming. I should have, but everything was moving so fast. From the beginning of this fiasco I never felt like I had time to put my thoughts in order. I couldn't understand why he was always in such a big hurry. I guessed it was

88

business. No loose ends. I tried to keep up with everything, I ran as fast as I could, but it left me breathless, face down in the dust of the past, while he was on a rocket ship to the moon.

The next day, I met Cliff at his lawyer's office and he told me what the divorce settlement would be. He encouraged me to take it so we didn't have to go to court, which he assured me, would not be a fun experience. I agreed with no argument. I was not a court person ∼ it takes a kind of patience for paperwork and sitting around listening to unbearably huge quantities of BS, that I don't have, and, besides, what he was offering was fine as far as I was concerned. We'd been together for 10 years but only married for four and I had this gut feeling of not wanting anything more from him.

After getting direction from Cliff I went to another office and met with the lawyer I'd chosen from the list Cliff had pro- vided. This guy (wearing a shiny suit) didn't like the deal and "formally" advised me not to sign the papers because he thought I "deserved a bigger settlement." After all, he said pointedly, Cliff had taken the best years of my life.

He was the perfect example of why I could not hang out in divorce-world one second longer than was absolutely necessary. I could not have borne having to speak with this person on a regular basis. This needed to be our last meeting.

I took a deep breath and said, "I'm fine with the settlement the way it is. Cliff has always been generous, more than fair." I knew if we went to court this lawyer would push me to the bitter end to get every cent he could, he'd probably manipulate us into

89

fighting, because he'd be getting half of whatever Cliff gave me. I didn't like *him* much more than I didn't like Cliff. I didn't want to play his game and I didn't want *him* to have any of Cliff's money.

How did he know which were my best years?

"Are you sure?" he pushed.

I just looked at him.

"Well, then," he was resigned, I could tell I was breaking his heart, "you'll have to sign this letter saying I warned you. This will protect me in case you change your mind later."

I rolled my eyes at the idea of me protecting him and signed his silly weird space-taker-upper. I wondered how long that piece of paper would stay in his files.

A few minutes later we were all sitting at a long conference table and I was praying no one could see my eyelid, which had suddenly started twitching about a hundred miles a minute. While I blinked to disguise my newest deformity, the lawyers and secretaries shuffled papers, put them in front of me to sign, page after page, which I did with exactly the same cunning and acumen as when I bought my house.

The lawyers divided us up, turning our 10 years together into nothing more than legalese with dollar signs: Cliff, party of the first part, would get the house and contents, we would each keep our cars; I could have my clothes and jewelry (oh, yes, all figured into the cost of the settlement. No one mentioned *his* clothes, not that it mattered as score was not being kept). I asked if I could have the Christmas decorations and he waved them away with a careless, "Fine, yes." I also asked for and got my Cuisinart pots and pans. I had already removed Shirley Temple, Beatrix Potter, and the quilts.

I rubbed my eye trying to settle it down, but it was more than that. No way was I going to cry in front of these people. I even joked, as if I did this every day, and it didn't hurt a bit. All this I did on the outside of my body, watching it like a movie, feeling my eyes well up with tears at the sad ending, thinking "Don't you dare ~ Dare ~ DARE cry."

Walking back to my car, the fake smile dropped off my face. Any idea of reconciliation was gone; the decision had never been mine to make. It was over when he said it was over. I just needed to get to the car. I felt a hundred years old. I had to watch how I walked or I would trip and fall down. Only one more day, I thought, and Cliff and I would have made our fourth wedding anniversary.

DEAD as a DOORNAIL. — Wm. Shakespeare

* * *

"How'd it go?"

Diana was waiting in the kitchen when I got home. She handed me a glass of wine. Next to her was a pink bakery box filled with chocolate éclairs. Lunch.

91

"How'd it go?" I repeated. "Just like you'd think. Horrible. Buncha' men yukking it up, doing business, long table, black leather swivel chairs, wall of law books. We were all in there together: me, my lawyer, his assistant, Cliff, his two lawyers ~ and two secretaries. It was like a party ~ or a wake. See this? Can you see my eye?"

I always felt lucky to have my own private nurse.

"No, what?" she held my forehead with her hand and peered into my eye. "Hold still."

"Look, right there, see how it's jumping up and down? What is that? Is that a tic?"

"Oh yeah, I see it. Yup, it's a tic. It's stress. You need a nap."

"I need a year's nap. They shoved papers at me. I just signed them all and got the hell out of there. I didn't even read them."

"So does that mean you're divorced?"

"I guess."

"Oh, you poor thing." She put her arm around me. "There is something wrong with a world in which he gets a new girlfriend, and you get a tic. Let's go out back and sit in the sun."

"Aren't I too young to have a tic?"

"No, anyone can get one."

"Will it go away? Do I have it forever now?"

So out to the weedy overgrown backyard of the rental house we went to do what we did best, lie on chaise lounges in the sun and drink wine. I was drowning my sorrows and trying to relax my tic while tanning, and Diana was being funny and making me laugh. We were stuffing our faces with chocolate éclairs and Gewürztraminer and trying to figure out why, when people kiss in the movies, some of them open their mouths really big (overly big) since, to us, this would activate the gag reflex, when Jeanie, a neighbor and one of our Tuesday Girls, came around the side of the house and through the gate.

She had a terrible look on her face. I could see something was wrong. Gently, because she knew how miserable I already was, she asked, "Have you seen your kitty?"

Her expression was telling me something; my heart stopped in mid-beat. The tic picked up speed.

"Noooooo?" It was a question. Pooh hadn't been home for two nights. I'd been walking the streets, calling for her, and then from the car ~ but no luck. I was going to check the shelter but then the divorce happened and I got sidetracked. Shelly said she had never disappeared while I was away. I thought Pooh might be lost; this was still a strange neighborhood for her, not her real home. She was probably mad at me for being gone so long. Then a different thought crossed my mind; she had felt a little thin. I looked up at Jeanie and held my breath.

"Well . . ." Jeanie paused. "I hate to say this . . . but I think maybe your kitty . . . is . . . dead ~ near the side of the house."

I got up, my vision blurred with tears, and followed Jeanie until I saw what she'd seen. My little yellow kitty was dead in the bushes next to the house. I felt my heart drain out onto the lawn.

Pooh was the solid self I'd been depending on, the rare thing I felt sure of and now she was gone. I went inside and got a dish towel to put over her.

"You should call Cliff!" the girls urged, with tears in their eyes. "He will want to know."

Of course, he would want to know, I thought ~ forgetting that, actually no, he probably wouldn't want to know.

The phone was on the grass between us; it had an extra-long cord that came through the house all the way from the living room to the yard. I picked it up and walked back inside carrying it. As I did I dialed Cliff's number even though I knew he didn't like to be bothered at work. I held the phone in one hand, the receiver to my ear in the other, and wandered around the house staring off at nothing while we talked.

"Can you come over?" I was choking back tears.

Things were really not going well.

"Now? Not really, I'm busy. The lawyers already took up my whole morning. How 'bout later?"

The divorce had interrupted his day. "It's always later. I need you now. It's important." All words he loved to hear.

"OK, you have my total attention, tell me what's going on." Silence. "Wait, hold on for a moment."

I waited, basking in his total attention. I wandered into the bathroom, looked at my hideous self in the mirror, and went back out to the sofa.

He was back. "OK, what's up?"

"Well," I started haltingly, "we just found Pooh dead at the side of the house." I wanted to add "and it's all your fault," but I didn't because I knew whose fault it was. It was my fault. I'm the one who left her here.

Deep breath of Why me? on other end of phone. "Dead? What happened? Was she sick?"

"I don't know, I didn't think she was sick, but she's . . ." sob, "all stiff there." I fell onto the couch.

His voice was distracted; he was busy. "Calm down. What do you want me to do?"

There is nothing more upsetting than being told to calm down for no reason when you have just discovered your kitty has died. I wasn't even screaming. "Can you please come get her? Can we bury her in the backyard at the house?" I asked, hunched over, elbows on knees, head down, looking at the floor.

"Okaaaaay." He knew he couldn't get out of it ~ just one more wretched thing to ruin his day. Poor guy. He was a very busy man. Cat issues had been my area of responsibility.

"Uh, when?" He was resigned to the situation. "Now?"

"Yes, now would be good. I can't just leave her there. I can't bury her at this strange house." I couldn't bury her at all, because I was not a cat burier.

"OK, I'm coming. I'll be there in a few minutes."

I went back out to the girls and drained my wine glass.

"Do you want us to stay?" asked Diana.

"No, it's okay. I love you. Don't worry. I'll be fine. Shelly will be home soon. I'll call you later." There was nothing anyone could say or do that would make this day better.

After hugging them goodbye, I went inside to wash my face and change my clothes. Thirty-five years old and I looked like the last person to leave the bar. I was brushing my hair back into a ponytail when I heard Cliff's car pull into the driveway.

While he went to look at Pooh, I found a pillowcase I'd embroidered with the words "Sweet Dreams" and took it outside. Cliff gathered Pooh's lifeless body into it and put her in the little space behind the driver's seat of his car. I started to get into the front seat, but he stopped me.

SWEET DREAMS

"You better bring your own car," he said "I have a meeting this afternoon."

Of course he did. What was I thinking?

The fairies looked at him & all
shook their heads at once.
The Brown Fairy Book

Like some short, miserable little funeral procession, I followed him out to the house, remembering the times we used to race each other home, laughing and happy and about 30 years younger.

Cliff dug the grave and we buried our little yellow kitty in the backyard of our dream house at the top of the hill under the oak trees where we'd been married that beautiful June day a lifetime ago.

I don't know how he stood there while I was silently sobbing, hearing the bell toll on the vows we'd taken on that exact spot. While Cliff looked on, I took some catmint from the garden I'd expected to tend for 50 years and planted it, along with my tears, above Pooh. I stood back, wiped my hands on my jeans ~ and that was that. We were divorced, our kitty was dead and buried; it was all over. There was nothing left for me to do but go.

I didn't say anything and Cliff didn't look at me. I turned and clumped back down the hill that looked out over the valley, past my house of broken dreams, past my vegetable garden and my rose bushes, past my orchard filled with blooms, whose roots were going to have to grow deeper without me there to help. Cliff just let me go. I got into my car, drove down the winding driveway, and saw my life disappear in the rearview mirror.

♪ ... And now I must confess, I could use some rest, I can't run at this pace very long... Jimmy Buffett ♫

Pooh's death was so awful it actually put me back on track. I only had to hold on ~ in this town where every street was a memory ~ for 10 more days. Then the movers would come and I could go. Because I finally knew, I was definitely going.

I counted the minutes and each one was an eternity. I quit going out at night and got some rest. I started pushing myself up San Luis Mountain every day; sometimes Mary and Shelly came with me. I went to the beach with my book and Diana. Things weren't going well between her and Paul. She didn't know what to do about it, and we commiserated.

I made lists and put my things into piles. I polished my pots and pans, wrapped dishes in newspapers and packed everything ～ my Marilyn Monroe telephone, my diaries and photo albums, boxes of books and my Fred Astaire albums ～ Tommy Dorsey, Doris Day, Shirley Temple, Frank Sinatra, Jimmy Buffett, Edith Piaf, Dan Hicks, and Patsy Cline, my Brazilian music ～ I wasn't about to leave those behind. One lucky thing about breaking up with Cliff: we never fought about whose albums were whose.

For the 400th time I thought, Why am I leaving home? Then I remembered. I was being pushed from behind, like the way a strong wind blows you down a road sometimes.

Cliff came over to say goodbye, all business, but still concerned about me in his own way. He said he'd take care of selling my car for me.

No house, no phone number, no address, no kitty, and now no car. Pretty soon it would be like I never existed in this town.

On the bright side, he'd brought along a chart that showed how I should budget my money. If I was careful and didn't "do anything stupid," and maybe "got myself a little job," it was his matter-of-fact opinion that I'd be okay until I figured out what I wanted to do.

Holly Oak would be paid for by the settlement so I wouldn't have a mortgage, and he offered to keep me on his insurance until I got settled and we'd finalized the divorce. He had it all figured out except for the part that didn't include him. I was kind of numb to what he was saying; nothing made sense and I couldn't for a moment be sure that I wouldn't do something stupid. When he left I went to the kitchen and threw his little chart into the trash.

I wasn't entirely brain dead. I realized many women had it much worse than me with children to raise and bills to pay and no help at all. I was lucky; I was going to get to start over relatively gracefully ~ but at that moment all I could think about was that I'd lost everything, including, most likely considering my age and the situation, my chance to have children. I couldn't see myself running out and getting attached to someone else. I probably wasn't feeling as grateful as I would someday, when it no longer hurt. One thing on my side, I had lived alone and provided for myself just fine before I met Cliff, and even during the time I knew him, and I had no doubt that I could do it again.

So every morning I spit in his coffee.
He doesn't know. I feel better;
everyone's happy.
Author unknown

The clocked ticked forward. I couldn't wait to get back to the little house on the Island.

The moving van arrived, was loaded up and drove away with everything I owned. It was finally time to say goodbye. I cried with my sisters and friends and understood exactly why cats instinctively hide themselves when they are sick and dying.

Saying goodbye to Shelly

Then I went to the airport and flew away.

The ocean is filled with tears,
& the sea turns into a mirror...
Tom Waits

Do what you can with what you
have, where you are.

Chapter Five
JUST LIKE STARTING OVER

In the evening she came to a large forest, & she was so tired from sorrow & hunger & from the long walk that she climbed into a hollow tree & fell asleep.

Brothers Grimm

Martha's Vineyard Island

Shore Front, Vineyard Haven, Mass.

98614-N

Summer 1982

When I arrived back on the Island, spring had turned to summer. I'd missed the Fourth of July, but the sidewalks were packed with flip-flop-wearing tourists in shorts eating ice cream cones. Trees hung over the roads dappling everything with bright yellow splotches of sunshine and shimmering green shadows. Hydrangeas bloomed and roses tumbled over arbors and walls.

I asked the cab driver to wait for me while I ran into Cronigs to get milk and butter, cheese, bread and eggs, apples, Stouffer's chipped beef on toast and mini crumb donuts, things to get me by. The driver pulled into my driveway. My yard had been abandoned for too long, the yellowish grass was short and weedy and needed help.

Cottage: A small single house typically situated near a lake or beach. *Oxford Dictionary*

I unlocked my front door, relieved to be there, dropped my bags on the empty living-room floor, opened all the windows to get the month-long closed-up-house smell out, put away the groceries, and threw myself on the bed ～ glad I made it back alive, sick at heart not to have Pooh.

And that's where I stayed, becoming one with the mattress, watching dust motes float in the sunrays coming through the windows, from that other world, the dangerous one, outside.

It took me another week to get out of my bathrobe, and the only reason I did was because the moving van was coming and I had to get everything ready. I was just back from the market, unloading groceries from the car, when Myron called to me from his garden.

"Welcome home, Susan! Glad to see you back! When you get a minute, come over and say hello. Come see Gwinnie's kittens!"

Oh, Gwinnie. Kittens! I'd forgotten. Now that everything was in bloom I could see a path through the blueberries, past my fenced garden, to Myron and Ellie's house.

"How about now?" I called back. "I have something for Ellie. Just let me get it."

I didn't want to go over without a present. I went inside and grabbed the heart-shaped rock I'd found on the beach.

Myron came out of his garden and followed me up to the screen door where Peggy was wagging her hind end on the other side. Ellie was folding sheets and towels on the table; she stopped the minute she saw me. She reminded me of my Girl Scout leader, Mrs. Hutton, who taught me how to put on pillowcases without using my teeth.

"Welcome home!" She wiped her hands on her apron and hugged me. It was like hugging a baking powder biscuit. "How was your trip? I was worried we weren't going to see you again."

Her blue eyes shone with kindness. I would have collapsed in her arms, but I didn't know her well enough and didn't want to infringe . . . and she was so little I probably would have crushed her.

"I just had a lot to do back there. There's a moving van coming tomorrow or the next day, bringing my furniture and stuff." I pulled the heart rock out of my pocket. "I have something for you."

She put the rock on the little shelf over her sink next to the birds' nests and acorns.

"That was thoughtful of you, dear. Happy to have you back, good to see your lights on again. Are you all unpacked and settled in? How did your kitty do on the plane?"

"Uh," I gulped, hating to say it, "she didn't come." I glanced over at Myron. "A terrible thing happened. She died while I was at home. I guess she was sick. I think she missed me when I went away." Talking about it made eye contact difficult and I busied myself scratching Peggy's ears.

"Oh no. Oh, my dear, I'm so sorry." She bent over and put her arm around my shoulders. I fought back tears at her touch; I cannot tell you how sorry I felt for myself. Myron faded away into the other room.

"Awwww. Poor thing. It's true; cats don't do well with change. They like their routines."

"I'm sure that was it." Sniff. "She had too many changes. I didn't know, she was my . . . first kitty, she was ～" throat-catching "～ only four." Tears welled up and spilled over.

Ellie passed me a tissue, put her hand on my arm and said, "Come with me now, let's go see Gwinnie. Her kittens are five weeks old and the loveliest wee kittens there ever were. Come now, this will cheer you up." She didn't say kittens, she said kit-tins.

Peggy led the way, her toenails clicking on the wood floor, through the door at the far end of the kitchen. I followed behind Ellie, sniffling and asking, "How many kittens did she have?"

"Five ～ three males and two females."

Gwinnie was stretched out on the sofa keeping her eye on the big cardboard box under the window. Inside the box, five little kittens were in a jumble of motion ∼ pouncing on each other, falling over, rolling on their backs, licking their paws and washing their ears, chasing their tails ∼ little puff balls with round eyes, pink noses, and short whippy tails. Gwinnie jumped off the couch and into the box where she lay down and began to lick her babies while they climbed all over her.

I crouched down to see them, glancing up at Ellie, and already in love. "Oh, look how cute they are! Five weeks old?"

"Yes, they'll be ready to go next week." Myron was back; she looked over at him, then back to me. "Would you want one? Is it too soon?"

"Seriously?" My heart leaped, "I would love one." My hands reached out to touch them. "They aren't already spoken for?"

"No, not at all, dear. You can have your choice."

"Oh my . . . two? Can I have two? Can I have the two black-and-white ones?" I wished for a yellow one like Pooh, but there weren't any. The two black and white ones had not stopped playing together.

"Help yourself," said Myron. "Have as many as you like! Take 'em all! We'll enjoy having Gwinnie's babies living right next door! We'll be in-laws!"

My heart was overflowing with sudden happiness. There were no people I would rather have as in-laws.

Kittens! I would not have to sleep alone!
I picked them up, light and bony as little birds,
and held one to each cheek, one male and one
female. Their fur felt soft on my face, their pink
feet swam in midair as they struggled to get
away, making tiny mewing sounds. It was good
they weren't quite ready to go yet; it would be
better if I took them home after my furniture got here. I needed
to get a litter box, kitty food, and toys.

After the moving van had come and gone, when I was half unpacked
and there was the barest semblance of order, I went and got the
kitties ~ and that's when my life got better.

At first they were shy and careful, peeking around corners
and into closets to learn their new home. But soon they
started wrestling across the furniture and boxes, rolling off, jumping
back up, and coming at each other on hind legs like little bears,
and sleeping in a basket on the table wrapped in each other's arms.
I thought I might name them Jack and Jill, or maybe Dick and Jane.
I called home to tell Shelly about them and she suggested Dilly and
Pickles; Mary liked Cat and Mouse. Now I was confused. One
day I called them Dilly and Jilly, and the next, Pickles and Dick.

When I finished unpacking,
the stereo was hooked up,
quilts were folded, dishes were
stacked on the shelves and in the
cupboards, and my clothes were
crammed into the tiny closet ~
when nails had been pounded
into walls and pictures had been
hung, lamps were plugged in, and

Windowsills for all my little things,
but still no curtains

Getting the kitchen organized

Cheery kitchen window

My "new" stove

Hanging paintings over the
rejected oak table

my exercise bike was in
a prominent position in the
living room (soon becoming
a massive coat hook), I
went to the nursery.

bought a couple of large tomato plants with little green tomatoes already on them, some leggy basil, a zucchini plant ~ and three lemon thyme plants because they were perennials and would come back the next year. I tossed out a bag of fertilizer, dug holes in the weedy garden and planted everything. It was late, the middle of July, but I was hoping for some sort of little crop if I could. I bought an apple tree, too, and they sent a man out with it and he planted it at the end of the garden fence and then he spread fertilizer on the poor lawn. It was a start.

YOU CAN BURY A LOT of TROUBLES DIGGING IN THE DIRT.

The pieces of my new life were in place, all except one ~ and that came about two weeks later when I went, again, to what I fear must sound like my home away from home: the liquor store. Let's call it a package store, shall we? Much more dainty. There was a six-week-old yellow kitten in a box near the door with a sign on it that said, "Free." In California, Cliff had a limit on how many cats I was allowed, but there were no rules here. I knew the second I saw him, that little yellow kitten was mine.

The guy at the package store said his name was William T. Aristocat the Third (Get it? Aristocat?), so I called him Bill (also Billy, Bilster, Bilbo, Bil-kee). I had given up on creatively naming the other two; they now had easy-to-remember names, Girl Kitty and Man Kitty (aka Girlski, Man-kee, Miss Pie, Mr. Bo-Bo, etc., etc., etc.). So now we were four (counting me) and there was strength in numbers.

I sat on the front porch feeling lucky, leaning against the front door, writing in my diary while the kittens rolled all over everything, tumbled down the porch stairs, climbed back up, crawled up my chest making motorboat noises in my ear, climbed on my diary and attacked my pen while I was trying to write.

Girl   Bill   Man

I could make a life here, feed the birds, make potato pancakes, listen to old music with my feet on the coffee table, read my books and raise my kitties. I would live in New England and have seasons just like I always dreamed about. And this dream, no one could take away from me. Maybe I would even fall in love again someday. Probably not, from my vantage point it looked impossible, but stranger things had happened.

I've got the keys to my castle in the air but whether I can unlock the door remains to be seen. ♥ Louisa May Alcott

Hearts get broken all the time. People get over it, and I knew I would, too. It didn't happen quickly though. I would wake up at night longing for something that no longer existed, more than just Cliff or the marriage or even my old life, I mourned for the believing thing.

I took refuge in books and nurtured myself using the potato-pancake-and-old-movie cure. But sometimes I'd be eating my potato pancake and crying at some sad ending, and the kitties would do something funny. I'd laugh, then recognize I was laughing ~ and the laughing would turn back to tears. Between the potato, the laughing, and the crying there was a chance of choking. I would have to let the potato fall out of my mouth onto my robe because I really didn't want to have to perform the Heimlich maneuver on myself with a kitchen chair. It only happened twice. Don't tell anyone. I guess now you know I am capable of anything.

If you've never eaten while crying you don't know what life tastes like. ♥ Johann Wolfgang von Goethe

And while you are tasting life, it's better if it's a soft potato pancake and not beef jerky or caramels.

Potato Pancake

Word to the wise: If you are boiling potatoes to make a potato pancake, you might as well start with five potatoes, because one potato pancake is never enough. It's food of the gods, good for breakfast, lunch, dinner, tea and snack. Great at 2 a.m. if you can't sleep, eat one and you'll go right back to dreamland.

To serve one: Take about 1 1/2 c. of "leftover" mashed potatoes and form it into a nice firm little pancake. Dip it lightly in flour, or sprinkle it; just get some flour on it because it makes it crustier. Melt a chunk of butter in a small skillet, & slide in the potato. Cover the pan and cook slowly until well browned (the goal is crunchy on the outside, soft in the middle). Get it good and brown, turn it over, add more butter if necessary, and continue cooking until the other side is dark and crispy looking. Put the potato on a plate, salt it, pepper it, add another chunk of butter. (This is no time for dieting.)

Butter! Oh isn't butter divinity?
Amy in *Little Women*

I got a fork and my potato and dragged the phone to the green sofa, turned on the TV and looked for a good old movie to take me far away from my troubles, to an inspiring world of shipboard love affairs, satin dresses, romantic train rides, dancing, singing and witty repartee, charm, beauty and hope, pretty houses with wonderful curtains and even a little bit of history thrown in

Chick Flick Immersion

Fabulous OLD MOVIES
Guaranteed to Comfort & FORTIFY the BROKEN HEART

In no particular Order

The More the Merrier
Christmas in Connecticut
Suspicion
ROMAN HOLIDAY
Hobson's Choice
The Quiet Man
Indiscreet
PALM BEACH STORY
Top Hat
BACHELOR MOTHER
The Bishop's Wife (1947)
Mrs. Miniver
Margie
THE LADY EVE
Ball of Fire
1935 David Copperfield

TRUST ME ON THIS

Also works as antidote to disheartening news reports.

for good measure. My tissue box was on the floor next to me, handy for tears at the sad or happy endings. I fluffed my pillow and pulled my grandmother's nap blanket over my lap and the kitties would walk on me or nap on me. During commercials I'd write in my diary or call Diana or my mom.

Although the world is full of suffering it is also full of the overcoming of it. ♥ Helen Keller

I did pretty much nothing except get settled for the first month after I got back from California.

At night, I curled into the orange armchair I brought from home and read *West with the Night* (Beryl Markham's beautifully written account of her life growing up in Africa and her 1936 solo transatlantic flight) and underlined my favorite passages.

I read the Bartlett's book of quotes and put stars next to the ones I liked best.

I read one of the old books Agnes left in the house, *The Best of Stillmeadow*, and fell in love with the author, Gladys Taber, and her stories about her lovely life in a 17th century farmhouse in Connecticut.

111

It turned out that I wasn't the only person who loved watching birds. Taber's wise words smoothed the tattered edges of my soul because all the things she thought were important in life, I thought were important too.

As long as I have a window, life is exciting.
♥ Gladys Taber

I finally started to paint a new watercolor . . . of my kitchen stove. I painted with the doors and windows open for the breeze and I could hear bees buzzing past the windows and cows mooing up the road at Pilot Hill Farm.

I made dog cookies and took them over to the Thompsons to thank them for my new kitties and while I was there I met Carlton Sprague, a young carpenter and furniture-maker friend of theirs.

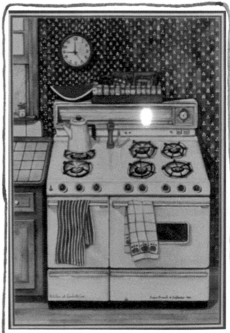

Had to make up the wallpaper and the counter but not much else. ♥

I began to wonder if we had birds in California ~

Why had I never noticed their singing before?

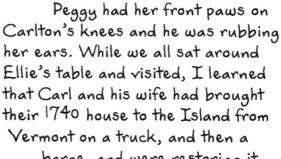

Peggy had her front paws on Carlton's knees and he was rubbing her ears. While we all sat around Ellie's table and visited, I learned that Carl and his wife had brought their 1740 house to the Island from Vermont on a truck, and then a barge, and were restoring it.

I almost felt bad when I asked him if he would put a greenhouse window in my kitchen, such a pitiful little job for a guy who moved a house, but he said sure, he'd come over and give me an estimate. I figured if I was going to live where there was winter, I was going to need an indoor place with light enough to grow something.

Every day I walked past the white horses in the meadow through the woods, under the trees, past the sparkling pond to the sea and the sailboats and the seabirds, where I looked at the sky and said, "Thank you, God."

Some days I would go before the fog had burned off, when it was still so thick and white that I could only see a few feet into the woods where trees and cottages were like ghosts in the mist.

Feed your soul with silence. That's where dreams are born.

113

With just the noise of my feet scraping pebbles on the dirt road, it was like walking in a dream. The sound of the foghorn echoing over the Island was otherworldly and hushed and I discovered this was exactly what I came here looking for.

AND IF YOU COULDN'T BE LOVED, THE NEXT BEST THING WAS TO BE LET ALONE. ♥ *L. M. Montgomery*

*   *   *

A month later, in August, my dad came and gave me something to think about besides myself. He packed his tools and drove his truck across country to the Island. He had married again, to a wonderful woman named Jeanie; she came with him, and they brought their little dog, Chief. I cleared some space and set up a makeshift bedroom in the attic.

Walking past the pond.

My dad went right to work, and spent his first week building a redwood deck, just off the kitchen door, with stairs going down to the lawn.

Then he tied a clothesline between the trees; I bought clothespins and hung our towels to dry in the air scented with ocean and pine and blueberry bush.

114

I made them oatmeal for breakfast with chopped apples, walnuts and cinnamon ～ and stuffed pork chops & sweet potatoes for dinner. For dessert I spread watermelon slices with sour cream & sprinkled them with brown sugar.

WE WERE VERY COZY. ♥

After the deck was finished, Dad and Jeanie wanted to see a little of New England, so I asked Ellie if she would feed the kitties while we were away which she seemed happy to do. We took my Honda onto the boat to the Mainland, and drove up to Lake Winnipesaukee in New Hampshire and found a little bed and breakfast in a farmhouse where they allowed dogs. It was a working farm next to a lake.

Billy

We visited the cows in the barn, ate blueberries and cream for breakfast, and prowled through shops and antique stores looking for old postcards and quilts.

And best of all, while we were there we went to a car dealership and my dad helped me trade

I STILL HAVE IT

in the Honda, which he wasn't wild about, for something he thought would be safer ~ a brand new, 1982, green Volvo sedan ($11,000) that drove like a tank and had been dipped in something called "Rusty Jones" (because in New England, something else new to me, cars rusted).

On the way home, we stopped in Plymouth to see the Mayflower and Plymouth Rock.

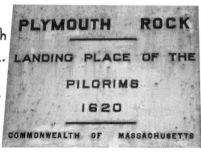

PLYMOUTH ROCK

LANDING PLACE OF THE

PILGRIMS

1620

COMMONWEALTH OF MASSACHUSETTS

We climbed the steep brick path at Burial Hill Cemetery and left flowers on the grave of William Bradford, my diary-writing ancestor. Boat whistles blew from the harbor below where we could see hundreds of big and little craft rocking at anchor. Church bells rang the hour, beech trees swayed and leaves whispered over crumbly old headstones leaning crookedly in the deep grass of this Colonial burial ground. Jeanie and I read the words and dates on the gravestones to each other out loud, trying to figure out who belonged to whom. My dad threw a stick among the stones, and Chief raced to retrieve it.

ll that history, I could feel it, the forgotten memories and shadows of days gone by . . . Someone putting a seashell on a windowsill, washing the face of a child, pulling a pie from the oven, made me think about how short a lifetime was and

about all the things that gave it meaning, and how, in my opinion anyway, the basic things about people, things of home and family really hadn't changed at all.

All we have to decide is what to do with the time that is given us.
♥ J.R.R.Tolkien

ack on the Island, we stopped at Nip and Tuck Farm and bought a glass bottle of cold fresh milk and drank it in the car on our way up to Menemsha where we celebrated my dad's 56th birthday on the beach at sunset, eating steamed lobsters with melted butter we bought at Poole's Fish Market and brought down to the water. We spread out on an old chenille bedspread and ate as the sky turned to pink then lavender and peach; sunrays streamed through the clouds and lit up every windowpane in the tiny cottages staggered along the hilly shore.

ince I was now the closest thing to a lobster-eating expert we had, I showed Dad and Jeanie how to use their teeth to bite the meat

out of the legs. We licked butter off our fingers as waves lapped on the sand flipping small shells and rocks, making tiny clicking noises as the water pulled away from shore. I almost expected to hear the sun sizzle when it touched the sea, creating rippling ribbons of crimson and sapphire as it slipped into the horizon . . . And when the last golden bit of it was gone, everyone on the beach applauded. I told my dad they were clapping for him ~ music to a Leo's ears. We drove home in my new car, not talking, with the windows down, the summer wind in our hair, the moon rising through the trees, and a tape of Patsy Cline singing "Tennessee Waltz," my dad's favorite song.

Look AT THAT MOON. POTATO WEATHER FoR SURE.
♥ Thornton Wilder, Our Town

I t was a wonderful visit. My dad, like Superman, coming to the rescue of his girl. He only told me how to live my life seven or eight times (and why not, I'd done such a good job of it so far), and ripping Cliff to shreds six ways from Sunday. At least my dad didn't, as in the old days, take my car away from me.

He hugged my shoulders, leaned his head to mine and asked what I was going to be when I grew up. Deep sigh, little voice, "I don't know, Dad."

He said, "Don't worry too much, grasshopper" (he got that from the 70s TV show, Kung Fu), "you'll figure it out."

A morning face only a father could love

But I wasn't sure. Not knowing felt like the huge, empty space of eternity. It had no end.

Watching their ferry pull away was hard. Dad and Jeanie stood up top waving until they were just specks and then they disappeared altogether. I wiped my tears & drove home. I went into my quiet house, kissed the kitties, did laundry, weeded and watered my tomatoes, turned on the music, and started cutting up the quilts I'd gotten in New Hampshire to make into curtains for the living room.

Dad on his new deck with Chief and Billy

August 11. 1982 Wed. 75° Overcast + rain. Dad + Jeanie left yesterday. And here I am. It'll be so lonely without you dear diary. The only good thing is that - in the silence - you hear birds sing.

In the quiet I realized I'd never lived alone in my life. I grew up in a house full of people. There'd always been family and best friends, roommates and coworkers, then the Tuesday Girls and Cliff, of course, and everything that had come with him: housekeepers, gardeners, the pool man . . . all those dinner parties and lunches with our friends. Now there was no one to cook for.

I was 35 and realizing for the first time that my sense of self had nothing to do with me and everything to do with the simplest of every- day routines in my old way of life: the lovely security I'd taken for granted, of the bed I woke up in every day, the guy I talked to when I took my clothes to the cleaners, the ladies at the supermarket, my favorite coffee shop, the route I took into town, the girls in the dress shop where I liked to shop, my house and the things I thought I owned . . . and most especially, the reflection I saw in the eyes of my parents, husband, and friends.

Without those things, I didn't know who I was. It was a complete surprise to find out I didn't take me with me when I left.

It gave a whole new meaning to starting over from scratch. The only thing I brought with me, the very thing I'd come to escape, was the sadness.

I had a little tea party
    This afternoon at three.
'Twas very small,
    Three guests in all,
    Just I, Myself & Me.

Myself ate all the sandwiches,
    While I drank up the tea;
'Twas also I who ate the pie
    And passed the cake to me.
        ♥ Jessica Nelson North

*   *   *

Cliff called to say he wanted us to be friends. It was just so that he could tell me how great Kimmi was, which he did, relentlessly. On top of that, he told me he was taking her to Paris. With Jim and Bev, (our friends) which, besides the fact that he was taking her to Paris, this was, of course, false advertising AGAIN since he hated to travel unless it was for business. I hung up on him. He would have to think of another way for us to be friends. That is if he ever thought at all, which I doubted.

Why is it that a woman
    can see from a distance
what a man cannot see close?
    ♥ Thomas Hardy

120

YOU HAVE TO BELIEVE WE ARE MAGIC, NOTHING CAN STAND IN OUR WAY... ♥ *Olivia Newton-John*

CHAPTER SIX

HYACINTHS *for the* SOUL

If, of thy mortal goods   thou art bereft,
& from thy slender   store two loaves
alone to thee   are left,
Sell one & from   the dole,
Buy hyacinths to   feed thy soul.

Sa'di, The Gulistan, 1258

In September, the blueberries ripened, and Diana came for her first visit to Martha's Vineyard. I knew her stay would go way too fast, and after she left, it would be fall and then winter and probably no one else would come until spring. I vowed to make this a great last hurrah.

I put purple asters and goldenrod (picked in the woods) next to her bed in the attic, and a book on her nightstand I knew she would love called *My Brilliant Career*. I made a few of her favorite things: a chocolate mousse pie, chocolate truffles, and chocolate-chip cookies, and brought home chocolate-covered almonds, ice cream and a can of Hershey's chocolate syrup. I made a big bowl of watermelon chunks and carrot and celery sticks for the health part of the visit, and a pan of cheese enchiladas because, after chocolate, she loved enchiladas best. I was getting my best victim back and I wanted it to be good. She needed to want for nothing.

KISS BORING GOOD-BYE!

On the way home from the airport, Diana asked me to stop at the liquor store so she could buy some beer. I explained the "dry town" situation, thinking she'd find it funny, but I said it too fast and she misunderstood.

"Is this a trick? I'm on vacation in a place where there's no alcohol? And you didn't tell me till now?" Her voice went up an octave with each word: "You might as well turn around and take me back to the airport."

I laughed, trying to get a word in "Don't panic, we have it, there's liquor, just not here. We have to go one town over to get it. There are bars and dance places and everything. It's totally normal here."

✳   ✳   ✳

Diana loved my little house. She called it a dollhouse and laughed when she asked, "What's the matter, couldn't you find anything smaller?" She liked that it had a name; no houses we knew of in California had names. She was happy with the nest I'd made for her in the attic. I told

"Good thing you didn't see this first." Diana

her about Agnes and brought her the baby book; we opened the little envelope so that I could show her the baby curls.

On her first morning, I was in the kitchen filling the kettle for tea when Diana came shuffling downstairs from her perch in the treetops, eyes half closed, hair in a tangle, face pillow-creased. She was up but not awake, and heading for the bathroom.

"Would you please tell those birds to shut up?" she mumbled, "How do you people sleep around here?"

DIANA

Ellie had invited us to "pop over" for tea, "elevenses," she called it, which, Ellie explained, was 11 a.m. tea in England. Like afternoon tea, only in the morning. She fed us berry trifle. Diana fell in love with Ellie, and with Myron and his red suspenders and his bookstore in the barn ～ and we both fell in love with elevenses.

I took Diana to all my favorite places that I knew about so far. We sang "She's Got Bette Davis Eyes" along with the radio on the ride up to Gay Head to watch the sunset. Singing in the car made us feel like we were 22 again. We talked to cute guys at the Square Rigger and danced until closing at the Hot Tin Roof.

We stopped at a farm stand called the Italian Scallion and got a pumpkin for the porch. We ate still-warm sugar donuts at Humphrey's Bakery (where we agreed that the screen door made the perfect summer-slamming noise), and bought zinnias in

Me, trying to juggle windfall apples in the Humphrey's driveway

the yard of the farmhouse next door where there were bouquets lined up in old coffee cans on a green-painted picnic table, with a sign that said "$4 each." We paid for the flowers using the honor system (choose your flowers, leave money and take your change from the shoebox provided).

We went to the Field Gallery so I could show Diana the whimsical dancing sculptures by a local artist, Tom Maley. We got a newspaper across the street at Alley's General Store, and spent the whole afternoon reading our books at Bend-in-the-Road Beach.

Of course, I wanted Diana to see my walk. We brought along some sugar cubes and fed them to the white horses out back, wondering out loud why they only had white horses and not brown or black ones and decided the white ones must be someone's idea of a fairy tale. We followed the beaten path around under the trees and through the woods ~ where a million spider webs, like tiny hammocks between twigs in the undergrowth, sparkled with dew ~ past cottontails diving into honey-suckle vines and Queen Anne's lace, to the pond. Out at the end, there was a thin layer of overcast that turned the sky a silvery blue

color, with just the palest apricot showing through openings in the clouds down near sea level. I was so proud of this place, as if it was all my idea, I loved showing it to her.

The woods were scattered with bright yellow goldenrod, and on our way back, under a sky the color of doves, I pulled bags from my pockets and we filled them with all the blueberries and huckleberries we could find. Not only were there wild blueberry bushes in my yard, I'd discovered they also lined the road ~ what we didn't eat while picking we brought inside, spread on cookie sheets and froze for winter.

We found this tiny sand castle on the beach.

Diana had broken up with Paul just after I left and was dating someone new. The whole time we were out there we hashed over the new guy, and of course, the past, the good, the bad, and the ugly, but mostly we just laughed.

During a rainstorm, which Diana reveled in because there was never any weather in California, especially in the summer, we sat facing each other at each end of the sofa, cross-legged with bed pillows on our lap, our diaries on the pillows, our teacups on the book-and-magazine-laden coffee table in front of us, and the kitties curled up around us.

Rain pattered the leaves outside the windows, while we watched Top Hat with Fred Astaire, wrote in our diaries, argued (in great detail) about who we would rather date, Richard Gere or Tom Selleck. We cleaned out our purses, looked at the pictures we carried in our wallets for about the seven hundredth time, and tried on each other's rings. I went and got my jewelry box and we sorted through that, trying it all on and discussing all the little memories that went with everything.

At 4 p.m. we had tea with chocolate mousse pie with a crust made with chocolate wafer cookies and coffee granules. After tea, we had wine, which, we laughed, made our event "twine." Being disciplined as we were, we decided it should never be twine at elevenses ~ elevenses would always be strictly tea. And cake. And also, the next time I was in California we'd have a Twine for the Tuesday Girls.

Cats are connoisseurs of comfort.
James Herriot

TEA?

A JOY SHARED IS A JOY DOUBLED

One day, as we were crossing a street in Edgartown on our way to lunch, Diana stopped cold and elbowed me, her eyes were piercing laser beams of speechless meaning, compelling me to look in the car that was stopped at the crosswalk, waiting for us to get out of the way. The woman behind the wheel, wearing giant sunglasses and one of those little babushka cotton scarves, was unmistakable: Jackie Onassis.

As soon as it registered, I moved quickly across the street, casually racing into the ice cream store on the corner so that I could whip around and watch out the window to see her drive by. But when I got inside the store, I saw that Diana was still frozen in the street, holding up the traffic that had begun to build, staring at Jackie. I had to go get her. I grabbed her arm and pulled her along, asking, "What is wrong with you?"

"It's history!" she exclaimed, her eyes like half-dollars. "Did you see who that WAS?"

At the Harborside we ordered wine, Cokes with lime wedges, crushed ice, and straws; cheeseburgers with toasted buns, sides of Thousand Island, and fries with tartar sauce (we had learned to dip our fries in tartar sauce and slather our burgers with Thousand Island when we worked at Bob's Big Boy, and had done it that way ever since).

THOUSAND ISLAND

Try this on your next
 Cheeseburger
 Stir together:
1/2 c. mayonnaise
1 tsp. catsup (enough to turn
 the mayo pale pink)
1 Tbsp. sweet pickle relish
 (or, to taste)
And tons of freshly ground
pepper. ♥ Use unsparingly.

We sat at a table under an umbrella next to the dock and watched the boats rock and send ripples through the water while we talked about what it would be like to be Jackie Onassis, rich and famous, with houses all over the world.

I shook my head, "No, thank you. I wouldn't want her life no matter how many houses she had."

"Wouldn't you want to be famous?" asked Diana.

"Not like that. She can't even go out on her porch to get the paper without cameras in her face. It would be great to have a famous name, so that you could always be first in line at the emergency room and get reservations in a nice restaurant, but not a famous face, because if I'm sitting in the emergency room, I don't want people taking my picture. And I

WE'RE THE NORMAL ONES ♥

really don't want anyone taking pictures of me in my bathing suit if I hadn't had time to suck in my stomach. Can you imagine having helicopters over your house, or having to get dressed up just to go to the market? Because if everyone knew who you were, that's what you'd have to do. It's not normal."

Diana dipped a French fry into her little pile of salt, then into the tartar sauce, and mashed it into her mouth.

"Don't worry," she said, "famous people don't go near the market," Chew-chew-chew. "They have maids do it for them."

"Yeah, but who wants maids around all the time?" I continued ~ taking bite of burger, long string of cheese looped from mouth to sandwich, pickle sticking out of bun, pulled it out, deposited in mouth ~ "What if you just want to lie on the couch and read your book? Wouldn't you feel guilty if there was a maid behind you scrubbing the floor?"

No worries, only fake drinking on the streets of Edgartown.

Well-behaved women rarely make history.
♥LAUREL THATCHER ULRICH

"No, I'd just go into the library or . . . perhaps, I'd pop out (now she was channeling Ellie who "popped" everywhere she went) to the veranda off the South Wing. Or maybe I'd get Jeeves to drive me to the beach."

I ignored her. "And if your husband is shot dead in front of you, every sadness you have is on the national news; then you're totally judged on what hat you wear to the funeral. Look at Rod Stewart's girlfriends. How embarrassing. Everything so public. Is it worth it? I don't think so. Or if you get addicted to something, heaven forbid, then it's party time for the newspapers. Look at John Belushi." I took the last swig from my wineglass.

BATHING BEACH AND SHORE LINE, EDGARTOWN, MASS.

"Yeah, and you wouldn't dare get fat," she said, seeing the light and coming over to my side, digging two fries into tartar sauce at same time. "I'd rather have what we have any day ~ chomp chomp ~ we can get fat in private." Licking off pink Thousand Island/beef juice as it rolled down wrist.

"We have more fun," I said, "We can go to restaurants with our books and be invisible. We are so lucky."

"Let's have another glass of wine."

Birds of a Feather

"Yes, let's! Let's drink wine and stuff our faces and watch how much no one cares. We'll have to think of other ways to get a million dollars besides being famous. We are going to need that, you know."

Then we started playing our favorite game, "what if we had a million dollars" and forgot all about being famous.

I don't know much about being a millionaire, but I bet I'd be darling at it. ♥ Dorothy Parker

Our week together flew by. On Diana's last day we came home from the beach to find that Myron had left two lobsters in a Styrofoam cooler on the front porch. I was so excited! I'd never cooked a lobster before, but, I thought, *How hard could it be? It's just boiling water.*

I got out Agnes's big speckled pot and put about two inches of water into it. As it was coming to a boil, I checked her *Joy of Cooking* and added 🥔🥔 salt and then sliced two lemons into the water. Then it was time to put the lobsters in the pan. They were flopping quietly in the sink. I took a step back. Hmmph.

Encountering a moment of truth, I fervently wished there was someone else to put the lobsters in the pan. I thought about calling Myron, but it seemed a bit much to drag him over, so I tried to get Diana to do it; after all she's a nurse, she should be able to handle these things. But she ran out of the kitchen crying, "absolutely one-hundred-percent NOT."

"But you're a nurse!"

"I'm not a *lobster* nurse," she yelled from the other room. "I save lives!" She wouldn't even come stand by me for moral support.

I thought, *What would Julia Child do?* Relentless brave intrepid cook that she was, skinner of rabbits, gutter of ducks. I stopped pacing, turned fast, grabbed the lobsters before I could think, and shoved them (still wearing the rubber bands that keep their claws tightly closed; I wasn't taking those off) into the pot, praying they would be quickly lulled to sleep in the steam. I tried to bang the lid on, but a red feeler escaped and the lid wouldn't go all the way down.

I was dying; this was sad, murder in the first degree. But it was too late now. I pushed the feeler in, got the lid back on, and ran . . . into the living room, holding my ears so I didn't have to hear the lobsters scream in case they did. We were the ones screaming, stomping our feet, holding our ears, saying, *No no no no no no nooooo.*

E E E K.

Never again would I do this, I didn't care how good lobster tasted. I was a lobster eater not a lobster killer. And this is the very good reason I will probably never have my own cooking show on TV. Julia is proof you have to be ready for any-thing. I am proof that not everyone is.

You're only given one little spark of madness. You mustn't lose it.
♥ Robin Williams

The next morning I took my one little spark of madness to the airport. After hugs and kisses good-bye, I stood watching her plane take off with my arms bent, hands together under my chin and fingers crossed in prayer mode. I never liked the people I loved to fly.

And then, I was alone again. In fact, the whole Island was suddenly alone; the summer people had packed up and left en masse on Labor Day weekend. Boats were leaving the harbor, the roads were swept clean of mopeds, bicycles, and traffic ~ parking spaces downtown, impossible to find all summer, were suddenly a dime a dozen.

I sat in the dappled light on the front steps of Holly Oak, holding Girl Kitty, watching Man Cat wiggle and roll in the sandy driveway, enjoying the last warmth from the summer sun. A leaf fell from the trees and skittered across the yard and I wondered again for the hundredth time how I'd gotten here and for the first time, I started to wonder why.

Glory be to God for dappled things.
~ Gerard M. Hopkins ~

But if you try sometimes you get what you need.

CHAPTER SEVEN
BABY STEPS
MY ECHO, MY SHADOW, & ME

Now the maiden lived all alone in the cottage. She kept herself busy by spinning, weaving & sewing and bringing cow parsley from the meadow. Grimm's Fairy Tales

AUTUMN

September. My first New England fall had begun, something I'd read about but never experienced. And once it was done, I knew I could never move away, because if I did, I would be homesick for Autumn for the rest of my life. The change was so magical and spirited and filled with color and movement I almost didn't notice I was alone.

Suddenly there was wonderful chill in the air, even in the warm sunshine, like hot apple crisp with ice cream. The light turned golden, the days grew shorter, Canada geese flew in V formation honking across the blue sky, and cicadas hummed all day long. Life felt bigger and brighter and more promising than ever before. I'd been a bit numb that first summer, but Autumn woke me up.

On my walk, the wind blew me down the road, clothes and hair flying every which way. Dry leaves crackled and crunched deliciously underfoot and kicked up delightfully. Leaves cartwheeled alongside of me. I had to run to keep up with them.

I took my clippers to the woods with me and snipped branches of foliage with colorful leaves, tangles of bittersweet, bayberry, rose hips, and wild asters and brought them home to make bouquets and

garlands of leaves to hang in the window.

If I'd grown up with all of this, perhaps it would have seemed normal, but I saw it as something in the realm of miraculous. I had the urge to bury my nose in note books, crayons and paper, buy new shoes and run and run in the wind. It was exhilarating and inspiring, it made me want to cook something, sew something, cozy up my house and light candles at night. I wondered how I had managed to live my whole life without this magical thing.

There's a back-to-school feeling in the air....

Standing out at the water's edge, watching the sea birds hurrying along the shore, racing in and out with the waves, it was so beautiful, my heart would be so full and I'd feel so lucky I would put my arms out as if to fly, and I'd wish so hard, I'd think, maybe this time, I might really do it.

And then, out there at the end, in the thinnest voice possible, I sang one of my favorite songs from *Funny Girl* ～ next to "Sadie, Sadie, Married Lady," it was the one I loved the best:

"...*I'm the greatest star, I am by far, but nobody knows it...*" arms flung out to sides, voice raised ～ in my imagination, I'm with Fannie Brice on that little stage in New York ～ "I'm gonna live and live now, get what I want, I know how . . . I can make 'em cry! I can make 'em sigh! Some-day they'll clama for my drama . . ." all in that Barbra Streisand New York accent.

If you cannot teach me to fly,

Teach me to sing.
J. M. Barrie

It would buck me up and I'd feel better. It became my theme music for starting over.

Delicious autumn! My very soul is wedded to it. ⚜ George Eliot

in the yard

...under a tree...

out on my walk

on the road

under foot

More than my wildest dreams...

Because Martha's Vineyard is an island, no matter which direction the wind comes from, and no matter what season, it has to blow across the ocean before it gets to us.

It filters through the many woods and meadows, not only carrying the fragrance of the sea but gathering perfume from everything that grows wild: goldenrod, clematis, wild apples and pine, blueberries, beach plums, asters and bayberry. It slips in and out of seashells, climbs tree trunks, dives into squirrel holes, slides along

Bittersweet & the sea ~ how could I not fall in love?

old porch rails, stumbles through the bittersweet, skips along picket fences, scoots beneath falling leaves, whistles past ancient grave-yards, flits over and under dragonfly wings, and steals all the wishes off the dandelion puffs, flinging them in every direction, wishes for all.

Then, when all the finest most magical of ingredients were gathered, the fragrance came to me. I'd fill my lungs with a deep breath of cold, salty, wind, standing barefoot on my dad's deck before bed, shivery with goose bumps, pulling my shawl closer, looking up at the sky full of stars and saying goodnight stars, goodnight woods, goodnight sky, goodnight moon, and then I'd go sleep the sleep of the pretty much wildly contented.

Three brown leaves danced with two yellow ones in a little whirl of wind. *French Folktales*

Girl, Bill & Man - there's a bird feeder attached to the window sill.

The days got shorter and wild swans flew over the house (you really can't make this stuff up). I made myself pancakes for dinner, put more blankets on the bed, and slept wrapped in kitties and feather quilts with the windows open for the chill and the faint smell of wood smoke.

The moon, like silvered glass, winked between the blowing trees, peeped through the window and was sometimes so bright it woke me up. Everything was new and different from what my life had been before. Everything went slower. Nothing was the same.

Bella Luna

In the mornings, none of us wanted to get up (the kitties and me), we just sank deeper into the bed, and in the early light we lay there in the quiet, wondering about everything, listening to the cicadas singing in the woods, watching the leaves fall outside windows, noticing tree shadows bouncing across the walls, and hearing the long boat whistle from the harbor reminding me always of where I was. I'd open whatever book I was reading and put my nose inside to smell it, and melt back into the story and then fall back to sleep . . . it was as close to being 12 as I could get.

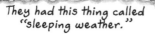
They had this thing called "sleeping weather."

☺ You are original and creative.. ☺

I made oatmeal or cream of rice  and shuffled around in my slippers with my tea. I'd pull out a clean sheet of water-color paper and paint all morning in my jammies with just the hum of the heater and the wind at the door. I would grab an old sweater and blow around the garden collecting the rest of the basil and the last three tomatoes, still green and on the vine, to ripen in my new green-house window. I'd read that soon we would get a "killing frost" and anything still in the garden would freeze and turn black. This was not something I'd worried about in my garden in California.

the quilt on the right was made by my great grandma

But here, everything seemed to be finite. There was a moment, and then it was gone in this new world of seasons. It was making me more respectful of time. Instant gratification seemed less interesting. Anticipation was more fun. Agnes had left behind an old wind-up clock that made a ticking noise and I put it on my art table. Who better to remind me of the passing seasons than Agnes? I wanted to celebrate. I dug holes and planted daffodil bulbs and made carrot-cake cupcakes and took half of them through drifting leaves, past the garden to Ellie and Myron for elevenses. I kept exploring the Island, went to Owen Park to watch the full moon rise, drove up Middle Road under the color-splashed canopy of trees, to look at the water, the rock walls, and the old houses and sang along with Olivia Newton John . . . "Come take my hand, you should know me, I've always been in your mind . . ."

In the village store someone says, "I heard the geese go over", & there is a moment of silence. Why this is so moving, I do not know. But all of us feel it. Gladys Taber

138

CARROT CAKE CUPCAKES

350° Makes 15 cupcakes.
You can double the recipe.

Flavor a dish with LOVE & it pleases every palate.
Plautus, c. 254-184 BC

Chock full of nuts & fruit, these moist & tender morsels don't fall apart when you eat them & with a little imagination could almost be classified as health food. The frosting is traditional cream cheese, which you can tint any color you desire. While baking they make your house smell like heaven.

2 eggs, well beaten
1/2 c. packed dark brown sugar
1/2 c. granulated sugar
3/4 c. canola oil
1 c. unbleached flour (not necessary to sift, just stir to lighten with fork before measuring)
1 tsp. baking soda

1 tsp. baking powder
1 tsp. cinnamon
3/4 tsp. nutmeg
1 1/2 c. finely grated carrots
1/2 c. sweetened coconut
4 oz. can crushed pineapple, drained
1 c. coarsely chopped walnuts
1/2 c golden raisins

Preheat oven to 350°. Put cupcake liners into two cupcake pans. See frosting recipe on next page and set out butter and cream cheese to soften. Put the pineapple into a sieve to drain.

Beat eggs in a large bowl. Add sugars and beat with hand held mixer until light and fluffy. Whisk in oil and mix well. Put in the dry ingredients and beat until smooth. Stir in remaining ingredients and pour batter into cupcake liners filling about 2/3 full. Bake for 20 minutes until toothpick comes out clean when inserted in center of cupcake. Cool slightly and frost with

Cream Cheese Frosting →

Cream Cheese Frosting

1/2 c. butter, softened
1/2 lb. powdered sugar
   (or 1 3/4 c. + 2 Tbsp.), sifted
   into bowl (to remove lumps)

4 oz pkg. cream cheese, softened
1 1/2 tsp. vanilla

Cream together butter and cream cheese. Stir in powdered sugar and vanilla and until smooth. If desired, divide the frosting into four bowls. Add one drop of food coloring to each bowl until you have the color you like (particularly pretty at Easter). Decorate with toasted coconut, candies, walnuts, or dragoons.

LIFE in the SLOW LANE

Yes, I had to have that goose

I chose blue wallpaper for my bedroom, blue with tiny white flowers, and made curtains for the windows from the white cotton lace tablecloths I'd bought in California.

I watched how Islanders prepared for winter, battening down the hatches, chopping and stacking wood, raking leaves, putting gardens to bed, storing yard furniture in their barns or sheds, and putting the storm windows back on. Stuff we never did in California. It was very festive! They put pumpkins and baskets of mums on their porches, hung dried corn on the door, and put funny homemade scarecrows in their gardens.

They packed up summer and put it away for another year. Into attics and closets went the beach towels, bathing suits, cotton dresses and shorts, and out came the winter wool, the sweaters and hats, and scarves to hang on door pegs.

October

Every season turned out to be an adventure and each one taught me something new. From the moment the first leaf blew off the trees I was right there in the yard with Agnes's rake, ready to scoop it up. I didn't want a mess, so thought I'd get a head start on the situation and keep on top of it despite the fact that even as I raked more leaves were falling. Large black crows cawed and flew low between the trees, eerie and spooky, the wind blew and the clouds tumbled through the sky.

I filled cardboard boxes with the brightest most blazing of leaves and sent them home to Bev and Sarah so they could see what I was seeing. Diana, being a Hawaii kind of girl, was not that into dead leaves, no matter what color they were.

"It is not everyone," said Elinor, "who has your passion for dead leaves." Jane Austen

At one time I had maybe 15 piles of leaves in the yard while they were still falling. I'm sure Myron looked out his window and laughed as I madly raked every day into November. One day the UPS man came by, looked at my bandaged thumbs, blistered from raking, nodded at my leaf piles, and kindly said, "Around here we just leave those things on the ground and hope the wind blows them into the woods. Clean them up in the spring if there are any left." Ohhhhh. The light comes on slowly. Ohhh. Oh. I see. Thank you.

The light came on slowly in my heart too. Six months after the divorce I was still analyzing what happened. Although, right here, for the purposes of telling this story, I shall try not to dwell on my still-grieving heart to the point of ridiculousness because of course that's exactly where it went. I wouldn't want you to think, by my not mentioning it, that I was callous, because I was anything but. I

My walk was alive with flying leaves

continued moving forward since I really had no choice, but the heartache caused much introspection. Luckily, I was in the perfect place for soul searching. Even if your heart wasn't broken, remote Martha's Vineyard, cut off from the outside world by a choppy blue moat, with long, lonely stretches of beach, stark changes of season and all the beauty that went with it, including the cold, dark winters, and the hypnotic rolling of the sea, might give a person pause. In my alone time, I read everything I could to figure out where I'd gone wrong so I wouldn't do it again. But answers didn't come overnight and neither did healing. Those things took time.

The wound is the place where the light enters you.
♥ *Rumi 1260*

Slowly I began to realize that it wasn't just the loss of Cliff or the dissolution of my marriage that caused the devastation; it was the loss of everything. My identity, my friends, my home, but probably most of all, the loss of my childhood dream of happily ever after which I had unfortunately pinned on Cliff. Cliff, I could get over, but the dream refused to die. Despite the fact that I already knew better, I continued to think perhaps a Prince Charming would come save me. Because the alternative, which was becoming more obvious to me every day no matter how deeply I put my head in the sand, was that no one was going to show up ~ I was going to have to save myself. What a nightmare. I felt so unqualified.

But there was a big, fat, un-deniable drawback to my old dream, a fatal flaw: no job security.

Prince Charmings weren't on every corner and where there was a Prince Charming, I began to see, there was very likely a woman living someone else's life. All terrible news.

Girl and Man, and there's my "Marilyn Monroe" telephone.

The disturbing question my dad asked, and I'd asked myself a hundred times, "What are you going to do with your life?" gnawed at me night and day.

Then I realized that if I still wanted the fairy tale, which I was pretty sure I did (with about 10,000 caveats), it would have to be reassembled from scratch and this time, for safety's sake, it had to be the kind of fairy tale that didn't depend on anyone but me. Next time I would have to make sure I owned the basket where I kept the eggs. But first I had to get some eggs.

Put all your eggs in one basket and WATCH THAT BASKET. ♥ Mark Twain

PEOPLE LIVE THROUGH SUCH PAIN ONLY ONCE. PAIN COMES AGAIN, BUT IT finds A TOUGHER SURFACE. Willa Cather

But I didn't want a tougher surface. I read a quote by Thomas Paine: "We have it in our power to begin the world over again." I believed this was true then and I still do.

There were good days and bad, and as time went on, more good than bad. I called the good ones "Red-Letter days." Like in California, I made lists in my diary of things that would con-stitute a Red-Letter day.

When I was little, each week when my mom put clean sheets on my bed, I would take a bath, put on fresh-from-the-dryer jammies, brush my teeth, polish my shoes for school the next day, go out on the porch of our house on Claire Avenue, look up at the stars and take a big breath of night air and then get between my crisp, sweet-smelling sheets feeling like a fawn or some other clean little woodland animal. That about sums up what I needed to do for more Red-Letter days.

From my Diary

A RED LETTER Day

Read a wonderful book, write a letter, listen to the birds, walk to the pond, nap with the kitties, soak in a bubble bath, wear something cute, paint, knit, sew, cook something wonderful, dig in the garden, watch an old movie, pick a few flowers for a little vase, sing out loud, listen to Tommy Dorsey & Frank Sinatra, make a healthy dinner, sleep with the windows open for sweet dreams.

So if times were bad or I was anxious, I would do a few of those things, and I would always feel better. Sometimes I even had Red Letter weeks.

The trouble is not that I am single & likely to stay single, but that I am lonely & likely to stay lonely.
Charlotte Brontë

Was I lonely? Yes, that was definitely the worst part. Worse than the divorce. Loneliness takes the courage right out of a person. I had never really experienced it before, but now that I knew what it was, I felt bad for all the lonely people in the world. It is a rotten, terrible thing. I cried a river into my diary and ran up a monumental phone bill. (Back then, we paid for long-distance phone calls by the minute.)

Although I wouldn't wish it on anyone, I still wouldn't change a thing of the gift that was given to me, because I didn't know it, but I needed to be alone. Because, as it turned out, that's where all the secrets were.

It's only a paper moon sailing under a cardboard sky...
Frank

Isle of Dreams

And you know what helps loneliness? Beauty. Your heart can be sad, but it will leap at the sight of the moon on the water, or when light flickers through the leaves and flutters like butterfly wings on the wall. You might fall back into sadness, but then, thank goodness, you see something else, even the smallest of things, a pink rose in a vase, an amazing line of inspiration in a book, kitty paws the way they fold over each other, and it leaps again.

Kitty paws

I walk. I prefer walking.
♥ Jane Austen

To ease the feeling of loss, I flew home at least once a year to see my friends and family, for weddings and birthdays and new babies, and for no reason at all because life went on in California. Despite my discomfort with flying, I had no choice. A person can't be without the people she loves forever. And I was lucky, because just like my dad and Diana, at one time or another, my family and all my girlfriends came out to see me. I had a wonderful time fixing up the house for their visits, cooking for them and taking them on Island tours, but sooner or later, everyone went home and I was alone again. Silence isn't always golden, you know. Sometimes it's just plain yellow—
Jan Kemp

145

ortunately, that first fall on the Island, I was offered a commission to paint 15 watercolors, subjects of my own choosing, for a friend of Cliff's who wanted them for his new restaurant in San Luis Obispo. It kept me busy and creative and practicing my art all winter, and it was a real job, doing the thing I loved the best, with the added bonus of actual money attached to it.

The commission would more than pay for the greenhouse window Carlton put in my kitchen. After he finished that, I asked him if hewould make a bookshelf carved with hearts for over my bed. He'd said, "OK, draw me a picture," so I did.

After Thanksgiving, which I felt lucky to spend with Ellie and Myron (and Peggy and Gwinnie), Carl came over and hung my new shelf over my bed. We talked

My new heart shelf

about maybe remodeling my kitchen and putting in real cupboards and a dishwasher. He said if I wanted, he could do it starting in the spring.

One cold end-of-November evening, after working all day on the paintings for the restaurant, and after my first glass of wine, I started stenciling a border around the top of the living room wall. It was a little red flower with green leaves and hearts in-between. I got out the bristly, stubby stencil brushes and the tiny jars of red and green paint, stood on the small red children's chair I used as a step stool, and began to work my way around the room, laying out the stencil, stabbing color into it with the brush, listening to the TV as I worked. Up and down, move the chair, around the room I went. I thought it was looking great.

More wine: *The Love Boat* was on TV, Captain Stubing was falling in love with a passenger and Gopher was worried because he thought the woman was a gold digger. I'd gotten tired of stenciling around the ceiling ~ it was going on forever and the blood was draining from my arm ~ so I stopped that and concentrated on stenciling the front of every stair that went up to the attic ~ brilliant idea, if I did say so myself, which I did. Because it looked fabulous too!

WHAT'S SHE DOING?

More wine: *Fantasy Island* came on while I stenciled the fronts of kitchen cupboards. De Plane! De Plane! And, WOW, how gorgeous can you get? I'm good at this! I should put an ad in the Yellow Pages, I should be a professional stenciler! I fixed cinnamon toast and stood there admiring everything. Then I poured another glass of wine and stenciled a flower on each of the panels in the kitchen door. Then I did the door to the basement.

DON'T ASK ME!

> 17 She believed in excess. How can you tell whether or not you have had enough until you've had a little too much?
>
> Jessamyn West, *Hide and Seek* (1973)

Around Johnny Carson time, when I found myself stenciling the same design on the splashboard in the bathroom, I had a moment of clarity. I stopped short and stumbled off to bed before I turned Holly Oak into Santa's Village East. The next morning I woke up to my new décor. There was no one to blame but myself. I made a cup of tea and wandered around the house looking at what I'd done and laughing at myself. I didn't hate it, but I had stopped in the

Luckily the room was small

More a picture of Bill than of the stencil, but you can see it at the top

bare nick oftime, and I still had to either finish the border around the ceiling, or paint over it. That's when I knew it was time for me to find something to do that would get me out of the house. I was a people who needed people.

WINTER

In early December, I found a part-time job at the gourmet food store on Main Street, wrapping cheese, and selling dried pasta, fresh herbs, bakery goods, salads, and flowers, three days a week, four hours a day, all winter long.

It was good to have a reason to get out of my bathrobe. I loved going to work amid the festive energy of small-town Main Street during the Christmas season. The bell over the shop door never stopped ringing as adults and kids in bright knit caps came blowing in bringing gusts of frosted air into the warm, coffee-scented shop. I wore a white apron over my sweater, stood behind the counter and wrapped wedges of Parmigiano Reggiano and Explorateur cheese in thick white paper. I sliced bread, boxed baked goods, poured hot cider and coffee, cut fudge squares, scooped peanut brittle and chocolate truffles into white bags, took orders for party trays, and said "Merry Christmas!" and "Happy Holidays!" Like almost every shop on Main Street, our store windows were outlined in twinkle lights and draped with pine boughs and cranberry garlands. Bing Crosby sang "White Christmas" while outside, snow floated down in big beautiful flakes, and the bells rang from the church around the corner.

A woman and her kitchen

How had I lived my whole life without snow? Just like my first vision of fall colors, I could not imagine ever getting used to a snowfall. Sometimes the flakes were light and airy and drifty and romantic, and other times they came at you with a vengeance, sometimes they were big as cotton balls, and sometimes they would fall straight down, sifting over the town like powdered sugar. The wagon from Fisher Farm, filled with happy people in bright scarves and hats and pulled by large work horses wearing thick leather straps with sleigh bells on them clip-clopped down my street in the snow. All of it was magic.

Cardinal

Frost is on the pumpkin

Miranda, my boss and the owner of the store, was 38, married, with two children, and so busy she could barely think straight. The second week I was there, she asked me if I'd like to cook for the store. We'd been talking about food and recipes while we worked. She knew I loved to cook, and she didn't care what I made.

Downtown side street

"Surprise me," she said, speaking my language. She just wanted me to keep the store stocked with brownies, cookies, pies, cakes, whatever I wanted to make.

"Homemade marshmallows?" I asked her.

"Yes," she said, "perfect!"

149

It was just what I didn't know I needed: new people to cook for, new victims. Having the oven on kept my house warm too. It was a win-win situation.

Homemade Marshmallows

The difference between homemade and store-bought marshmallows is the same as the difference between a homegrown tomato and one you buy at the supermarket in February. Basically, night and day. They are important for the perfect cup of hot chocolate.

Makes 64 – 1" square marshmallows. You will need a candy thermometer.

1/2 c. powdered sugar
1/2 c. cornstarch
3 pkgs. powdered gelatin
  (or 2 Tbsp. + 3/4 tsp.)

1 c. water
1 3/4 c. granulated sugar
3/4 c. light corn syrup
1/4 tsp. salt
1 1/4 Tbsp. vanilla

Lightly spray a 9" x 9" baking pan with vegetable oil. Sift together powdered sugar and cornstarch onto a piece of waxed paper and use a spoonful of it to dust the baking pan; set the rest aside. In a large, wide mixing bowl, combine the gelatin with 1/2 c. water and set aside. In a medium saucepan, combine the granulated sugar with corn syrup, salt, and 1/2 c. water. Cook over medium heat until sugar melts, stirring occasionally. Turn heat on high and cook till candy thermometer reads 250°. Slowly, in a thin inter-mittent stream, pour hot mixture into gelatin, beating with electric mixer on low speed. Turn the mixer to high, beat for 15 minutes, add vanilla and beat another minute. Pour into baking

Snow Flowers

pan. Sprinkle the reserved powdered sugar-cornstarch mixture over the top, and set aside at room temperature for 6 hours or overnight.

Cut into 1" squares (cold water on the knife helps) and make sure to roll each marshmallow in the powdered sugar mixture. Keep in an air-tight container. Give them away in small bags tied with holiday ribbons, along with chocolate bars and graham crackers.

So most mornings when I didn't have to be at the store, I got up, looked to see if it was snowing, turned up the heat, made tea, fed the cats, and watched the nuthatches, cardinals and squirrels vie for space at the feeders. I listened to music, turned on an old movie, or talked to friends on the phone while mixing up batters for goodies for the store. I popped carrot cupcakes in the oven and painted pictures for the restaurant guy in San Luis until the timer went off.

When it snowed I'd go out and run around, put out my tongue to catch flakes, and come inside to the delicious smell of cupcakes or my grandma's molasses cookies. I'd read about snow angels and one day, checking first to see that no one was watching, I dropped into a thick blanket of snow and made my own. Then of course I was caked in snow and realized why people stopped doing this at a certain age. Fortunately my live-and-learn exercises in the snow did not include putting my tongue on a metal pole, but I did fill the yard with snow people, and made sugar on snow with maple syrup. I had a whole missing childhood to make up for.

THE MAGIC OF SNOW

In the afternoons I'd drive to town to drop off my baked things at the store. Working there made being at home much less lonely. Being around Miranda and her friends was fun, but I felt like the new kid in school. She and her friends had known each other forever and they were always stopping in, talking about things they'd done, bringing back her kids' sweaters from play dates, grabbing her to go to lunch.

They had shared memories, had seen each other through thick and thin, they knew each other's moms which I always thought was the mark of true friendship. I had that too, that lovely, wonderful connection with best friends, just not here.

My new greenhouse window in the snow

Now that I had to be at work, I could no longer stay home just because it was snowing. I had to learn how to drive in the snow, and remember rules like, If you hit a patch of ice and start to slide, stay calm, take your foot off the gas and don't step on the brake.

In December, when days were shortest, it would be pitch dark at 4:30 p.m. When the street-lights came on, the flakes caught the light and came flying at the windshield like long white needles. It was very beautiful, especially when James Taylor was singing, ". . . Though the Berkshires seemed dreamlike on account of that frosting ~ with 10 miles behind us and 10,000 more to go, oh, oh, Oh . . . There's a song that they sing when they take to the highway...a song that they sing when they take to the sea . . ."

If Martha's Vineyard had a voice it would sound exactly like James Taylor.

More discoveries for my first winter on the Island: There was something called anti-freeze and you had to put it in your car. It actually wasn't a choice. Otherwise the water in your radiator would freeze. Then the needle in your car would point to the H, and you would be in trouble and get the humiliating What's-wrong-with-you-lady? look from the man at the gas station. The good news is that it would only happen to you once.

Other things I'd never heard of included black ice (which isn't black), mud porches, wind chill, hoar frost, and snow tires ~ I had never used a snow shovel, or scraped ice from a windshield, but I was now a pro when it came to storm windows. In California, we swam in the pool on Christmas Day. We never put our yard furniture away "for the winter." I was surprised to find out how much body heat could leak out the top of your head. It came to me as a revelation that the real reason Laura (on *Little House*) wore that ruffled cap to bed was not to look cute but to keep warm.

Brrrr

In a way it was like being a child again, with a lot of "firsts" waiting to be discovered. I woke up to snowlight coming through the lace curtains in my bedroom, as holy and quiet as a confessional window, and lay there thinking of more questions: Are kitties allowed out in this? Do things freeze in the basement? Will the car start? Are tennis shoes okay in the snow? If I slip off the porch on my way to work and break my leg, how long will it take before I freeze to death?

And I was still trying to figure out how to dress. The things I had weren't really warm enough. I couldn't get enough sweaters under my jacket, it was too small. I needed something more, some sort of professional winter coat,

William T. Aristocat III

153

especially for my walks. I looked around to see what others were wearing. One woman ❄️ came into the store wearing a full-length puffy down coat that ❄️ looked very warm, so after work, I went down to Murray's (a clothing store for men and women) to see if they had one. They did, but only in white, so that's what I got. Unlike past coat purchases, there was no question of looking cute in this. Proportionally it didn't work, my head looked like a peanut. Wearing a knit hat with my white coat, I looked like a re-frigerator with a cupcake on top. But I was warm, and that was all that mattered. I thought.

L I V I N G &

It was 4:30 and dark when L E A R N I N G I left Murray's wearing my new coat. Big flakes of snow were swirling out of the sky, landing softly on my hair and eyelashes, ❄️ which tickled like the bubbles in champagne. Main Street was ❄️ busy with bundled shoppers hurrying in and out of stores. Santa Claus's arm cranked up and down, clanging his bell at the red Salvation Army bucket in front of Mardell's and tiny white lights twinkled in the old linden tree.

It was positively, ridiculously, adorable ～ it warmed the pro-verbial cockles ❄️ of my heart. Vineyard Haven ❄️ reminded me of one of those little towns in an electric train set. There was a wreath on every shop door and a piney smell from the Christmas tree lot next to the Capawock Theater. I picked out a skinny tree while street carolers sang, "Come on, it's lovely weather for a sleigh ride together with you ..."

Popcorn garlands on the tree but still no curtains

remembered last Christmas in California. It was hot, and I could barely see, my eyes were swollen into slits from crying, and now, only one year later, here I was, on the other side of the country, living in a Norman Rockwell painting. Only it was real. Children actually skated on ponds and slid down hills, red, blue and green hats popped against the white snow, colorful scarves flew out behind them in the wind.

— Snug as a bug with an outside view of the greenhouse window. —

When you're stuck in a spiral, to change all aspects of the spin, you only need to change one thing. ♥ Christina Baldwin

got all my presents wrapped and sent home and after dark on Christmas Eve I crunched through the snow out to the horse meadow. The blanket of white spread before me sparkled with starlight and seemed lit from within, as if the moon was under the snow. The next day all of us, the kitties, the birds and me ∼ had homemade blueberry muffins for Christmas breakfast. I ate mine, hot and

buttered and dusted with cinnamon-sugar with a cup of tea while watching Miracle on 34th Street and reading an article in Cosmopolitan titled, "What to Do When Your Lover Leaves." "Number Three: Don't overreact and embarrass yourself." Ha! Too late.

155

New Year's Eve

Say good bye to 1982, the longest year of my life.

NEW BEGINNINGS

Every night I turn my fears over to God. ♥ He's going to be up all night anyway. ♥ *Anon.*

NEW YEAR
WISHES

Get dressed every day
Finish paintings for SLO
Don't redecorate while
drinking
Don't talk to Cliff while
drinking
Drink less
Be grateful
Be more creative
Do sit-ups
Practice self-reliance
Be a better person
Figure out what you want
to be when you grow up

BE TRULY GLAD. THERE
IS WONDERFUL JOY AHEAD.
1 PETER 1:6

Dear Diary...

Jan 19, 1983 6 p.m. Freezing ～ so cold I can't even tell you. Glass storm door frozen shut, phone broken, talking to myself. I've had a cold for the last three days. It's a ridiculous 18°! With wind chill, it's 10 below zero. The cats hate me 'cause I won't let them out. We're trapped like arctic rats. So far today I've eaten toast, chocolate cake, potato pancake and chicken legs. I'll be 300 pounds before this winter is over. Heard on the news: John Ghiorse (weatherman and new best friend) says tomorrow's temperature will SOAR into the upper 20s. He actually said, "soar." Wonder what they're doing in California?

All through January and February I kept busy, working on the paintings for the restaurant in SLO, fishtailing down the snowy streets to keep Miranda and the store supplied with salads and baked things, reading like crazy, talking on the phone, and trying to keep warm. I loved the quiet, the birds, the snowfall, and lighting candles in the purple twilight.

156

Walking in a winter wonderland

If the road wasn't too icy, I would walk out to the water streaming hot breath the whole way, past the boarded up fishing shacks to the wild and windy shore where there was snow on the sand, a very strange concept, and come in breathless, my nose and face numb from the cold.

In March I had an idea. I thought maybe I should try selling my art on the Island. So I took two paintings down to the store and asked Miranda if I could hang them on the big empty wall above the stairs. It seemed like a natural. I did all these kitcheny home-type paintings of stoves and flowers and quilts and this was a food store with a big empty wall in it.

If you do it with heart, it's art

I should never have done it. I didn't mean to put her on the spot, I could see she was embarrassed and I was instantly sorry. It was sort of like asking a woman, "When's the baby due" and hearing her say, "I'm not pregnant." Awful, fall-through-the-floor stuff. She glanced at the paintings, but didn't meet my eyes and said she thought if she did that for me, she would have to do it for everyone. She was sorry, and was perfectly wonderful and nice, but I was mortified. I'd had enough rejection to last a lifetime.

Painting I did for the restaurant

Based on that one person and that one experience I deduced that my art was too unsophisticated for the East Coast, and, in fact, true or not, I could see that my art was about as sophisticated as a soda cracker (with or without the chicken noodle soup). These people went to New York all the time and they knew what real art looked like and mine wasn't it. The jig was finally up. It was a quick lesson for me, or so I thought, that my paintings would not be the way forward on Martha's Vineyard. I could take "artist" off my list of things to be.

You'll be surprised to hear this wasn't the end of the world for me. There is something to be said for low expectations.

On the way home I stopped at the Thrift Shop and got rid of the white refrigerator coat. The two months I'd owned it was more than enough. Like everything else, it was part of the learning curve. Besides the fact that it made me look like the Pillsbury Doughboy, I'd also begun to notice that it whisked with a sound that grated on me like sawing cardboard with a serrated knife. I would get home from a walk or the post office and be so overwhelmed by the sound of whisssssssk, I would rip it off as fast as I could and leave it where it fell on the floor till I had a glass of wine and a nap and could face that noise long enough to hang it up. It had to go.

I donated it to the Thrift Shop and replaced it with an oversized man's brown leather bomber jacket. It came halfway to my knees, I could fit two sweaters under it; it cut the wind, had big pockets inside and out, and best of all, it didn't make noise.

March 27, 1983 Sunday
The little plans I tried
to carry through
Have failed..
I will not sorrow.
I'll pause a little
while,
and try again tomorrow!

I don't know where I'm going but I'm on my way. ♥ Voltaire

CHAPTER EIGHT

A New Kind of Love

But once in a while the odd thing happens,
once in a while the dream comes true,
& the whole pattern of life is altered.
Once in a while the moon turns blue.

W. H. Auden

SPRING
1983

The PINKLETINKS ARE SINGING on MARTHA'S VINEYARD

At the end of March I sent the 15 new paintings to California to be framed by my old friend Dan at the art store. He would make sure they got to the restaurant. I received a check for $3,500 from the restaurant owner. I proudly put it in my bank account thinking at least California liked me.

But none of my minor setbacks mattered. Daily I fell further in love with Martha's Vineyard because of things like this:

Fall inspirations

Roses and dishes I painted for California

I was the third car back in a line of traffic that had come to a complete stop, seemingly for no reason, on both sides of State Road. At first I couldn't see what the holdup was, but after a moment I saw a mama duck and her three fuzzy yellow babies waddle out from between the cars, cross the street, scramble up the embankment one by one, skedaddle over and around a clump of daffodils and tumble into the undergrowth on the other side.

159

How could you not fall in love with a place where traffic stopped for ducks? Not to mention wild daffodils just growing willy nilly by the side of the road. I felt like elves were running ahead, setting up scenes like these just for me, because this kind of thing happened all the time.

"...Ma Nature's LYRICAL with her yearly miracle, Spring, Spring, Spring..."
Crosby & Astaire

Top driving speed on the Island is 45 mph, and there are no traffic lights.

Even place names on the Island were magical: Music Street, Merry Farm Road, Beetlebung Corners, Squibnocket, Cedar Tree Neck, Dog Fish Bar, Beaten Path, & Herring Creek Road. In California, the street Cliff and I had lived on was "Linda Way."

I was out working in my garden, listening to the blackbirds sing, planting lettuce, thinking that Island earthworms were about six times the size of the ones at home.

I was on my knees, my face close to the ground, I dug in with the trowel and suddenly a large worm, too close to snake-size for any normal person's comfort, leaped out, spring loaded, like from a jack-in-the-box. I jumped back and screamed. I looked over to see if Ellie, out hanging clothes on her line, heard me. She didn't seem to have noticed.

Blossoms from my "orchard" (that's what I called my one little apple tree) blew across the garden like tiny pink butterflies. I walked over to say hello and laugh with Ellie about the worms.

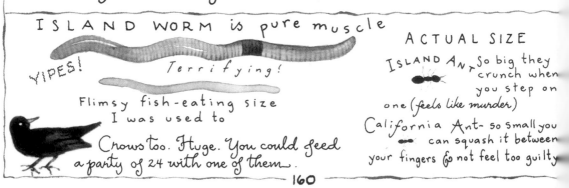

ISLAND WORM is pure muscle

YIPES!   Terrifying!

Flimsy fish-eating size I was used to

Crows too. Huge. You could feed a party of 24 with one of them.

ACTUAL SIZE

ISLAND ANT So big they crunch when you step on one (feels like murder)

California Ant- so small you can squash it between your fingers & not feel too guilty n her darling English accent, she looked up at the sky, and said, "Look, dear, it's all dashes and dots." Clouds were moving fast across the bright blue sky in small puffs and little streaks. Looking at her the way she was ~ the long skirt, the homemade apron, the striped socks, the lilac hanging over the wall behind her, that precious dog ~ I wouldn't have been a bit surprised if there were fairies living at the bottom of her garden.

The whole Island smells like lilac in the spring

There are people who take the heart out of you & there are people who put it back.
ELIZABETH DAVID

Myron brought over his rototiller and dug up a rectangle of lawn under my greenhouse window so that I could plant flowers, which I did, out in the soft May sunshine. I planted fox-gloves and hollyhocks next to the house, interspersed with forget-me-nots, daisies, and catmint, scented geraniums and sweet peas and a couple of baby boxwoods, and something I'd never seen in California, a peony.

Myron gave me a glass jar with about an inch of bleach in it and told me about Japanese beetles and the damage they can do and

how it's not good to spray, and that I should just flick the coppery green plant-eating machines into the jar. When I had gotten as many in the jar as I could stand to look at, I was to dilute the bleach with water and pour the awful contents into the woods.

161

I said thank you for the rototilling and the jar with a gift of pillowcases I embroidered with watering cans and flowers. We didn't have giant worms or Japanese beetles in California. But, there were no gophers on Martha's Vineyard, so I felt way ahead of the game.

BEACH FINDS

Every day on my walk I searched the shore for colorful heart rocks, beach glass, and bricks, all shaped by the sea . . .

— *to add to my growing collection.* —

One fine spring day, as promised, Carlton came with his tools and started to remodel my kitchen. He was about the same age as me, maybe a couple of years younger. We got to know each other a little at a time while he pried up the old linoleum and ripped out cupboards. He was a serious, kind, self-effacing, funny, quirky, original, creative, shy, New England sort of guy, who never once, in all the time I knew him, made me feel illogical. He was one of seven children, born and raised on the Island. He and his tall, beautiful dark-haired wife, Tammis, had two little children and a dog, one of Peggy's corgi puppies they called Bess.

He also kept a flock of about 40 white doves in his garden. When he released them from the aviary he built for them, the flock would fly as one, like a small, white murmuration, dipping and turning in

162

In spring the Island was a carpet of yellow.

precise unison through the sky over the Island, sometimes over my house, like nature's Blue Angels, up and over the town, around the church spires, dazzling white birds. I would see them dipping and diving and say, there goes Carlton's doves.

Despite this tendency to make magic, Carl was down to earth and loved old things and tradition as much as I did ~ old books, old art, old people, and old architecture. He did much of his carpentry in an old-fashioned way, using hand tools and not a lot of electricity. His sensibilities and mine were in perfect sync, but he could actually make things happen. I would describe what I wanted, and he would ask me to sketch it for him and then he would build it. And once we got started, we really never stopped.

For the next few years, while I peeled apples, kneaded bread, chopped vegetables, folded clothes, arranged my heart rocks on a windowsill, put away groceries, made lists, painted and talked on the phone, Carlton was pretty much a quiet fixture around the house, sometimes inside, sometimes out. I would cook for the store and he would be my taster. We would finish a house project, a few months might go by before he was back and we were on to something new.

In addition to my heart shelf and the greenhouse window, he remodeled the kitchen: made new cupboards, a shelf for my cookbooks, and a small pantry; he laid down a hardwood floor, tiled my counters and hung my pots and pans between the cupboards over the sink where they could drip dry (saving me lots of cupboard space). Carl built a wooden porch at the front door with two benches that faced each other. Before the white paint on the railings could dry, the kitties, ever curious, walked in it, leaving paw prints on the benches, adding the finishing touch.

Carlton building my cupboards.

163

Carl only laughed when I followed him around filling the cupboards while he was still finishing them.

As time went on, Carl added wainscoting to the living room and then wallpapered it. He built a guest "house" in the backyard, and en-larged my bedroom. He fixed the roof when a hurricane blew a tree onto it, and reshingled the whole house. He also made me a hutch, and a wardrobe with a secret drawer. Sometimes when I went away, if he was going to be around, Carlton took care of the kitties.

Because he came early and stayed late, he saw me at my worst: just out of bed, uncombed and un-brushed; dripping sweat on my exercise bike; hunched over while painting at the dining table; napping on the green couch with my mouth open catching flies, burning croutons

Seventy mph winds knocked over the tree. Thank goodness it missed the porch. I was in the garden digging potatoes when I saw it go over and ran for the basement. My first hurricane.

Every time I asked for a heart Carl gave it to me. ♥

or pine nuts, or stuffing my face with the refrig-erator door wide open. He most likely heard every word I ever said to Diana on the phone and never batted an eyelash. There was a word to describe Carl. I learned it in Mexico: "simpatico."

164

BEFORE & AFTER

I liked the size of the kitchen so we didn't change the footprint. The window in the door (which led to the basement & the back door) allowed a view into my new "pantry" which Carl made, just one can deep to fit behind the back door when it was open. I measured

the spaces; one shelf was exactly the height of three cat food cans, another was for Perrier bottles, which you had to have in the 1980s if you were any kind of self-respecting gourmet-type person. Carl put in a hardwood floor & a red stripe in

my white tiled counters. Pans & colanders could hang over the sink & drip dry, and there was a new shelf over the stove for tea & spices. But best of all, Carl surprised me with a special little under-the-cupboard shelf for my cookbooks. I chose red wallpaper with tiny white dots. Plus, I got a dishwasher!

Bees do have a smell you know, & if they don't they should, for their feet are dusted with the spices from a million flowers. Ray Bradbury

Shouldn't all towns have a big old tree in the middle loaded with blossoms and buzzing with honeybees? There should be a law; it would give Congress something productive to do, and a way to use our tax money that I personally could endorse: trees.

BUT IN CAMELOT, CAMELOT! THOSE ARE THE LEGAL LAWS.

The great old linden tree that shaded half of Main Street was dripping with clusters of cream-colored vanilla-scented flowers. Under it, tables were set for a bake sale to benefit the Garden Club. Candy boxes had been recycled and filled with different kinds of cookies displayed on doilies. There were coconut cakes, poppy seed cakes, powdered sugar lemon bars, rhubarb tea-cakes, custard pie, chocolate pie, and all kinds of breads, sweet, crusty, and seeded. Customers came on foot and by bicycle and business was done from a cigar box while bees landed

Downtown, church bells, and a rainbow ~ the elves at work again.

on the rims of Styrofoam coffee cups. I bought a sugar donut and sat on the bench behind the table, tossing crumbs to the birds. In this sun-dappled summertime ambience of picturesque small-town charm, I pulled my pencil and notepad from my bag and sketched a this little dog that sat so still, totally focused on getting anything from that table.

166

On the new life, which our growing fashion of summering by the sea is bringing to Martha's Vineyard, it is to be hoped that the pleasant traces of the old ways may be well preserved. ♥ N. S. Shaler 1874

In June, I saw my first fireflies, and felt like I was in kindergarten from the excitement. They were twinkling in the balmy dusk amid the ferns and clover at the edge of the woods. Clearly no stone was left unturned in the planning of the universe. I recognized them immediately. If there is any real sort of fairy thing, this must be it. I supposed J.M. Barrie got his inspiration for Tinkerbell from the fireflies. Pretty sure Walt Disney was into them too.

In short there's simply not,
a more congenial spot,
for happily-ever-after-ing
than here in Camelot. ♥

Slowly, the Island was working its magic on me. Sometimes after work, I walked down to watch the ferry come in. I can tell you, if you are ever sad and feeling lonely, it is a most uplifting thing to do.

All this and daffodils too.

Flags flew, seagulls cried, sailboats leaned in the wind and scooted through the foamy blue water. The ferry was huge and white, and the visitors and vacationers came down the gangplank single file wearing shorts and sandals, having escaped real life on the Mainland, to come to the otherland of Martha's Vineyard where the Island fairies waited with scenes of delight to cause wonder and joy in the hearts of all.

167

There were shouts of "Welcome home" and "Welcome back."
Arms were flung wide for hugs and kisses. I watched while
dogs leaped and barked to get in on the action, grandfathers hugged
their sons, children ran to grandmothers, babies were passed around,
children chased in and out between the adults. This event of kisses
hello ～ and then, after the ferry reloaded for the trip back, everything in reverse, and kisses good-bye that sometimes included
tears ～ had gone on for as long as people had been coming to the
Island and was so filled with love and tradition, that no matter
how I'd been feeling before, the vision of it warmed my heart to
the correct and true temperature and all was right with the world.

Sometimes I would walk over to Mad
Martha's Ice Cream for an orange
sherbet and chocolate chip sugar
cone. On my way home, I'd see
station wagons, just arrived,
loaded with kids, beach umbrellas,
and ice chests, careening down Main
Street, with the smiling faces of yellow labs and terriers hanging
out the windows.

I'd stroll through the old neighborhoods of two-story white houses,
built along narrow lanes originally made for horses and carriages,

overhung with hundred-
year-old trees, lined in
hydrangeas nodding their
heads over picket fences
in front of graceful, old
gardens full of charm and
history. And I fell even
further in love. I was all
so beautiful. ❤

ISLAND CHARM

Let yourself be silently drawn by the strange pull of what you really love; it will not lead you astray.

Rumi 1207-1273

I loved gingerbread!

19 People from a planet without flowers would think we must be mad with joy the whole time to have such things about us.
   Iris Murdoch, *A Fairly Honorable Defeat* (1970)

Felt strangely drawn to old doors

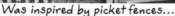

Was inspired by picket fences...

enthralled when they were smothered in roses

espite the beauty around me, I still spent way too much time thinking about my pitiful past. An article in *Cosmopolitan* said it would take five years to get over a relationship that had lasted 10. I found that totally unacceptable. In five years, I would be 41. I didn't have that kind of time.

> Your senior years will be happy and successful.

Much as I loved the gourmet food store, I couldn't work part-time forever and I had developed a Carlton/house habit that wouldn't be cheap (however, as it was done incrementally, one, which would be me, tried not to notice). And I had *plans*. I needed to go to Europe someday. I was determined to find my way forward. I refused to curl up and die there alone with nothing to show for it. I couldn't abandon my heart to the past of all places.

My relationship with Cliff had controlled my life for 10 years (my own choice I reminded myself), I wasn't going to let it continue, in absentia, for another five.

A SHIP IN HARBOR IS SAFE, BUT THAT'S NOT WHAT SHIPS ARE BUILT FOR. ♥ *John A. Shedd*

I finally went to a psychologist for help. She told me (while I blubbered into a tissue) that I had a right to be sad, that she would worry more if I wasn't sad, that it was normal to withdraw ~ to feel invisible and self-conscious at the same time ~ my self-worth had been dependent on Cliff, our home and his gold stars of approval, now it was gone and what had passed for self worth had gone with it. She told me it was okay to grieve. She said it wasn't my fault, I'd lost my identity and it would take time to make a new one. She put her arm around my shoulders, hugged me and said I had to forgive myself. She said it was a huge opportunity to be a blank slate. She said I should feel lucky because now I could be anything I wanted. She gave me a phone number and suggested I take a course in meditation that was just starting up.

I didn't feel that lucky and I didn't understand why I had to be the one to be forgiven, but I went ahead and forgave myself anyway. And I knew it was the right thing because, for some reason, it made me cry.

AFTER A YEAR IN THERAPY, MY PSYCHIATRIST SAID TO ME, "MAYBE LIFE ISN'T FOR EVERYONE." *Larry Brown*

TRIED & TRUE
Recipe for
STARTING OVER
HOMEMADE & FROM SCRATCH

4 c. silence
SEASONED WITH
1 lb. bird song
3 pr. flannel jammies
2 gal. telephone, room temp.
75 bottles of wine (to drink with)
700 lbs. girlfriends
1-5 kitties (or, to taste)

MIX WELL. LET SIT SIX YEARS.

Meditation? Well, I thought, I had tried wishing on the moon, on hay trucks, first stars, falling leaves, rainbows, hummingbirds, eyelashes, ladybugs, birthday candles, shooting stars, and blown dandelion puffs. I'd thrown coins into fountains, ripped apart fortune cookies, read horoscopes, had my handwriting analyzed, got my palm read, had psychic readings, pulled on wishbones, and had never EVER put new shoes on the kitchen table. (Such bad luck!)

BLOW ALL OF THE FEATHERY REMAINS OFF A BLOWN DANDELION FLOWER WITH ONE BREATH. YOU WILL GET YOUR WISH.

It was all fun, but it hadn't gotten me anywhere. I did exactly what the books said and followed my heart down the road less traveled where I went out on a limb, hoping and praying for the thing that would tell me who I was and where I was going. And so far I had nothing. So why <u>not</u> try meditation? I knew what Cliff would call it: "Mumbo jumbo." But, there was nothing to lose. It wasn't like I was busy. The only other alternative was to give up, and that was not going to happen.

Where troubles melt like lemon drops, away above the chimney tops, that's where you'll find me...
♥Judy Garland

In Agnes's Bartlett's Familiar Quotations, I'd starred a quote by Georgia O'Keefe: "I'VE BEEN ABSOLUTELY TERRIFIED EVERY MOMENT of MY LIFE AND I'VE NEVER LET IT KEEP ME FROM DOING A SINGLE THING I WANTED TO DO."

So, ah, I realized, terrified is normal. Even for the genius class.

Since I came to the Island I'd been reading everything I could to learn how to live a fulfilled life and hadn't had very much luck. What I really wanted was something easy, with a straightfor-ward, no-nonsense title like *The Secrets of Life* ～ a plain, simple, practical guide (preferably a pamphlet), a 1-2-3 shortcut, first you do this, then you do that. Like a recipe, with basically guaranteed results, two cups of this, a tablespoon of that, put it together, and voila!

Instant enlightenment. Some people seemed to have found the answer. <u>Someone</u> must have written it down, and I was determined to find it. This "blind struggle" I'd been experiencing for years (as Louisa May Alcott called it) was making me crazy.

I never found that easy 1-2-3 book I was looking for, which is one reason I wrote this book. No two people find their path in the same exact way. What rings one person's bell is sure to be a lead balloon for someone else. I'm sure my experience won't help everyone, but at least I can say I wrote it down.

The books I was reading gave wishy-washy advice like "Be happy," "Be yourself," and "Live in the moment," none of which helped. I understood that part. I could actually do everything on that list just by making myself a bowl of hot salted Tater Tots. There had to be more to it than that.

So, I started reading autobiographies, biographies and diaries of people I admired to learn how they had overcome obstacles, discovered who they were, moved ahead, and made something of their lives.

Joy is not in things, it is in us.
Benjamin Franklin

It didn't look like I was going to be having kids, or be married, or any of the normal things. So what was it going to be, just sit here and molt? World without end, amen? I could die here like Agnes and be forgotten and no one would care for my baby book either. Well, that was just unacceptable. My mother had worked much too hard on that book.

☺ In all the world there is only one you.

173

The stories I was reading were inspiring; the struggles of people who'd made something wonderful of their lives gave me hope and helped me understand that no one is born with all the answers.

Perhaps the beginning is just to say nice things are going to happen until you make them happen.

Frances Hodgson Burnett *The Secret Garden*

(My favorite authors had been hinting the truth to me since childhood.)

But the very best discoveries of all came slowly and from the most unexpected place: my quote books. After starring my favorite quotes in *Bartlett's* and enjoying them so much, I wanted more, so I began collecting them, and after a couple of years I had a shelf full of them. It didn't matter the subject: Quotes from the Garden, Quotes from the Kitchen, Quotations for Women, Quotes for the Lovelorn, Quotes from Yesteryear, Quotes for Artists, Quotes from Victorian England, Quotes from the Bible, or Native American Quotes, I wanted them all, looked for them in every bookstore I visited, brought them home and read them like novels. Another gift from Agnes, that amazing bit of inspiration I found in her house.

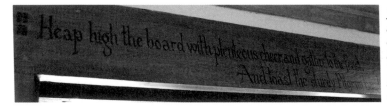

I painted this quote about Thanksgiving over the door in my kitchen, celebrating "the sturdy pilgrim band whose courage never ceased."

I took quote books everywhere with me, out to lunch, and when I traveled, reading them cover to cover, continuing to circle and star my favorite lines. In these books I found every important thing ever said, by all the smartest people who ever lived; practical words of wisdom from the ages, from all countries, on every subject, since the beginning of recorded time. Everything that needed to be said had been said. The books were distilled genius ~ witty, charming, inspirational, genius. For an unschooled person in a hurry for answers, these books were perfection.

STARS for DISTILLED GENIUS

It is not easy to find happiness in ourselves, and it is not possible to find it elsewhere. **Agnes Repplier**

One can never consent to creep when one feels an impulse to soar.
Helen Keller

Laziness may appear attractive, but work gives satisfaction.
Anne Frank

If A is success in life, then A equals X plus Y plus Z. Work is X; Y is play; and Z is keeping your mouth shut.
♥ALBERT EINSTEIN

Quote books introduced me to authors I hadn't read before, like Mark Twain, who said, "If everybody was satisfied with himself there would be no heroes." I read so many wonderful quotes by Mark Twain, I became curious about him, so I read his autobiography, fell madly in love with him, wished to date him and have his children. I didn't love him because of Tom Sawyer and Huckleberry Finn, but because of HIM. I traveled to his beloved house in Hartford, Connecticut, stood on his porch surrounded by everything he had described and all the things he loved, including his bed with the carved angel heads, and cried like a baby. I cry like a baby writing this, I love him so much. This was the first house of one of my heroes I was able to visit, but it would not be the last.

Me in front of Mark Twain's home on Farmington Ave. in Hartford, CT. Thrilled to the tips of my toes.

The young Sam Clemens. Adorable, or what?

CLOTHES MAKE THE MAN. NAKED PEOPLE HAVE LITTLE OR NO INFLUENCE IN SOCIETY.
♥Mark Twain

175

Inspiring
HEROES
Try hard & never give up

If I could be half as brave as these people, I would be happy.

— Helen Keller —

It's not in the stars to hold our destiny but in ourselves.
♡ WM. SHAKESPEARE

— Mark Twain —

Catch on fire with enthusiasm & people will come for miles to watch you burn.
♡ John Wesley

Eleanor Roosevelt

YOUR WISDOM WILL BRING YOU MUCH RESPECT IN LATER YEARS

Louisa May Alcott

Albert Einstein

Anne Frank

Benjamin Franklin

Elizabeth von Arnim

here were quotes from some of my favorite authors, like Elizabeth von Arnim and Lucy Maud Montgomery that were so wonderful and smart I became curious about them and wanted to know how they got to be so brave and how they learned to think the way they did. (This was before Google. We're so lucky now, we have instant answers to any curiosity. Read a line, wish to know more, run to the computer and voilá the world and all that brilliance is right there waiting.)

— Abigail Adams —

ver time, through my quote books, I discovered many people who became my heroes, because these were people who fought for truth, justice and the American way, even if they were not Americans ∼ people who even in the darkest times and with the most impossible obstacles, never gave up. I read about people like Anne Frank, Helen Keller, Eleanor Roosevelt, Albert Einstein, Benjamin Franklin, Gladys Taber, Abigail Adams, Julia Child, Louisa May Alcott, Ralph Waldo Emerson, Beatrix Potter, and many more. There should really be an exclamation point after every one of those names. They lit a little fire inside me.

Gladys Taber

Julia Child

— Beatrix Potter —

George Bernard Shaw's definition of a gentleman: A man, but more often a woman, who owes nothing & leaves the world in debt to him. ♥

Reading their perspectives on life made the world seem a saner place. Inspiring dreamers and do-gooders who, like the old movies, and the words to the old songs I loved, were like antidotes to the demoralizing chaos that populated the Pandora's box in my head ~ and increasingly, the daily news of war and homelessness, and grotesque talk shows where relatives and best friends were encouraged to physically fight each other and pull each other's hair on air (and worse), and soap operas where if it could go wrong it would go wrong. Even the weather report, each prediction of a storm threatened a new "storm of the century." This kind of noise seemed to be getting louder all the time; I didn't see how we were supposed to take it. How were people expected to get through a day, with all the worrying we had to do?

The modern rule is that every woman must be her own chaperone.
♥ *Amy Vanderbilt*

It was easy to see why they were doing it. There was money to be made.

I read Amy Vanderbilt's quote and realized what had to be done. Slicing & dicing wasn't only for food. It was for TV, movies & books, too. Choose your poison carefully is what I thought Ms. Vanderbilt was saying.

I do not ask for any crown but that
which all may win;
Nor try to conquer any world,
except the one within.
Be Thou my guide until I find, led by
a tender hand,
The happy kingdom in myself & dare
to take command. ♥
Louisa May Alcott

Feed your life from the well of SWEETNESS ♥

The stories of my heroes provided me with MUCH better things to think about. Important things, meaningful things, real things, that mattered and didn't depend on ratings. Learning about them, reading their words made me want to be a better person.

I also learned that my heroes had heroes of their own. They had stood on the shoulders of those who came before them, learned from them, were inspired, took what they learned and wove it into their own originality, and made something brand new for their own times. Everything was connected. Everything stepped us forward in thought and genius. If we could see through the fog of cultural bombardment, it was there. And what I understood everyone to be saying en masse was, "If I can do it, you can too." My heroes had all been children at one time, blank slates like me. It was easy to see that I was made up of exactly the same basic material as the people who built the Golden Gate Bridge and the Statue of Liberty, heart, blood, bone and dreams. And desire, too.

☺THE COURAGE TO BE GREAT LIES DEEP☺ WITHIN US.
3, 7, 22, 25, 39, 40

When there's an original sound in the world it makes a hundred echoes. ♥ John Shedd

I wanted more than anything to be an echo, "a cheerer of men's hearts" as Emerson put it. I wanted to lift up in the same way I was being lifted. Little by little, between the quote books and biographies, I began to find the practical advice I was seeking. One particular theme appeared in almost every quote book I read, which boiled down most succinctly to this:

Seek not outside yourself ~
Heaven is within.
♥ Mary Lou Cook

I read quotes relating to this theme so often I started keeping a separate notebook for them. Everyone was saying it, people born hundreds and even a thousand years apart were all saying the same

179

thing, the Bhagavad Gita, the Bible, Shakespeare, Marcus Aurelius, Louisa May Alcott ~ it was too much of a coincidence that these and so many others should all be credited with different versions of that same exact message: that heaven lies within. But that's what they all said, I read it again and again, and so I began to trust this message. Now all I had to do was find the "within" they were talking about, because if that's where heaven was, that's where I wanted to go.

* * *

TRAVELING TO THE NEW COUNTRY of "WITHIN."

Where there's a will there's a way.

My mom

There were four of us in the meditation class and the first night was dedicated to each of us figuring out what our dreams actually were. As our teacher said, "It's hard to make your dreams come true if you don't know what they are." That was me to a tee.

Those questions ~ What are your dreams? What do you want to be when you grow up? ~ always left a huge empty space inside me, my own personal black hole. The wind whistled through it. People said, "Think big, dream big" but I could never think of anything big enough or good enough to fill that space ~ nothing I actually thought I could do. Could I wish to be an astronaut? No. I didn't want to be an astronaut. But what then, a movie star? No, don't be ridiculous. A bank teller? No. But what?

All I want is a dress with puffy sleeves. L.M. Montgomery

Our teacher helped us boil the question down to something small and real and practical. She asked that we make a list of the things we *didn't* like in our lives, and then, she said we should rewrite the list and change the negatives to positives. "And then," she said, "I'll teach you how to meditate on those things and you will find that you can have them. You don't even have to believe me, just follow the directions, give it a try, and see for yourself."

FINDING YOUR DREAMS

So, "I keep procrastinating on writing a cookbook" (for example) becomes, I choose to write a cookbook. And, "I hate being alone so much" becomes I choose to have more friends. I did what she said, and here's what I got:

I choose to be loved.
I choose to walk out to the water every day.
I choose to have a beautiful garden.
I choose to give myself one gold star a week.
I choose to eat healthy.
I choose to write a cookbook.
I choose to have meaningful work that will be flexible
and pay enough so that I can go to California when I want.
I choose to have a fireplace, to exercise, to be surrounded with friends, to have a best girlfriend on the Island, to call my mom more often, and to go to England on an ocean liner like Fred Astaire. Oh yes, of course, and I choose to change the world.

What you seek is seeking you. RUMI

And there they were; reasonable, down-to-earth dreams that seemed relatively attainable and not too much to ask. I already had my small, real and practical house, a wonderful walk, and my three kitties, if I got those other things too, my life couldn't help but be happy. My dreams tumbled into that huge empty place of unknowing and filled it right up to the brim. For the first time in my life, I knew what I wanted.

Books. Cats. Life is Good.
≈^^≈ Edward Gorey

Neglect not the gift that is in thee.
I TIMOTHY 4:14

I COULD SEE ~ THEY WERE ALL SAYING IT ~
THE SECRET WAS WITHIN.

During the following six weeks of classes, I discovered that, for me, the key to making my dreams come true ~ the one that opened the door to the gift of "within" ~ was meditation.

My quote books were telling it all.

Except for the point, the still point,
There would be no dance,
And there is only the dance.
♥ T. S. Eliot

At first, when I closed my eyes to meditate, it was hard to concentrate. My mind was like a run-away two-year-old going off in all directions; I had to chase it down and bring it back over and over again. It was difficult to be still. I found it so frustrating that I almost quit the course, but I thought, then what, I had nowhere left to go, and the second week was better. Which is why they call it a practice. They gave us guided tapes to use at home; the voice in my ear telling me to "Close your eyes, take a deep breath, now imagine . . ." made it easier. I did what I was told to do: meditated twice a day ~ 20 minutes, morning and night ~ and went to one meeting a week.

THE FUTURE BELONGS TO THOSE
WHO BELIEVE IN THE BEAUTY
OF THEIR DREAMS. ♥
♥ ELEANOR ROOSEVELT

My experience in learning to meditate was like the movie *The Secret Garden*. Up until they opened the door to the walled garden, the film was in black-and-white, but on the other side of the door, it turned to glorious Technicolor.

> THE AWAKENING OF CONSCIOUSNESS IS NOT UNLIKE THE CROSSING OF A FRONTIER—ONE STEP AND YOU ARE IN ANOTHER COUNTRY.
> ♥ADRIENNE RICH

By the end of the six weeks, tears of joy leaked from my eyes. In the quiet I began finding a connection to everything that mattered, God, spirit, hope, love and the shiniest star of all, faith . . . I felt just like I did out at the end of the dirt road on days I thought I could almost fly.

FOR TO HAVE FAITH IS TO HAVE WINGS.
♥ J. M. Barrie

Meditation is cumulative. It changes nothing if you do it for a day. All the power is in the repetition. To make it work, you have to practice, and it's slow, like learning to play the piano, but the difference is, it does not require talent or any sort of aptitude, or even any real interest. Just practice. And in the next few months and then years, a little at a time, things in my life began to shift.

HEROES   MEDITATION   NATURE

KEYS to my CASTLE

In the beginning I had difficulty with something they suggested we say at the end of every meditation: "I choose to be true to myself." I didn't know what that meant in the same way I wouldn't have understood a phrase spoken in Japanese. So far I'd only been what I thought others wanted me to be and my foundation had all the attributes of quicksand. It was hard to be true to something when you didn't know what the something was.

I want to do something splendid ... something heroic or wonderful that won't be forgotten after I'm dead... I think I shall write books. ♥ Louisa May Alcott

It was a time of waiting, and to anyone whose ever had to go through a waiting period, you know it seems like it will never end. Especially when you have no idea how it will come out. But when you look back, the waiting was the very sweetest part, like fresh corn, just picked in July, the first of the season, when the kernels jump from the cob into your mouth.

YOUR WORK IS TO DISCOVER YOUR WORK & THEN, WITH ALL YOUR HEART, GIVE YOURSELF TO IT. ♥ Buddha

"You just think lovely wonderful thoughts," PETER EXPLAINED, *"and they lift you up in the air."* ♥ J. M. Barrie

New wainscoting & green wallpaper

And while my mind was flying around in the cosmos and practicing meditation, the rest of me stayed on the ground, reading my quote books, riding my exercise bike, making living room curtains out of old quilts, taking walks to the water, reading *Enchanted April* (a heavenly book Myron left on my porch), writing letters home, painting the straw hats hanging on my door, writing in my diary, planting roses, filling the bird feeders, making tea breads and salads for the store and working downtown three days a week, I decided that what my little house needed was a one-room cottage guesthouse in the back yard.

I painted the hats on the back of my door

184

Quilts for my windows to keep out the cold

The Summer House

Oh, you won't know why, &
   you can't say how
Such a change upon you came,
But once you have slept
   on an island
You'll never be quite the same.

Rachel Field

"Build a house?" exclaimed John. "For Wendy." said Curly.
"For Wendy?" said John, aghast, "Why, she is only a girl."
"That," explained Curly, "is why we are her servants."

♥ J. M. Barrie

After Carlton finished the kitchen and put the wainscoting and wallpaper in the living room, I asked how much it would cost for him to build a guesthouse in the backyard. I wanted a place where my friends and family could stay when the weather was good so that they wouldn't be upstairs in the dark attic.

I drew a picture and asked Carl to make it the size of two king-sized beds; half the floor space would be taken up with a built-in platform bed and the other half would have a chair and a rug and a place to hang clothes. He looked at the drawing and said he could do it for $2,000. So much cheaper than remodeling the attic, so I said, "Yes, please!"

I asked him to frame the house and leave it unfinished inside so it would smell green like freshly cut wood. No bathroom, no electricity, no insulation, just a simple summer house (which very quickly became known as "the shack"), almost a box, candle

CUTEST LITTLE THING

lit, with a peaked roof and lots of windows so that my guests (and me, too) could sleep under down comforters in the moonlight, smell salt air, hear the wind in the trees, the splashing of summer rain on the leaves, the foghorn, the chirping tree frogs, the singing birds, and the chorus of crickets in the fall. It would be like camping in the woods without mosquito bites or bears.

— Welcome to the Hotel California. —

The end is nothing,
the road is all.
♥ *Willa Cather*

My guests could be out there with nature and the fireflies, and read their books or write in their diaries by candlelight and oil lamp. I saw myself bringing them tea and English muffins in the morning. It would be soooo romantic. Diana would love it. Jane would love it. Everyone would love it. I could even loan them a kitty!

Carl built the summer house close to the deck, just outside my back door (so everyone could easily get to the kitchen or the bathroom). When it was finished, I

— View from window at foot of bed. —

painted the floor green, gave it some rag rugs, and hung bunches of dried flowers from the rafters over the bed. Carl added a large stone for the front step and put up

All the windows were different; the two at the peaks were stained glass, this one opened in.

186

a window box, which I filled with pink geraniums. I carried home small white rocks from the beach, a few at a time, to make a little border for the flowerbed, and hung a straw hat on the door. It was the perfect place to experience the change of seasons. When you looked at the two houses together, the shack was kind of like the caboose to Holly Oak. For a surprise, Carlton carved a sign for it that said "Branch Office."

For the rafters

God and nature, the whole world and the stars too...

Carl stripped this branch, put it in a corner so guests could hang their clothes.

The only photo I took of the inside was this old Polaroid, which doesn't do it justice, but here it is, with dresser scarves & lace placemats for window valances.

And then I learned something else about meditation. The quiet was fertile ground for creative thoughts to grow, and came with the gifts of acceptance, bravery (to a certain extent, everything had its limits), and gratitude (which had no limit), and more than anything, it seemed to be putting a foundation under those drifting, disconnected, frightened feet of mine.

Sadness is but a wall between two gardens ❧ Kahlil Gibran

"It's impossible," said pride.
"It's risky," said experience.
"It's pointless," said reason.
"Let's do it anyway," said the heart.
♡ Author Unknown

CHAPTER NINE

Isle  of Dreams

A very little key will open
a very heavy door.
Charles Dickens

The Nor'easter Fall 1983

The way to read a fairytale is to throw yourself in.
W. H. Auden

There were no nor'easters in California. But there were on Martha's Vineyard ~ wild storms that hit the Island at any time of year, sometimes with hurricane-force winds strong enough to knock over anything that got in the way.

In the winter there were raging blizzards where snow blew in all directions at once. I'd fall asleep to the whistling wind and the comforting sound of the snowplow going by out front (a sound very much like hearing your parent's voices murmuring in the living room when you're nine and falling asleep), and wake up in the pale blue light of winter, excited to peek out and see a wonderland where every twig and leaf was sparkled in snow.

Sometimes lightning and thunder, pouring rain, and howling wind tried to beat through my front door. In a bad nor'easter, the Island lost electricity, the ferry boats stopped running and we'd be cut off from the Mainland, floating alone and vulnerable in a great stormy sea. But that's what had gone on here for hundreds of years; people just hunkered down to wait it out. When it was over, everyone  would pick up the downed branches, move the trees off the road, drag the yard furniture back from where it blew into the woods ~ or, depending on the time of year, dig

A disconcerting sight.

out their neighbors, blow away the snow, and move on. I could already see that life would be a little bit too humdrum without a good solid nor'easter to shake things up every once in a while. That elemental thing of nature added spice,

Surf After a Storm, Oak Bluffs, Mass.

Blow, winds, & crack your cheeks! RAGE!
Shakespeare

was grand drama, took the hum from the drum.

AND SO IT CAME; the sky turned black, the wind whistled, and the air was littered with leaves. I called the kitties, got the car windows closed, pulled the laundry off the line, filled the bird feeders, and brought in the porch plants while small branches crashed down in the woods around us. There was a flash of lightning, a crack of thunder . . . and the rain began beating in waves against the windows of Holly Oak. The lights blinked and then went out and I said to myself, cringing at the thunder while digging around in the junk drawer looking for a flashlight, *Tell me again why you think you need to be here?*

'Twas a Dark & Stormy Night
not fit for man nor beast

The electricity had been out for hours. The lines were down which meant no phone, no TV, and no stereo to distract me — and no heat — just candlelight, and spooky storm noises that sounded like someone trying to break in amid flashes of cold blue lightning where if you caught a glimpse of your face in the mirror, you looked like you had a flashlight shining under your chin.

Thank goodness for the old gas stove — it had a beating heart, the pilot light burned softly no matter how bad the storm, providing warmth for the house and a cup of tea with honey and lots of milk to soothe my thunder-jangled nerves.

Chicken stock simmered away in the candle-lit kitchen, fogging up the greenhouse window, while a sweet potato roasted in the oven for my dinner. But it was still cold . . . I was wearing wooly slippers, flannel jammie bottoms, three sweaters, a shawl and a hat. I tried not to let the sound of the storm unnerve me, but when I went to the kitchen to put the kettle on, the candles flickered and my shadow leaped up the wall — I caught it out of the corner of my eye — jumped back and almost had a heart attack. Which made me talk to myself out loud, "Good God, Sue, get a grip."

The corners of the room were so deep in shadow Stephen King could have been standing there with his dog Cujo at his side, their bloodshot eyes gleaming right at me, and I wouldn't have seen them. I wondered: Did our foremothers flinch at every crack of thunder? Did Abigail Adams shrink back in her long skirts?

191

I didn't think so. Girl Kitty and ☁ Man were rolled into balls in their various nooks, Billy was 🌧 hiding under the bed. Either I needed to join Bill or I needed to change the subject and do something else besides think about the storm.

I pulled my shawl tighter and carried a candle over to the bookcase, holding it low so that I could see the books, thinking to myself, *If I did write a cookbook (as had recently been included in my meditation), not making any commitments or anything, but just pretending, what shape and size should it be?* I touched the spines, pulling one or two out to look closer. *Hmmm. I thought, I guess I could make it any size.*

Imagination is more important than knowledge.
♥ Albert Einstein

This kind of question had stopped me for years. Silly, little, easily surmountable details like *What size should this cookbook be?* kept me from trying. I had no idea how to write a book, and I didn't know anyone who wrote books. A voice in my head said it was a joke to try. But then again, my girlfriend Jane thought I could, and she was much smarter than that voice. And what else did I have to do on a dark and stormy night? It couldn't hurt to think about it.

I pulled out a few books of different sizes, turning them over. I chose one with a shape I liked and set it on the table. I lit Agnes's old oil lamp with the cracked chimney and put it, along with every other candle in the house, on the table with my

There is something special about painting by candlelight that takes you back a couple hundred years.

192

art things. I pulled my chair up close to the table and in a circle of candlelight, I measured the book, and with a pencil and ruler I drew it on a smooth piece of Bristol board. And there it was, the shape of the book, on paper. I sat back surprised; my first roadblock was gone in about sixty seconds. How odd, I thought, that was way too easy.

Lesson #1: To begin, begin.

I hoped that the Bristol board choice of paper would be okay in case of actual publication. It seemed like the smoothness would work better for cookbook pages than my usual textured watercolor paper. But more questions kept coming: Should I leave white space around the sides of the page and write the recipe in the middle or should I bring the border right against the edge of the paper? What kind of pen should I use? How do I lay it out? What's the best way to ensure straight lines of copy? I had no idea. I had to guess.

Lesson #2: EVERYONE GUESSES. CREATING IS NOT A SCIENCE; IT'S EXPLORING THE UNKNOWN BY YOURSELF WITH-OUT A ROAD MAP. IF IT WAS EASY EVERYONE WOULD DO IT. And there ain't no crying in baseball.

One thing I did know: my book would have drawings on every page just like the recipe cards I'd made for Jane's wedding present. So what would be the best way to do that? How could I wrap the text of a recipe around a painting of a bowl or a slice of watermelon with my typewriter? What if I wanted to put falling leaves down a page between the words? Because there were no computers or Photoshop which would have made it all very easy, I decided I had two choices: either I had to draw the bowl or whatever art I wanted to include on that heavy art paper, run down to the basement and somehow roll it into the IBM Selectric I kept on a big table down there, then try to type around the art, which sounded ridiculous from the start, especially when I thought about putting leaves between the words, OR I could handwrite the whole thing, which made much more sense, at least to me.

Lesson #3: One Thing Leads to Another. My mom ♥

I had always loved handwriting. Since grammar school I'd played with lettering in different styles ~ blocks and italics, script and printing, round letters and thin, far apart or close together, arched and shadowed. I scribbled on backs of envelopes, inside the covers of my address book and all over my notebook at school, every kind of fancy and plain letter. I never took a calligraphy class, but I always got an A in handwriting. So I thought, Why not a handwritten cookbook? Recipe cards were handwritten; letters had handwritten recipes in them, Jane's cards were handwritten. Handwriting and cooking went together in an old-fashioned "real" way. It was almost traditional, a grandma thing. It would make my book "handmade."

Writing I Love You in all the ways I could, for my 2nd grade Mother's Day Card.

I heard interesting dialogue while watching an amazing movie made in 1927 called Metropolis and wrote it down: "The mediator between the brain and the hands must be the heart." Because they're connected. That's why old handwritten letters are so wonderful, and like little bits of history. You could tell things about people from their handwriting. Secret personal things like their humor or their fears. With no machine between the hands and the heart, a letter could send kisses or tears across continents.

Lesson #4: Follow your heart.

194

All the cookbooks I'd ever seen were typeset, so I wasn't sure anyone but me (and Jane, I knew she would like it) would go for this idea of a handwritten book. I figured if I ever got far enough along to show it to a publisher, if they required it to be typeset, then so be it. That would be fine with me. I was sure they would know how to get the art between the words. But in my secret heart, I thought the handwriting made it more personal, like a letter, and the more I thought about it, the more I loved the idea of a handwritten book.

L e s s o n # 5
THERE AIN'T NO RULES AROUND HERE! WE'RE TRYING TO ACCOMPLISH SOMETHING! ♥THOMAS EDISON

Here's what's cooking:
MOLASSES-RAISIN DROP COOKIES
Recipe from the kitchen of: GRANDMA
3 CUPS UNSIFTED ALL PURPOSE FLOUR
2 TSP. CINNAMON, 1 TSP. GINGER, 1 TSP. B. SODA
1 CUP SHORTENING, 1 CUP LIGHT BROWN SUGAR, PACKED
2 EGGS 1/2 CUP LIGHT MOLASSES 1/2 CUP BUTTERMILK
1 1/2 CUP RAISINS, SEEDLESS, 1 CUP CHOPPED NUTS.
SIFT TOGETHER FLOUR CINNAMON, GINGER, SODA
SET ASIDE. IN LARGE BOWL E MIXER BEAT SUGAR
+ SHORTENING UNTIL FLUFFY. ADD EGGS E BEAT
UNTIL LIGHT. AT LOW SPEED BEAT IN MOLASSES

+ BUTTER MILK. GRADUALLY ADD FLOUR
MIXTURE BEATING JUST UNTIL BATTER IS
SMOOTH. STIR IN RAISINS + NUTS.
REFRIGERATE 1 HOUR
PREHEAT OVEN TO 375° LIGHTLY GREASE
COOKIE SHEETS. DROP DOUGH BY ROUNDED
TEASPOONS 2 INCHES APART ON SHEETS.
BAKE 12 MINUTES OR UNTIL COOKIES
ARE LIGHTLY BROWNED. REMOVE TO WIRE
RACK COOL COMPLETELY.
MAKES 3 1/2 DOZEN.

My grandma and my mom sent recipe cards in their letters.

I'd always painted at my dining table ~ paper, brushes, paints, ruler, pens, and the water pot I'd bought at Disneyland (infused with Disney magic I hoped) were all there along with my dictionary. My chair faced the two front windows of the house, and was about five steps from the teakettle. There was a basket on the table just the right size for a kitty to curl up in. It was like my own brand of Feng Shui. Old movies were one clicker-button away. "La Vie en Rose" could play on a whim. The phone cord stretched from the kitchen wall to the table. I could paint and talk on the phone at the same time. Who could ask for anything more?

Lesson # 6: **Never get too far from the tea kettle.** ♥

*U*nder oil lamp and candlelight on that stormy night, I started my first page ~ a one-page love story about my new home and fall, the roadside stands and apple season in New England.

I marked quarter-inch increments in pencil down both sides of the paper. I connected the marks with a ruler, lightly penciling straight lines across the page, generally leaving space for the watercolors if I knew where they were going to be, going back and erasing the lines if I needed to. On a separate piece of paper I wrote in quick longhand what I wanted to say about the arrival of fall. When I thought the words were good enough, I copied them in my best handwriting in pencil onto the lined Bristol board. Then I wrote over the pencil with a Rapidograph pen. When the ink was dry I erased the pencil marks.

I'd been inspired by a recent visit to a roadside stand where I bought several different apple varieties; I had them lined up in front of me. I drew each one onto the paper, filled my jar with water, swirled my brush in apple reds, Granny-Smith green, and Golden Delicious yellow; painted stems and leaves, left light spots where the candles reflected and shadowed the edges for roundness. I wrote down the best uses for each apple, which ones were tart, which were juicy, which were good with cheese, for baked apple, for pie and for eating And that was it. Page one of my "cookbook" was done. It took maybe four hours. I didn't really time it. I was lost in the absolute joy of doing it ~ and never noticed the storm.

APPLE ❧ SEASON

Here in New England we celebrate the arrival of Fall in many ways ~ its an exhilarating time of change signaled at first by a quick drop in temperature, then a gradual turn of the leaves from their Summer greens to the magnificent golds and reds of Fall. It's a time to prepare for the cold to come, to make the garden secure with rototilling and mulch, to finish the last freezing and canning for the Winter supply, to put the pumpkin on the porch and the wreath of dried flowers on the door. Time for cozy dinners of soup and bread and indoor games by a toasty fire. It is also Apple Season ❧ and is heralded by the many busy roadside stands with their big baskets of juicy apples for sale. I want to give you just a few examples of the different tastes available and some of their uses:

Granny Smith · Golden Delicious · Cortland · Delicious ·

Tart hard apple ~ use in pie & apple crisp ~

Sweet, fine-grained, use in Salads & for baking ~

Soften-tender apple ~ a use for baked apple ~

Crisp and juicy good with cheese, for McIntosh flavor breaks ~

McIntosh   Jonathan

good eating wonderful with cheese

tart and juicy good for applesauce

Let the beauty of what you love be what you do. ♥ Rumi

The next day, I did a second page, a recipe for Apple Crisp, which I laid out the same way: measured and drew lines on a new sheet of paper, wrote everything carefully in pencil, washed my drawings with watercolor as I went along, and then I thought, since there was space on the page, I should include one of the quotes I'd been collecting. I thought people were bound to love these quotes as much as I did if they just knew about them. I had just read one by Ogden Nash about gardens that I thought was cute even though it had nothing to do with apples ~ I liked "horticultural ignoramus" and could relate very easily from a gardening point of view.

So that's what I put at the bottom of the page. I wrote over the pencil with ink, waited for the page to dry, erased the whole thing, and there it was, page two. I set both pages up on the hutch for viewing.

APPLE CRISP

375° Serves Six

An old standby with a deliciously crunchy top. Serve it either hot or cold ~ pour thick cream over or serve with ice cream. ♥

Meat 4 medium, peeled, sliced, tart apples (Granny Smith)
3/4 c. firmly packed brown sugar
1/2 c. flour
1/2 c. oats
3/4 tsp. cinnamon
3/4 tsp. nutmeg
1/3 c. softened butter

Preheat oven. Butter a square baking pan. Place the apple slices in pan. Mix remaining ingredients and sprinkle over apples. Bake 30 minutes or until apples are tender and topping is golden brown. ♥

"My garden will never make me famous,
I'm a horticultural ignoramus,
I can't tell a stringbean from a soybean,
Or even a girl bean from a boy bean."
Ogden Nash ♥

I wanted to include my very best recipes, tried and true.

I thought to myself, Look at that. It's not so difficult; the trick is to think small. I shouldn't think of a whole book at once, that's too big, too scary. I should think of it as one page at a time. And if I make each page the very best I can, when I put them all together to make a book, it will be the best book I can do. It's not think big, like everyone tells you, it's think little, the same way you cross the beach in the sand, slogging along, one little step at a time, until you've made it.

197

And that thought carried over to, Maybe it's not a "lifetime" ~ that's not how to think about it. It's just today. If today is the best I can make it, the lifetime will take care of itself. If this hour, right now, had kitty petting, dinner cooking, and book reading in it, and the next had a bubble bath and a call to my mom, and the next had painting with a cup of tea, an old movie and a walk in the woods, if I put all those hours together, what a lovely Red-Letter life that would make.

And I remembered the wonderful quote by the prolific "Author unknown:"

All the flowers of all the tomorrows are in the seeds of today.

Of course, doing these pages was a leap of faith. Full belief in myself wasn't going to come all at once or be easy. I still had a lifetime of work to do in that regard. I started and stopped on the book several times, thinking, No one will ever want this. I quit for months before I realized, You're right, they probably won't, but no one will ever get the chance unless you finish it. The war between the old me, and the thing that wanted to be born went on for a while, it was a fight to the finish. But meditation had the upper hand whether I was conscious of it or not. With meditation, you don't really have to be there, you just have to do it.

The Secret of Success is Constancy of Purpose.
♥ Disraeli

A word grows to a thought ~ a thought to an idea ~ an idea to an act. The change is slow; the Present is a sluggish traveler loafing in the path Tomorrow wants to take.
Beryl Markham

* * *

Over the months and then years, Cliff (remember him?) stayed true to his word and did not let me "get away." But I didn't make it easy for him. In the beginning our phone conversations were short and businesslike, tying up loose ends from our marriage, often ending with me hanging up on him. After his last trip to Europe in the summer of 1983, he called and mentioned AGAIN how spoiled I was (while I was standing there on an island in the Atlantic Ocean with the phone in one hand and toilet brush in the other and he was unpacking his Paris suitcase). I said, "Don't say things like that. Why are you calling me? I'm not spoiled. I'm working. I'm trying to do things. You're the spoiled one (no, you are, no, you are, etc.). Go away and leave me alone, I don't want to talk to you. Anymore. Ever. Again." Clunk.

Dear Susan-
I heard this song the other day by some guys who were young when we were- it reminded me of you.

There are places I remember all my life
Though some have changed.
Some forever, not for better,
Some have gone and some remain.

All these places had their moments
With lovers and friends I still can recall
Some are dead and some are living.
In my life I've loved them all.

But of all these friends and lovers,
There is no one compares with you,
and these mem'ries lose their meaning
when I thinnk of love as something new.

Though I know I'll never lose affection
For people and things that went before,
I know I'll often stop and think about them,
In my life I'll love you more.

Your bud- Cliff

LESSON #7

Never allow someone to be your priority while allowing yourself to be their option. ♥ Mark Twain

A few months went by and then I got a letter from him where he typed all the verses to the John Lennon song In My Life. He signed it, "Your bud, Cliff," complete with hand drawn hearts and arrows. Your bud.

What was I supposed to do with that? I put it in my diary, along with everything else. Barfastarfard. (Only readers who've digested Arf and Arfy will understand the word, but insert whatever expressive expletive you like, because I know you know.) I did not want any more glimmers of false hope confusing the issue.

He didn't stop calling. At first I was lying when I told him, "If that's what you want, then okay, I'm your friend." But as time went on, I got used to him still lurking and it did get easier. In fact I began to think of the divorce as a horrible relief, kind of a joke gift. I really wasn't born carrying the hating gene or the revenge gene. I had wicked thoughts here and there, but I

Me in painting mode. Carlton made the hutch behind me. Man Cat's asleep on the couch. I wish I could jump into this photo and close that drawer. Why is it open? I don't know.

pretty much figured everyone was doing the best they could despite the brainlets that some of us had been fitted with, including me of course. He couldn't help the way he was and neither could I.

> ⭐ "Holding on to anger is like drinking poison and expecting the other person to die." –Gautama Buddha

The thing was, for some reason, it seemed we were each kind of still addicted to having the approval of the other. That gold star thing we did for each other was difficult to give up. When he called, which wasn't every day, just once in a while, he was nice, he would send me music tapes, and have roses delivered with little notes; he even asked for his favorite stuffed chicken breasts recipe. Once, when I was home in California, he bought me a divorce ring. It's not like I could magically forget him. Or even that I wanted to. Yes, I realize there was a conflict, an emotional tug of war between my heart and my brain, and the voice inside that said, Please, shut up, you are driving us crazy, but that's the way it was. And I felt safe, so far away, where he couldn't get me even if he wanted to.

EVERYTHING WAS ACTUALLY

JUST RIGHT

Don't think I don't know that you're yelling at me, "Stop talking to him! Never talk to him again!" I can hear you from here just like I could hear Diana from there. I think you had to be on the experiencing end of what was going on. But really, deep inside, I was actually quite safe from him when I was on the Island, almost a rock.

IF ONLY THE BROTHER HAD HIS HUMAN FORM, IT WOULD HAVE BEEN A WONDERFUL LIFE. ♥ Brothers Grimm

I wasn't thrilled when he married Kimmi; that was a terrible day. But I cheered right up a couple years later when they got divorced. After Kimmi came more girlfriends, first Lauren, and then Amber ~ who had the mesmerizing slow-blinking eyes of a ventriloquist's dummy and became famous (the stuff of legend) for buying a purse, scandalously costing $700 (over $1,600 in today's money), that put me and all my SLO girlfriends into free fall of shock and awe. We lit the phone on fire on that one. Diana called her Charlie McCarthy.

I was always a little down when he fell in "love." The interchangeable girl would stay home and fold his t-shirts and he would be so happy, it was irritating. He would perform false advertising and take her places. I always felt a stab of joy when they broke up, which was inevitable considering the degenerate teenagers he was attracted to, not to mention he was still drinking the stud-muffin water over there and all his relationships were doomed because of it.

I carried on, one foot in Martha's Vineyard and the other in California. It sounds wonderful, to be in love with two places, but it meant I was homesick no matter where I was. When I was in California, I wanted to be on the Island, when I was on the Island, I wanted to be in California. I wasn't doing justice to either of my two lives. There was like a line of demarcation somewhere over Kansas that I crossed for years, flying from old life to new and back.

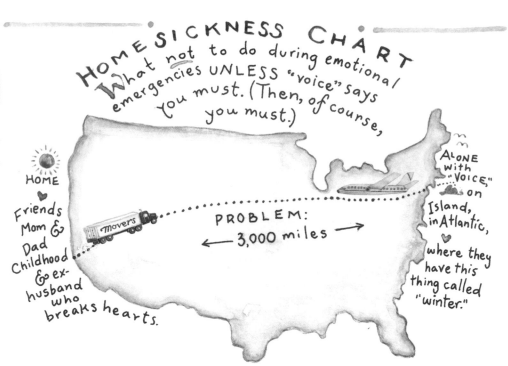

HOMESICKNESS CHART
What not to do during emotional emergencies UNLESS "voice" says you must. (Then, of course, you must.)

HOME

Friends Mom & Dad Childhood & ex-husband who breaks hearts.

PROBLEM:
← 3,000 miles →

ALONE with "VOICE" on Island, in Atlantic, where they have this thing called "winter."

movers

Sometimes I'd yearn so much for California it hurt. I longed for my old life, the old familiar things.

I missed January lunches at my favorite restaurant with my best friends outdoors next to the ocean under blue skies and fair-weather clouds. I missed my mom and laughing with my sisters. I missed crazy, unexpected things, like for instance, the fabric store, Dan and the art store, my hairdresser, Copeland's Shoes, even my dentist. I missed driving 70 miles an hour on 101 with the windows down and the music up, and that curve in the road as you round the bend on your way home from Cambria going south and

January late lunch in Shell Beach, CA. They may have only one season, but it's a good one.

S KY, BE MY DEPTH;
WIND, BE MY WIDTH
& MY HEIGHT;
WORLD, MY HEART'S SPAN;
LONELINESS,
WINGS FOR MY FLIGHT.
— Leonora Speyer

see Morro rock and the whole long stretch of coastline shining in the sun where your heart just flies to the moon from the beauty, and I missed my spot on the beach. Mostly little things, things I took for granted before. And of course there was always Cliff — still a crazy attraction, but the reason I left in the first place and the reason I had to stay gone. California was dangerous, I never felt totally safe when I was out there.

B ut the Island tugged my heart back, even from far away, like a magnet. When I was in California, my heart leaped at the smell of eucalyptus and all the things I missed, but soon I would ache for the quiet, the wild and changeable weather, old houses and red leaves flying past church steeples, and the bells, and my little spot behind the counter at the gourmet food store, the smell of the sea in a storm, my house where the only people I had to please were the kitties and me, the total privacy of it all.

And the seasons. Each so completely different than the other. Each so hopeful in all its fresh newness in the change where no mistakes had yet been made. They were becoming my anchors, almost the

only truly dependable things I knew, because, no matter what, after a long gray winter, the snow *would* melt, spring *would* come, the flowers *would* bloom, the sun *would* shine, it always, always happened that way. So life affirming! (I kept waiting for it to not happen, but it always did, and I was always surprised like when opening birthday presents.)

There are only two ways to live your life. One is as though nothing is a miracle. The other is as if everything is. ALBERT EINSTEIN

Attention lavished on my old life left little room for social progress in the new one: I had acquaintances on the Island; Ellie and Myron were my friends. There were people I could say hello to at the market, and regulars at the store where I worked, but no best friend, no Diana. I missed that teatime-girlfriend-talk beyond words. People were nice but their dance cards were full. True blue best friends who know all your flaws and like you anyway don't grow on trees and all mine were too far away.

Should I stay or should I go?

So all went well & happily for a time, but then
she began to be very sad & sorrowful, all day
long she had to go about alone; & she did so wish
to go home to her father & mother & brothers & sisters.
♥ *The Blue Fairy Book*

I came very close to leaving the Island and moving back to California; once I even put my house on the market. It was late March of my third year. Diana was thrilled when I told her. Within two or three days I had to call her back and say, "Ooops, never mind," because a real estate agent came to show my house and was met there by Judy Belushi (John's widow), who was looking for a house to buy.

As it turned out, Holly Oak was smaller than she wanted ~ and thank goodness, because immediately, with Judy and the agent still in the house, the thought of selling it became so real, and scary, and wrong, that I instantly took it off the market, at least in my mind, before the agent even got out the door. Take my kitties away from the only home they'd ever known? To where?

But Judy and I hit it off and she ended up staying for about three hours. We drank wine and ate apples and cheese and talked and laughed about the things women always talk about: our families, where we grew up, our experiences.

It wasn't long before she asked what brought me to the Island and told me she was planning to live here full time, and we discussed how strange it was that both of us unexpectedly lost the lives and the people we thought we had, how we both gravitated to the Island to start over and how hard it was to do. I told her how I'd coincidentally come to the island on the very day that John had died and that I was at the Kelley House when all of their friends came for his funeral. We marveled over the small worldness of things and compared the fatal flaws of our two ambitious husbands. We talked about what could have been, if only . . .

She was still in mourning; I could just imagine how it was for her, she and John had been high school sweethearts, he was her first love, they went to the prom together. It must have been like hitting a wall. Sadness filled the room as dusk began to fall. I got up and turned on some lamps. After she left I felt so bad for her . . . at least Cliff's fatal flaw wasn't fatal ~ I still had the opportunity to kill him myself if I felt like it. I could call him up and yell at him for ruining every-thing. Judy couldn't do that. She was totally on her own. That made me the lucky one.

I'm nobody's sugar mama now ~ I'm lonesome ~
I've got the lovesick blues. ♥ Patsy Cline

It's Raining Men
Hallelujah?

SITTIN' HERE EATIN' MY HEART OUT WAITIN' ~ WAITIN' FOR
SOME LOVER TO CALL... *Donna Summer*

Diana was always calling and harassing me about my love life, or lack thereof. Our conversations went much like this one in 1984:

"How much longer are you going to hole up out there? It's time for you to get back home and fall in love with someone gorgeous."

"Please. Not gorgeous. They're trouble. In fact, they're all trouble. But I figured it out, what I need is a 6'2" Leo, like my dad, who can cook. I get along great with my dad. I really don't think I should bother with anyone else. I'm thinking about placing an ad."

"Wow, I'm impressed. That's so scientific of you. Why do you want him to cook? You cook."

"It would be nice if we had something in common. And, mean people don't usually cook. It's like a little test. Anyway, you'll be thrilled to hear, I actually went on a date."

"Oh, God, now you'll probably marry someone out there and pawk the cah on Martha's Vineyard for the rest of your life. What do you mean you had a date?"

"Yeah, well, fat chance of pawking the cah around here. Wait till you hear."

"Oh, thank God. Okay . . . Go."

"For starters, the guy picked me up in a topless orange dune buggy."

"Oh, that's probably not good."

"It had a long curved antennae with a little flag tied to it and it sounded like it had a lawnmower engine for a motor."

"Where'd you meet this guy?"

"He came into the store a couple of times and the other day he asked me to go for a drink at a new place in Edgartown. I never saw his car. He looked normal, although perhaps a little too clean ~ but I wanted to go to that restaurant. So, against my better judgment, FOR YOU, I said yes. Thank you very much."

"You need me there. You can't do this alone. You're no good at it."

"Obviously. He came to the door reeking of Beeman's gum."

"What's wrong with that? I love Beeman's gum."

"You come date him then," I said, laughing. "Anyway, so out the door we go, and there's the dune buggy in my driveway. Day-Glo orange. With words painted on the back that said, "Feelin' Groovy." What could I do? It was too late. I had no choice but to get in. Instead of normal seats, it had slippery orange plastic chairs shaped like half an egg screwed to the metal floor. It was so low, I was practically sitting on the road, my legs were straight out in front of me. I felt like Wilma Flintstone."

I continued over her laughter and her yabba-dabba-dooo comment.

"It was a beautiful night, so he drove down Main Street ~ which was crammed with summer people, walking, eating ice cream, standing in line at the movie theater, going in and out of the stores, all dressed up for dinner in their summer Island finery. Traffic was bumper to bumper. I guess he wanted to be seen, and he got what he wished for because that engine was so loud everyone turned to look at us. I would have lain on the floor if I could have gotten any lower than I already was. To talk to him I had to scream above the noise of the engine all the way to Edgartown and THEN he parked right in front of the restaurant ~ which was a sidewalk café, and there were all these people and I had to climb out of the orange dune buggy, basically get up from the ground, totally blown to smithereens, and literally crawl to my feet. I wanted to die."

Diana was practically hysterical. "Oh my God!"

"There's more . . . He was wearing ironed jeans with a perfect crease in them, bright white tennis shoes, a big diamond pinky ring and clear polish on his nails. He was better put together than me."

It's always something . ♥ Roseanne Roseannadanna

"Oh, no," she snorted.

"Oh, yes." I replied, accusingly. "That's it. I'm done."

She sputtered a protest.

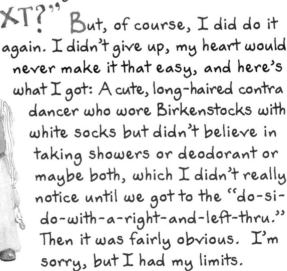

17905
NO REFUNDS
HOT TIN ROOF
DOUBLE ID REQUIRED
JOHN SEBASTIAN & JESSE COLIN YOUNG
Sunday July 8, 1984
Early Show 7:00 P.M. $7.00

"No," I said, "really. I can't do this again. Please don't make me."

"NEXT?" But, of course, I did do it again. I didn't give up, my heart would never make it that easy, and here's what I got: A cute, long-haired contra dancer who wore Birkenstocks with white socks but didn't believe in taking showers or deodorant or maybe both, which I didn't really notice until we got to the "do-si-do-with-a-right-and-left-thru." Then it was fairly obvious. I'm sorry, but I had my limits.

208

Another guy I met at a dance place called the Seaview hollered in my ear over the music that he didn't have a checking account, didn't believe in banks, taxes, or voting. He kept his ratty old passport in his back pocket and proudly showed me, under the table, what he said was $11,000 rolled up in a dirty ball in his front pocket. I had to fight to keep a good expression on my face. He actually asked me if I believed in big families. The world is already way too crowded right this second, I thought, escaping out the door when he went to the bathroom.

Psychotics, say what you want about them, tend to make the first move.
♥ DAVID FOSTER WALLACE

Adventures in BEING SINGLE

Another of my "dates" got falling-down drunk on Harvey Wallbangers (vodka, orange juice and Galliano, who wouldn't be sick?) and threw up in the parking lot at the Hot Tin Roof, which was probably a life-saver, or else all that booze would've killed him. That's when I began to realize it was going to take a pretty special man to take the place of no man at all. You can't just go around handing out trust like it's nothing.

There were others: I danced, several times, with tall, dark, sexy . . . and married. Or twenty-two. Or both. The dancing was excellent, Bruce Springsteen: Glory Days, Dancing in the Dark. Tina Turner: What's Love Got To Do With It. And Elton: I Guess That's Why They Call It The Blues. Fun

The Edgartown Yacht Club Christmas Party. Snowy freezing night, almost to the door, threw my gum into the harbor, my bracelet went with it & not a thing could be done.

209

It wasn't all a one-way street, there were also some very cute guys that would not give me the time of day ～ feeding my fear that probably no one I wanted would ever want me.

There was one large guy with a beer belly and one eyebrow that stretched across his entire forehead, and a long chin beard who showed me some serious interest. In conversation, when I asked him what he wanted out of life, he cocked his head pertly, chin hair wagging, and said, "You." I had just met him. The very last thing I wanted him to want was me. Anything would have been better. His friends called him "Goat," if you can imagine. Probably because of the beard ～ nicknames were popular on the Island. I could not see myself dating a guy named Goat. My whole life I would have to say, Dinner, Goat! Or, Goat honey, the car sounds funny. It wasn't going to happen.

And there were assorted gentlemen who came back from the restroom with white powder on their noses; one of whom talked to me seriously about the benefits of free love and wife swapping. It was the 80s, a confusing time if ever there was one.

It's not like I didn't try.

I wouldn't want to marry anybody who was wicked, but I think I'd like it if he could be wicked & wouldn't.

♥ L.M. Montgomery

I thought maybe I'd hit it big (for about a minute and a half) when I met a tall aristocratic-looking man named Stuart (I looked away from the orange pants with embroidered blue whales on them, knowing it was a cultural thing and you shouldn't judge a book by its cover). He was a handsome (but not unbearably), unmarried, so he said, banking executive, with a house on another island that shall not be named (it wasn't Nantucket).

But in conversation at the bar of the Harborside, he described his golf game in minute detail (you can just imagine how fascinated I was; maybe if I played golf or knew one thing about it, I would have liked it, luckily he didn't notice). Then we got to talking about the celebrities who lived on Martha's Vineyard. He told me Jackie Onassis would not be welcome on "his" island because she had had a "Catholic husband" (he really said that, out loud, in casual conversation with a virtual stranger and did not even care; and even though her "Catholic husband" had been dead for 20 years, she was still tainted in his eyes) and Woody Allen also would not be welcome and he actually thought this was how it should be. Then he called his neighbor (on his crummy island) a "redneck." We kind of got in a fight when I asked him to define redneck. He got huffy and told me the people who lived on *his* island were the people "who founded this country" and I rolled my eyes and told him those were their descendants living off the fat of the land, a pure accident of birth. I pushed my chair back, stood up and asked, "How do you expect to change the world if you hold onto ugly, divisive views like those?" As I shakily gathered my purse and sweater, scared of myself and scared of him, the vile little (he'd shrunk) man said, "The way to change the world is to get rid of emotional, know-it-all women like you. The last thing this world needs is more strident, pushy women."

Eeeeek. Needless to say it didn't work out between the Lilliputian and me. Wharfut arfuh parfig, I thought to myself. Can you imagine being married to him?

Very few men care to have the obvious pointed out to them by a woman. ♥ *Margaret Baillie Saunders*

So I started giving up on men and that type of a future. Dating was like a shoe that didn't fit. Maybe I was too set in my ways. Maybe I wasn't supposed to fall in love. Not everyone gets to. I still looked, was still interested, but I didn't trust that part of the dream anymore. When asked out, I would automatically say yes, because I was no good at making up quick lies, I would get caught, I'd see hurt in their eyes and feel terrible. So I learned to just say yes, then, most of the time, I would call them back, and say, "I forgot, I can't, I checked my calendar and just remembered my mom is coming for a visit." No one felt bad. Everyone was happy.

It was dangerous business hanging your heart on the line for all to see. I'd already been through that and it had been a disaster.

For she fears that one will ask her for eternity & she's so busy being free.
♥ Joni Mitchell

oh the power

Besides, I had more than my share of blessings. I could decorate my house any way I wanted (free reign for the doily mentality); I had complete control of the clicker and could have pancakes for dinner, in bed, if I wanted. When the birds were singing and morning light filtered through the lace curtains in my tiny blue bedroom, it was like waking up in a field of forget-me-nots. No one said get up, so I could lie there as long as I wanted & write in my diary for hours.

Dear Diary

This goes on for six pages! Did I think I would forget?

Counting my Blessings

I had a job I liked that kept me reading cook-books and in the kitchen creating new recipes. I had projects. I had even sort of started writing my own cookbook. And I had a growing sense of peace coming from my daily meditation. These were enough miracles for me; a person shouldn't be greedy.

I put on my favorite T-shirt with a black and white, snarling, wolf-like dog wearing a spiked collar. I wore it out gardening and to the market over a white lace skirt. On the front, in black letters it said, "Too Mean to Marry." When guys saw it, they seemed to think I was flirting with them. At the market, one guy looked at my shirt, raised his eyebrow, looked me in the eyes and said, "Really?" The communication situation was bleak. But the flirting was good.

I still have it. Worse for wear, but so far I can't bring myself to throw it away.

An Arabian proverb says there are four sorts of men:
He who knows not and knows not he knows not: he is a fool—shun him.
He who knows not and knows he knows not: he is simple—teach him.
He who knows and knows not he knows: he is asleep—wake him;
He who knows and knows he knows: he is wise—follow him.
OR. He who thinks he knows but who knows NOT. *Lady Isabel Burton*
Get used to him he is everywhere

Alone too much, now talking back to quote books.

DIANA'S ADVICE TO THE LOVELORN:
When you see crazy coming, cross the street.

213

NOVEMBER 1984

Painting baskets was good therapy.

Coast to Coast

In the same kingdom, near the castle, lived two brothers, both country boys, so clever, their hands could make anything they wanted.
♥ FRENCH FAIRYTALES

Holly Oak continued to be ever so much more interesting than the guys I was meeting, by far. I was constantly being inspired by it, or from books and magazines I was reading, for it. I was happiest when I was puttering around, making things to decorate it. One day, I looked over at the far end of the living room and thought, as I had so many times before, I wonder if Carlton could take that window out and put a fireplace there instead?

I loved what Gladys Taber wrote in her book about her fireplace at *Stillmeadow*, the pre-Revolutionary war farmhouse where she lived in Connecticut. She described it in detail, the way it would have looked when it was

DON'T YOU THINK?

first built in 1690, and how it would have been used for cooking, with hanging iron kettles, and everyone would gather at the wide hearth and tell stories around the flickering firelight. She wrote about the time a hurricane knocked out her electricity and how she fried an egg in a small iron pan in the embers at the edge of her hearth. I wanted to do that, too, fry an egg in the embers during a storm. Maybe the sounds of crackling flames and settling logs would keep me company while I painted and keep me warm when there was thunder and lightning. Maybe it would be like having another person living in the house.

Since I was going to California for a month. I asked Carl if he could build the fireplace while I was away, so I could have it for winter. His brother Eric was a stonemason, and of course Carl, as always, said the magic words I loved to hear, *Yes, I can*. We decided that inside the house, the fireplace and hearth would be made with used red bricks, framed in wood, with a mantle. And outside, the chimney would be made of different-sized stones.

I hadn't been to California in a while. Miranda had a girlfriend who needed work and would be filling in at the store while I was away. Carlton would watch after the cats. I was thrilled to be going home. A. I had lost six pounds, and B. There was a family reunion at my mom's ~ and C. I was staying with Diana and she was having a party for me. I was excited to show everyone the pages I'd done for my "book" and see what they thought.

The Plane Crash 1984 . . .

while the mouse is away...

BILLY HAD THE VOICE

WHICH IS HOW I REFERRED TO THIS INCIDENT EVEN THOUGH IT WASN'T REALLY A PLANE CRASH, IT WAS CLOSE ENOUGH FOR ME.

I was 37 and had been flying in planes since I was 19. During those years, I did everything I could to make it less stressful. I tried Valium to make me sleep. I tried cocktails. Neither of these lessened my anxiety. I would arrive at my destination wide-awake but tired and/or hung over, and spend the first two days in a fog. By the time I moved to the Island, I'd given up anesthetizing myself and flew cold turkey, pure as the driven snow. Even meditation didn't help with the adrenalin overload. I had more or less learned to live with it. It was the price I had to pay to live in two worlds.

I don't have a fear of flying. I have a fear of landing too fast. Marty Ingalls

So, healthily stone-cold sober, excited to get home to California, with every nerve ending standing at attention, and my hands in a cold sweat, I boarded the plane in Boston and made my way back to my lucky seat. The plane was almost empty; I was alone in my row. There was one chatty guy on the aisle about three rows up who'd turned to talk to the stewardess perched on the arm of the seat across the aisle from me.

I had my foot pillow, my hand pillow, my headphones ~ every-thing I needed for survival. I was wearing a heavy gray wide-wale corduroy skirt (good for hand sopping) and wine-colored boat-necked sweater with a white blouse under it, along with my thin green plaid wool scarf to ward off airplane-fear chills. I had my meditation tapes, but I didn't think they would be loud enough to distract me from the takeoff noises, so I also had Creedence Clearwater. ♪♫ I was as ready as I could be, strapped in and buckled up, although we hadn't started moving yet.

The chatty guy in front reminded me of Bob Newhart. Every-thing about him was beige, his shawl neck cardigan, his plaid shirt, his slicked hair with a side part, his wide forehead and his long sideburns. He looked at the stewardess and then me and said in a clipped Midwest accent, "I have a cute flying story." I was thinking, since nothing ever strikes me as cute on an airplane, and I could see I was going to be inflicted with this story, Please make it good. WE HAVE CLEARANCE, CLARENCE. ROGER, ROGER. WHAT'S OUR VECTOR, VICTOR? ♥ The Flight Crew; AIRPLANE

"I've never been a great flyer," he said, with a little stutter, "but I was on a plane once; we'd been cleared for take off (Oh no, I thought) ~ and, just like on this plane," he nodded up front, "there was a big movie screen, like that one." (I look up front and there's a big movie screen. I'd never seen one in a plane before. It was new, and already I didn't like it.)

He continued, "The takeoff was televised to us passengers from a camera in the nose. We could see it all, heh-heh-heh." (I wasn't comfortable with his story so far. There was nothing funny but he was laughing and I didn't really want to watch us take off on a big screen when I knew it was me in the plane. I decided that when the time came I'd close my eyes and not look.)

"Well," he went on, "everything was fine, we began to taxi down the runway. We started picking up speed, racing along faster and faster, the nose came up, and we were just about to leave the ground when suddenly," he chuckled, "for absolutely no apparent reason, the captain SLAMS on the brakes and slows the whole thing down so fast we're all thrown forward in our seatbelts. I can't see WHAT'S going on, and then the lights go out, and the little overhead doors pop open and the oxygen things come dangling down. I don't know what to do, I mean, we were on the ground, did I need oxygen? I'm grabbing at it when we come to a screeching stop. The doors fly open, the evacuation slides inflate, everyone's panicking, passengers are screaming and crawling over the seats and each other to jump out of the plane! It was a mess. I broke my leg in the crush, but, as it turned out, there was really never any danger."

(Oh, okay, no danger, just a broken leg, screaming, crushing, and death by adrenalin.) I was staring at him, sending invisible laser arrows into his face.

He wasn't done. "There'd been some problem with the airspeed indicator not working right or something that got way outta hand. Anyway we all got free tickets for another flight anywhere this airline flew, and I got a free trip to Paris, heh-heh-heh." Self-satisfaction swept across his beige face. He was giddy from the cuteness of his story. He got a free trip to Paris.

I just looked at him. WHAT ???

This was the voice of a loser and I was on a plane with him.

218

But there was not one thing I could do about it. Our plane's jet engines were beginning to squeal, like it was in neutral and the captain had it floored. It felt like we were shuddering at the end of a fully stretched-out rubber band waiting for it to be let go. I did not want to do this.

I turned to the stewardess for confidence building. I said to her and the beige man, "When I hear a funny noise or we're in a lot of turbulence I look at the faces of the stewardesses. If their expressions are calm and cheerful, I feel a lot better."

"Ohhhh, no, don't look at me," she said, rolling her eyes and looking SO MUCH like Carol Burnett playing Eunice it was unnerving. "I'm the first one to fall apart."

Oh, my God, two chowderheads and me, the only normal one. Help!

It was too late; I was basically trapped in my seat. It was our turn to taxi. I was in a cold sweat, not looking at the screen in front of me, eyes closed tight, music blasting in my ears from my Walkman. I thought, *if we can just make it into the air, we'll be all right, we'll have lift.*

We hurtled down the runway, the overhead bins were rattling, the plane was vibrating, we were going a thousand miles an hour, the nose lifted, the floor of the aisle slanted up ∽ it was time to leave the earth, goodbye cruel world. And suddenly, un-believably, at the last possible moment, the pilot SLAMMED ON THE BRAKES, putting my heart into the ear section of my head. The nose of the plane came down hard as we continued streaking down the runway, the engines screamed into reverse ∽ I lurched forward in my seat, held tight by the seatbelt. It was déja vu all over again. My eyes flew open, my hands were dripping wet. I wanted to kill that guy and his story.

Frozen in my seat, I turned my head and looked sideways at the stewardess strapped in across the aisle from me. She wasn't calm, she wasn't the picture of mental stability; she was scared to death. She turned her head and looked at me. We stared into each other eyes as we bumped along the tarmac clutching our armrests for dear life. (I'm always amazed at the amount of information women can pass between themselves with no words spoken.) The pilot was stopping the plane as quickly as he could, but he said nothing to us, there was no reassurance or explanation. The man had zero bedside manner.

The plane finally came to a stop; I waited for flames to burst up the sides of the windows. Nothing happened. The plane slowly turned and started back to the gate. The doors didn't open; the evacuation slides didn't come down. Should I be worried about this? I didn't know. I saw no flames. The pilot wasn't talking. I sat there, numb and waiting.

Finally, the captain got around to announcing in his best Casey-Kasem-goes-to-Texas voice, "We-hel-hel, ladies and gentlemen, THAT was unexpected, but as you see, we have aborted the flight. Don't you worry, we're goin' back to the gate. Just as we were about to take off, there was a report from the plane behind us ～ that little ole' engine door back there was wide open and we were losin' oil." He didn't say "oil," he said "awl." "Sit tight, he continued, "we're goin' back to the gate to get 'er checked out."

TEN FOUR, GOOD BUDDY.

The moment we came to a stop I got out of my seat and asked the stewardess, "Can I get off this plane?"

She said, "Really? Are you sure? I don't know if we can let you do that. I'll have to ask the captain." And up front she went. I was already packing up, because if I had to break out a window, I was getting off that plane.

She returned down the aisle. "He says it'll only take a couple of hours to fix. Really, it's not that big . . ." I was shaking my head through every word she was saying, she stopped, took a deep breath and said,

"He says if you really want off, you can go, but we can't give you your checked baggage."

aggage? I didn't care about no stinkin' baggage. I didn't even care, at that moment, that I would be too late for my flight to SLO, thereby missing my Tuesday Girls welcoming committee that had practiced, "Here she comes just a-walkin' down the street," to serenade me when I got off the plane. I could not continue on this broken plane. Why? Because it was broken. I didn't want to be on a fixed plane. I wanted one that had never been broken. Number one, I needed to get off, and number two, I needed a DRINK.

You will do foolish things, but do them with enthusiasm. ♥ COLETTE

got off the plane enthusiastically ～ not embarrassed. Didn't care, was happy. Went to the bar, got a table, opened my diary and began to write. Drank two Jack and Gingers with straws and crushed ice and sat there writing until my adrenalin was sufficiently diluted with alcohol. And what did I write, in my frenzy of fear, now that I had embarrassed myself off that plane and wasn't going to arrive home on time, had no way to get to LA, all my clothes were on the plane, and I had to call Diana and tell her I'm sorry? I wrote about how cute the guys in the bar were and how sad I was that Diana wasn't there to get any of them for me. This, in a nutshell, is why the diaries must be destroyed.

Only good girls keep diaries. Bad girls don't have time ♥ Tallulah Bankhead

　　I was an idiot.

considered trying to find a train station, but it would have taken me hours in a phone booth to sort it all out, and since I didn't have my toothbrush or anything like that, and all my things had now flown to LA on the broken plane, I had no choice but to make reservations on the next plane. I could do this because of the bourbon. It wasn't even a nonstop flight, but I was too toasted to care. I slept through the stop in Chicago. We arrived into LAX too late for a connecting flight to SLO. I found my luggage there waiting for me and took a cab to a hotel. The next morning I rented a car and drove to San Luis Obispo. Seared to the bone with flying in airplanes.

Diana and I managed to kill off most of that memory very quickly. I stayed with her; we set up a long table outside on her deck and had a party for the Tuesday Girls. We made a flourless chocolate cake and roasted garlic with hot bread and linguini in clam sauce and wine and bourbon and salad and every other thing we could think of. Everyone was there, babbling conversation and filling their glasses. Shelly, just getting over a cold, stuck her head out the door with a perplexed look on her face and said to us, her self-appointed godmothers (poor thing), "What is it for a cold? Red or white?"

Debbie, Janet, Diana, Me, and Sarah

It is much easier & often more pleasant, to be a warning rather than an example.
♥ ELIZABETH VON ARNIM

I showed them the pages I'd done for my "cookbook," feeling a little embarrassed, but needing to know what they thought about the idea. Diana loved the pages and immediately copied down the Apple Crisp recipe; Sarah said she thought a book like that would

Looking at my paintings

be a "huge hit." Everyone said nice things and made me feel really good, but then I realized: What could they say? They were my friends, and everyone knows, when it comes to this stuff, you can't trust your friends. (It was always much easier for me to relate to the reasons this book-writing thing wouldn't work, rather than reasons it could.)

Shelly and I drove down to LA for Thanksgiving at our mom's. The whole family was there: Mom and Grandma, Dad and Jeanie, brothers and sisters, aunts, uncles, in-laws (we called them the outlaws), and the grandchildren.

THANKSGIVING
Togetherness

Mom with grandchildren

Dad with grandchildren

Grandma with my four brothers, my nephew, & our cousin with Mom.

Dad and (wonderful) Jeanie

The Fabulous Eight, blinded by the sun, but in for a penny in for a pound.

Family Love

We put our feet on the coffee table, looked at photo albums, ate lots of good Thanksgiving starch, took more pictures for the next family reunion, and laughed our faces off, telling old stories about camping,

Nieces, Tricia & Karis

223

"Oh, they ran through the briars & they ran through the

and killing the neighbors, go-cycles, and the dangers of drinking horsewater.

Making Gravy

Heirlooms we don't have in our family, but stories we've got.
♥ ROSE CHERNIN

We went out dancing to a country-western bar; all of us Stewart girls loved being two-stepped and twirled by our handsome, can-fix-anything, cowboy brothers. We sang Good Night Irene ♫ at the end of the night, for the grandmother none of us ever met, my dad's mom, Irene Murray Stewart.

Our Boys

MY MOM'S DANCING SHOES

Like always when we were together, my brother Chuck played the guitar and we sang the songs ♪ he'd written. We knew all the words.

SISTERS
with Mindy-cat.

☺ A happy and harmonious family is important to you. ☺

brambles & they ran through the bushes where the rabbits couldn't go..." ♫ JIMMY DRIFTWOOD

224

This was one of our favorites, we were crying with laughter at his lyrics. (FAMILY HUMOR, RIGHTLY SHUNNED BY OUTSIDERS BUT PRICELESS *from* THE INSIDE.)

I'm So Lonesome In My Saddle ♪ Since My Horse Died

(Don't you love it already?)

It's so lonesome in the saddle
since my horse died.
My boots are worn from the dirt
when I do ride.
And my cows just roam around,
can't herd 'em up,
can't chase 'em down;
and all I own is brown,
since my horse died.

Yes, an' it's lonesome in the
saddle since my horse died,
and it all just rubs me wrong
along my backside.
Ain't got no to in my to an' fro,
got no giddy in my up an' go,
but what's worse
now wouldn't ya know,
there ain't no yippie in my
tai-yi-yooo-hooowoe.

and my saddle is flat
an' much too wide;
makes my legs stick way out ~
un-com-for-ta-bly ~ to each side!
Well, this saddle is still my home,
but this ain't no way for
no cowboy to roam!

Oh! The Wit! The Talent! The Charm!

Looking at my brothers I think it might be okay if mamas DO let their babies grow up to be cowboys. ♥

225

When I told my grandma about my almost-plane-crash and how worried I was about flying back home she gave me the same sage advice she got from her grandma: "Worry's like a rocking chair. Gives you something to do, but it won't get you anywhere." I always loved it when my grandma spoke Iowa to me. When she was happy about something she was "tickled," really happy and she was "tickled pink," and when she heard something amazing, she rolled her eyes and exclaimed, "Land!" (Land what, I always wondered. Land o' Goshen? Land Ho? I never knew what land.)

A HOUSE NEEDS A GRANDMA IN IT.
♥ Louisa May Alcott

Driving back to San Luis, I noticed how much the area had changed from my childhood. From Los Angeles to Santa Barbara, the coast was almost completely cemented in ~ cities and towns, homes, commercial buildings, driveways, sidewalks, acres of asphalt in parking lots, freeways, and overpasses. Where the Pacific ended, the asphalt began. Poor trees. Poor birds. I felt my heart magnet tugging me back to the Island, to the woods and the pond.

That which is not good for the bee-hive cannot be good for the bees.
🐝 MARCUS AURELIUS c. 161 AD

IT ISN'T AS IF WE HAVEN'T BEEN WARNED.

The battle for conservation is part of the eternal conflict between right & wrong. ♥ John Muir

Reading this was the first time I realized there was a "battle!" And that it was eternal!

226

Diana & me

Back at Diana's ～ just before Cliff came to pick me up to go to his mom's ～ I had an epiphany. I realized that for the entire time I had known him, I had behaved as if it was my job to keep him entertained. I had filled every waking moment between us with talk ～ ideas, dinners, and parties ～ afraid of even a single second of silence. He didn't ask for it; it was just what I did because I was young and so afraid of boring him. I never noticed this about me before, and now that I did, I found it nerve wracking. I'd been wearing myself out. When I read this Chinese proverb in one of my quote books, "OUTSIDE NOISY, INSIDE EMPTY," I decided to stop it.

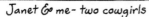
Janet & me- two cowgirls

I wasn't mad at him ～ just at myself, for always taking so long to figure things out. I realized this might be what they meant by "Be true to yourself" in meditation. So, when he picked me up, I got in the car and said hello, but that was all. I listened ♪ to the music on the radio. I didn't fill the void. I was happy and ♩ calm to the point of serene. It was nothing against him; I just didn't feel responsible anymore.

He didn't even seem to notice, and then a funny thing happened: He started talking and didn't stop. I just listened and smiled and he was funny and happy and went on and on. It was such a relief! It was probably a relief for him too. And a new thought for me to ponder, that I didn't necessarily have to put into words every single thing that crossed my mind. That would take some working on.

227

I showed Cliff's mom and dad my apple pages. Betty gushed and I blushed, and she said, *Oh Susie!* And sent my heart to the moon. Cliff and his dad liked them too despite the obvious doily mentality that was going into making them. But of course, I had the same problem with them as I did with the Tuesday Girls. They loved me; they would probably lie to spare my feelings. What they were saying felt beyond wonderful, but I couldn't really trust it.

Cliff and I drove over to Arroyo Grande to walk around a couple of acres he was looking at, high on a hill with a view of the ocean. Cliff loved real estate more than food; he loved building things. Views inspired him ~ he was on his third house since the one we built together, the one I thought we'd live in till we died. He was still sure of himself, drove too fast, and talked while looking at me instead of the road. But I didn't care. I was happy. I could smell the eucalyptus trees and the sea. He slipped in a tape and turned up the music: "Rocket Man." That wasn't fair, and he knew it. He said I was sweet. I told him I wasn't as sweet as I used to be.

✳ ✳ ✳ TRAIN TRAVEL 101

My month at Diana's was almost up. It was time to make reservations to go home ~ time to face the airplane again, and I was dreading it. In my years of travel I'd experienced turbulence at 30,000 feet over two oceans and the Rocky Mountains; had taken off and landed on tiny islands with short runways, had circled in and out of blizzard-blurred, precipitous mountain ski villages at 12,000 feet in twin-engine props. (The things you do for love!) I'd been ~~brave~~ trapped in a four-seater in fog so thick we could have been going straight down and I wouldn't have known it. I'd watched the sun set while stacked up in a jet-plane parfait, going in circles over New York. I'd given it plenty of time to prove itself, but nothing about flying was fun; none of it added joy to my life. It wasn't making me a better person. The best I could say was that I never actually lost consciousness. This last episode on the runway wasn't a big deal by some standards, not even a real crash, but for me it was the end. I figured it would add twenty years to my life if I never flew again ∽ from stress reduction alone.

NEVER LIVE FASTER THAN YOUR GUARDIAN ANGELS CAN FLY.

Maybe if there were more women pilots, it would have been different. But in those days, the people flying planes were the same people I'd seen riding dirt bikes until their teeth were black with grit and mud, who thought you didn't need brakes with go-carts that went 35 miles an hour, the

What's your vector, Victor?

same ones who jumped off roofs wearing a piece of canvas as a parachute, went head over heels into hospitals from their Harleys, did hard belly flops in the pool on purpose, kept real rabbit's feet in their pockets (the feet of rabbits!!!), loved the Three Stooges, liked to bite eyes and mouths out of their bologna (which to be fair, I liked to do too), spit on the sidewalk (which I would never do unless there was a bug in my mouth), and weren't that good at telling the truth or at monogamy (just for starters). How could I trust them? I was surprised they would get into planes with themselves. (By the way, I don't want to scare you, but in case you haven't noticed, with rare exceptions, these are the same people running the world today.)

Sometimes I wonder whether the world is being run by smart people who are putting us on Or by imbeciles who really mean it. ♥ Mark Twain

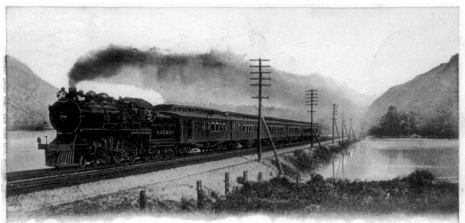

I decided I was all grown up and didn't have to get on airplanes anymore. Mark Twain had traveled the whole world without an airplane; if it was good enough for him it was good enough for me. I made reservations on Amtrak to take the train home. I reserved the smallest compartment called a "roomette," packed my jammies and my pillow, lots of decorating magazines, a biography about Zelda Fitzgerald by Nancy Milford, two new quote books, my diary, and my Walkman, with music and meditation tapes to keep myself busy on the four-day trip across Texas to New Orleans, through Atlanta then up to Boston. There were shorter, faster three-day routes through Chicago, but I was too late. They were all booked.

There was a good-bye lunch at Café Roma across from the train station. My girlfriends, my sisters, my brother, Stephen, and his wife Katie laughed and drank rosé and ate carpaccio at a table with a white cloth, under the eucalyptus trees, surrounded by bottlebrush and jasmine.

All too soon, the train came clanging into the station. They walked me over and we all kissed and hugged at the door to the sleeping car; the attendant took my bag to my room; put it away and hung my jacket in the closet for me. I waved to everyone from my window as the *Coast Starlight* slowly lumbered out of the station with my face pressed against the glass until we rounded a bend and I could no longer see them. Good thing I had a little room with a door because tears ran down my face as the train lazily wound through town, crossing

Café Roma, next to the SLO train station, has best carpaccio in the world.

over beloved territory, neighborhoods where my friends lived, past my favorite supermarket, my favorite coffee shop, and streets I'd driven a thousand times. As we curved into the foothills, I could see my old house and the orchard on the hill. We chugged through Price Canyon to Pismo Beach, to the sparkling blue Pacific and points south. I put my face in my pillow and cried my heart out to be leaving it all, already missing everyone.

By the time I reached LA and transferred to the *City of New Orleans* for the trip east, I was okay again. My mind had made the transition. I longed for the Island and my other life; I couldn't wait to see the kitties. I wondered how Carlton was doing on the fireplace.

I adored the train. It was heaven not to be at 32,000 feet, so human, so real, no one was in a hurry. The view was a thousand times better, and I enjoyed talking to the other passengers and the crew in the dining and lounge cars. I found out all the trains had names ~ besides the *City of New Orleans*, there was the *Empire Builder*, the *California Zephyr*, the *Southwest Chief* and the *Lake Shore Limited*, to name a few. And there was history: The oldest line had been in service since 1894. ♪ Isn't it ROMANTIC . . .
♪

America the Beautiful, SEA TO SHINING SEA

I could see the moon and the stars from my pillow at night. The sunsets were amazing as we chug- ged along over hill and dale, and the sunrises even better, streaked with pink and lavender. From my quiet, private room with a view, time stood still as

Sunrise Across the Desert

Over the River and Through the Woods

I watched America fly by my window at the civilized speed of between 80 and 100 mph. I could see kids playing baseball in parks and people sitting on porches, and I learned something about every state we went through. There were rushing rivers, red rocks, and corn-

fields with farmhouses and white barns, herds of antelope and wild horses, snow-capped mountains and deserts and tiny towns with brick or white clapboard houses, and little meandering dirt roads near the tracks, speckled with wildflowers, that went off to no-where. I had all the time in the

Streaking Through Autumn Leaves

world to read my books as the gentle rocking of the train made my eyes flutter closed, then open, then closed again. The compartment was muffled and quiet. I could pretend it was 1942 when the porter brought me coffee in the morning. There were no mobile phones then, if I wanted to make a call, I had to wait until we got into a station.

here was no connection to the outside world and no one could find me. It was four days of heaven. The Murphy bed came out of the wall of my compartment and took up the whole space, running the length of the window; there was a sliding door that locked and a heavy curtain that zipped. There was an electrical outlet in the room, and I made a note in my diary: Next time, bring an electric tea-kettle. (And chocolate, cookies and carrots.) It was a lot like camping.

A ROOM WITH A VIEW
So civilized!

Red Rock Canyon

Sunset in the Dining Car

Farms and Cornfields

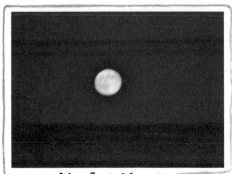

Your Basic Moonrise

The Lounge Car

Twas in the lounge car with my books, wrapped in my lucky green scarf, writing in my diary, and drinking tea at a table by myself. The train had stopped in front of a tiny one-room train station in Meridian, Mississippi. Out my window I saw a very large guy carrying a leather satchel get on board. He came into the lounge car and plopped himself down at my table (everyone shares tables on the train). He was probably around 50 with a big, open, craggy sort of face. He started talking to me in a friendly, outgoing, California-like, "Where-ya-goin'? Where-ya-from?" kind of way. Very talkative.

I was a little careful ~ I was trying to figure him out. There was something different about him, he didn't seem to fit in and I wasn't sure why. I watched him for clues: He was a really big man, a self-possessed person who took up a lot of space on his side of our table. And he was wearing enormous diamond rings, one on each of his huge hands. I'd never seen a man wearing rings like those, ever, not even women wore rings that big. I thought they were odd. A lot of expensive sparkle for a train. Not that anyone would try to rob him; he was too big to rob. He was telling me he lived in San Francisco and New York, but he didn't fly because he hated heights.

Stranger on a Train

I asked him suspiciously, my eyes slightly narrowing, "How can you live in those two cities and hate heights? Don't you have to go into elevators? How about the bridges?" He said, no, everyone brings everything to him. That did it. I thought, Okay, he's a drug dealer. Who else boards the train in the middle of nowhere, lives in two of the most expensive cities in America, has people bring him things and wears diamond rings the size of Nevada?

At his age, with those rings, I thought, he was probably the leader of the syndicate, the kingpin, murder incorporated. Suddenly aware of the danger, stranger on a train and all, I looked down at my diary, and thought, *Stop talking to him.* If I had to, I thought, I could stab him in the hand with my pen.

Right then a young man came up and asked if he could have his picture taken with this big guy. And as nice as could be, the drug dealer smiled a great big all-American smile and said sure. The kid handed me his camera, and asked if I would take their picture. I heard a murmur of excited voices and noticed that everyone in the car had turned to watch when the big guy put his arm around the young man. *Probably not a drug dealer,* I thought. These people all knew who he was. Now I had to ask him, "What do you do?"

"I'm a football coach."

Hello View, way better than at 30,000 feet.

I said, "Ohhhhh," relieved, shaking my head at myself. (Despite the strong influence of Cliff and my brothers, I didn't watch sports and knew none of the famous people in football.)

I said, "What's your name? I'm sorry, I won't recognize it because I don't pay much attention to sports, but I have a friend who does." My girlfriend Lorrie loved football; she would know this guy.

"That's okay," he said. "It's John Madden."

Which meant nothing to me; this was before he did commercials and I'd never heard of him. But I got his autograph for Lorrie. And I found out those suspicious diamond rings were Super Bowl rings.

He was extremely outgoing and friendly, just as nice as a person could be. We got to visiting, and I ended up sitting with him for a day and a half. He was a king all right, king of the train; everyone loved him, passengers and crew alike, and spoke to him and joked with him like they knew him. His table in the dining car had a "reserved" sign on it when we sat down. (I've traveled the train for years since then; I've never seen them do that for anyone else.) RESERVED

We stepped off the train on the longer stops and stretched our legs. I became his personal photographer; everyone wanted their picture taken with John and he could not have been sweeter to every one of them. Too bad I didn't think to get my own picture. He was very engaging; he went to college at Cal Poly so he'd lived in San Luis Obispo and knew it well. He asked what I was reading; I showed him the quote books I was marking up. He pulled one of them to him, his eyes scanned as he turned a few pages. We had a long talk about inspiration. He was very much into the subject; he told me how he consciously worked to inspire his players.

Nothing jazzes me up like football. I've acquired more passion over the years, not less. Not to love it wouldn't make sense. ♥ John Madden

He asked about the headphones and Walkman. I told him I was learning to meditate; he asked if he could listen to my tapes. We sat across from each other at a table in the lounge car as the beautiful Virginia countryside rolled by outside our windows. He listened to my meditation tapes with his eyes closed while I put stars next to quotes in my book. (It was the marriage I always wanted!)

He was one of the most down-to-earth, interesting ~ and interested ~ people I'd ever met. When I asked about his family, he told me he had children and was happily married to the same woman since 1959.

I had to know, "How do you stay married when you're gone all the time?"

He didn't blink an eye. "I don't leave my wife stuck at home with no life of her own," he said. "I asked her what she wanted to do, and she said she wanted to open a store. I told her to go for

Our country is particularly blessed with wonderful old barns.

it. She's her own person, and I want her to be happy. It's what she wanted, it gave her purpose, and now she's as excited to wake up in the morning as I am."

How could you not like him? Plus he said this:

WHAT'S THE TOUGHEST THING IN A PROFESSIONAL FOOTBALL GAME? IT'S BEING THE MOTHER of THE QUARTERBACK. 🏈 *John Madden*

By that time, for me, all men were suspect, especially pilots and anyone rich or famous, so I couldn't help but wonder if this big successful guy was faithful to his wife. Needless to say, I didn't ask, but I was pretty sure he was. Maybe it was me, but he was a perfect gentleman the whole time. He treated me like a person; he gave me hope for all mankind. I read this in my quote book and thought it fit perfectly for John . . .

The intellect of the wise is like glass; it admits the light of heaven & reflects it.
♥ *Augustus Hare*

I never saw John again after he got off the train in New York. I heard that he started traveling in his own bus soon after that, but even so, from then on, I always looked for him whenever I boarded a train.

BOSTON & HOME

While the train wound through the city and came to a long, slow, civilized stop at the end of the line, I gathered everything back into my suitcase. I stepped off into cold and windy South Station, crowded with bundled-up Christmas shoppers and commuters. I loved the train,  I loved the trip, I loved the station, I loved the people. I thought nothing would make me truer to myself than continuing to do this for the rest of my life. I caught the bus down to Woods Hole, then rocked across the water in the big white ferry under a navy-blue sky filled with glittery stars to the lit-up, white-washed shores of the fairy-tale island. It was December and I was HOME, where I belonged.

So lucky to be the One you run to see ♫

In the evening ♪ when the day is through...

TIME AFTER TIME

Vineyard Haven Harbor Lights

HOLLY OAK

When the cab turned into my driveway, the first thing I saw were the Christmas lights Myron had strung across the front of the house. I laughed out loud, so happy to be home. He'd left lamps on for me, too. I opened the door, Girl Kitty took one look and fell over on the floor, wiggling on her back and making little crying noises, wanting me to pick her up, which I did, wrapping her in my shawl and holding her close. Man Kitty was stretching like a Halloween cat on the back of the sofa, and Billy was curled up in a pile of quilts in a basket next to . . . are you ready? My new fireplace. It was done and even better than I hoped. I loved it. There was a small fire all built, all I had to do was light a match. I didn't

It changed the whole house.

think I would sleep that night, because Santa had already come and because there was no way I could go to bed before I decorated the mantle. There were flowers and a poinsettia on the table and a welcome-home card from Ellie and Myron. I lit candles and turned off the lights; the fire crackled and glinted on the dishes in the hutch, Man Kitty rubbed against my legs and I picked him up in my arms like a baby, surveyed my cozy realm and felt house-crazy with love. I kissed the wall next to me and thought, *Home. I hope Agnes can see this.*

You're probably wondering about the gun over the fireplace. I got it the year after the fireplace went in, during my "woodsy, Thanksgiving, pilgrim, patriot, minuteman, pioneer" phase of New England decorating. My sister Shelly was visiting and we took a road trip to Brimfield in western Massachusetts for the annual antique show.

The show takes place three times a year, on acres and acres of farmland where dealers pitch tents and put up displays and turn the miles of countryside into a huge flea market. A person can find every wonderful thing their heart desires at Brimfield.

If you ever need chairs, they have 'em!

Normally I would go looking for hooked rugs, flowery old china dishes, wooden cooking spoons, striped mixing bowls, teapots, mugs, embroidered dishtowels, quilts, hand-painted flour sifters, silver serving spoons, interesting fireplace equipment, and cute glass lamps with pretty silk shades, anything that fit my idea of beauty, was useful and practical and didn't cost an arm and leg. It was the secret to having a house that didn't look like everyone else's. Thrift stores, junk shops, antique stores and Brimfield, where originality lurked in every corner, were my cup of decorating tea. The thrill of the hunt and fun of discovery.

"Isle of Dreams" was inspired by pages of vintage stickers I found at an Island yard sale.

But this time, my eyes fell on an old rifle. It wasn't very expensive and it was made of such beautiful old wood, smooth and

240

BRIMFIELD Treasures

Old postcards

VALENTINE GREETING

This simple little valentine
Is just to say to you
That if it rains, or if it shines,
My love for you is true.

Pretty china dishes

Etched & hand-painted glasses

Perfect bread basket for Thanksgiving

Salt & Pepper shakers

Champagne glasses like Cary Grant drank from in the movie Bringing up Baby.

Vintage books

You have to have potholders, why shouldn't they be cute ones?

Old quilts!

Embroidered dishtowels make perfect gifts

Tiny vases fit on windowsills.

mellowed from the years, I thought it would be just the right Autumn Thanksgiving touch for over my new fireplace. The man who was selling it didn't think it worked, and I believed him. It didn't use bullets anyway, it had to be packed with gunpowder or wadding or something like that, something that neither I, nor anyone I knew, had, which meant I probably wouldn't accidentally kill myself with it. I think I remember the dealer saying it was from 18-something, but I had no idea. I just liked the way it looked and it was priced right. So I bought it.

I EVEN PAINTED IT.

And that's when the fun began. If you EVER need an easy way to meet men in festive surroundings, go to a flea market, buy an old gun (a rifle is best because it is most noticeable, try to get one that doesn't weigh too much) and carry it around with you the rest of the day.

So empowering! Guys were drawn to it like bees to honey ~ handsome guys, funny guys, full of flirty little jokes ~ all curious and asking about the gun, "Going hunting?" Or "Having trouble at home?" Shelly and I had the BEST time with that gun, we laughed and joked all day long. We felt like the most popular girls in high school.

Then again, maybe it wasn't the gun ~ could have just been Shelly!

Naturally, we became very attached to the gun and hated leaving it in the room later when we went to dinner. And although it wasn't light, we DID take it back to the show the next day to carry it around some more. It would have been wrong not to. The gun was like having Diana with us . . . going out and getting guys and bringing them back to us. It is the shy person's way of getting herself spoken to without having to do anything but tote a gun. Feel free to steal this brilliant idea!

Heap high the board with plenteous cheer & gather to the feast. And toast the sturdy pilgrim band whose courage never ceased. ♥ Alice W. Brotherton

242

Chapter Eleven

NOTHING VENTURED NOTHING GAINED

Don't just wait & trust to fate
& say, that's how it's meant to be.
It's up to you how far you go,
If you don't try you'll never know.
And so my lad as I've explained
Nothing ventured, nothing gained.

Merlin, Sword in the Stone. The Sherman Brothers

Despite all the encouragement I'd received in California, procrastination on "the book" continued for at least another year. Nothing slows down a dream faster than when the dreamer finds ten thousand reasons why it won't work. There were no deadlines, no one was waiting for it; only a few friends knew I was doing it. It seemed like such a big project, like it might take forever, and probably all for nothing, but it finally occurred to me that the time was going to pass anyway, I might as well try to have something to show for it.

TALKING? IT'S THE MOST LOQUACIOUS OF ALL.

And yes, I replied to the voice in my head, if I wrote a book there was a pretty good chance it would go nowhere, but if I didn't write it, going nowhere was a definite. Plus, the way things were going, I worried I would end up as a bag lady; I was running out of money.

Contemplating the whole bag-lady scenario further, and still with no idea of what I wanted to be when I grew up, but with strength from meditation and comments from family and friends spurring me on, I made the executive decision not to go back to work at the store and instead to put all my concentration into doing the book. But even so, with every page, I had to fight the insecure voice inside that said I was wasting my time.

You can get what you want or you can just get old. ♥ BILLY JOEL

LIFE ISN'T ABOUT FINDING YOURSELF. It's ABOUT CREATING YOURSELF. George Bernard Shaw

WINTER 1985

Resolved to take fate by the throat & shake a living out of her. ♥ Louisa May Alcott

I choose to write a beautiful cookbook

····· STILL TUCKED INTO MY DIARY ·····

But all the magic I've ever known, I had to make myself. Shel Silverstein

All that winter I pulled myself from my warm bed, put sweaters and slippers on over my jammies, and made a fire. While I fixed a cup of tea and put food down for the kitties, I watched the quiet snow fall around the bird feeders outside my kitchen window and the little feathered dustups when the red and brown birds fought each other for a foothold ～ the squirrels on the ground below benefited from the seeds that fell from the feeders in this peaceable kingdom.

My little house had become like one of my grandma's nap blankets, wrapped around me, keeping me safe, protecting me from the outside world. It was a climate-controlled, pancakes for dinner, chicken soup for breakfast, jammies in the afternoon, a firelit tea house of the Vineyard moon. Old movies kept happiness on an even keel, Frank provided the dance music, cats contributed antics for out-loud laughing.

I took my cup, pulled my shawl tighter and settled in to paint pages about decorating the guest room and breakfast in bed. I painted things from around the house ～ my quilts, hats, baskets and jars, and food of course. I hoped my book would be like my favorite childhood books, like a children's book for grownups, with pictures and quotes and stories to go with the recipes, and all the good and wonderful things about home.

I used the edges of teacups, saucers and platters as templates to make arched lines. I wrote down the story of the lobster boil on the beach that I helped Miranda prepare for her customers, the Tuesday Girls' Easter

Egg Coloring Party, Shelly's Valentine Cookie, my mom's Rainbow Jell-O, and Jane's Summer Salad, and I told the story of my parents' "Come as You Are" parties when I was little. I added quotes about the thriftiness of our New England grandmothers, and put in garden tips such as the benefits of planting garlic with roses.

I don't want anyone reading my writing to think about style. I just want them to be in the story.
♥ WILLA CATHER

I never thought of myself as a writer. In my diary I once wrote "how does a person write, how do they begin?" Not noticing that I was writing. It was just something I did, in letters and diaries, for as long as I could remember, as routine as breathing and sleeping and just about as noticeable. And never a thought toward "good" writing or "bad" writing. Just writing was all. And now I can see, reading over my diaries for this book, the difference. OMG. But I digress.

me in great ways ~ wonder how a writer writes. What starts them where do they begin?
9:22 am Jan. 17, 1978 Tuesday

Did I know what I was doing? No, I never did. I didn't have to worry about style because it never occurred to me to have one. I used to think when other people did things, they knew what they were doing. I'd never done this before; I didn't know how, and I lamented about it all the time. But, in order to satisfy the inner longing that was never going to leave me alone ~ I had to keep trying.

Jane's Recipe

Now I know the comforting truth, which is, until they've done it, *nobody knows how.* I had a new mantra, "eyes on the prize" ~ I said it over and over.

The real magic is believing in yourself. If you can do that, you can make anything happen. ♥ J. W. von GOETHE

Believing in myself was difficult. But I learned that I could get by without believing as long as I kept on doing. And my quote books gave reassuring advice such as:

Every artist was first an amateur.
♥ *Ralph Waldo Emerson*

As my pile of pages grew, they started to actually *look* like a book; I could even turn them like real pages. That was very encouraging, so when I had about 15 pages I decided to try to find out how many pages a publisher would need in order to consider my book for publication. I looked in one of my books, saw the publisher's name McGraw Hill, thought they sounded sturdy, called Information and got their number in New York. I rang them and asked if I could speak to an editor. I was on hold for a moment; then a man came to the phone.

I said, "Hello, you don't know me, but I'm wondering if I could bother you with a quick question."

"Okay," he said.

"Well, if someone was writing a handwritten, watercolored cookbook, how many pages would a publisher need to see before they'd know if they were interested?"

He answered kindly, pausing for a moment, "Well, let's see . . . 50 would probably be good."

I thanked him and said goodbye. For all I knew he was the janitor, but it didn't matter, he had given me a goal.

I needed 50 pages. I thought, *That's doable. And if worse comes to worst, and this thing doesn't go anywhere, I'll frame the pages and have 50 Christmas presents to give away.*

That's what turned the tide, the idea about the Christmas presents. Now I couldn't lose, I was no longer doing this for "nothing" ~ it was a win-win.

Making a path for the children.

While icy winds blew across the Island, I painted and talked on the phone, to my mom (who filled me in on all the family news, but worried about the cost of long distance calls; and thought I was alone too much), and my dad (*Hello from Smallville, how's the car holding up, grasshopper?*), to Diana and Shelly and Janet and all my girlfriends, and my brothers and sisters. Cliff called too. Sometimes I'd feel sad after talking to him, so I'd turn the stereo up loud and let Edith Piaf sing, "*Non, Je Ne Regrette Rien*" (French for, "No, I regret nothing"), and march around my house flinging my arms out and go from sad to formidable. That song is a great backbone stiffener, in case you ever need one. ♪

Where words fail, music speaks.
♥ HANS CHRISTIAN ANDERSEN ♪

My stack of pages kept growing ~ when I wasn't painting, I was scraping ice off the windshield and slip-

Wouldn't want them to step in snow.

248

sliding through the snow to get groceries to test recipes ∼ or washing vegetables, doing dishes, filling bird feeders, or letting the cats in and out, because, as it turned out, cats do like to go out in the snow, just not for very long.

For months, I'd come back from the market, and turn into the driveway to see my house half buried in the snow. The wind took bites out of my face while I struggled to get the grocery bags out of the car and up to the porch . . . but inside it was warm and smelled like piecrust or chicken stock or caramelized onions. I painted, went into a trance, blinked, and the day was gone.

I was a girl with a fireplace and a new camera that could take selfies.

On days when the ice had melted and the ground was bare, I escaped into the fresh air for brisk walks into the white-washed woods and out to the sea. And I meditated every day and marveled at the billions of stars I could see in the dark, icy sky above the Island at night. It occurred to me that maybe all this quiet and aloneness was the reason I'd been drawn to the Island. Between the constant good weather, and my friends and family, the distractions in California might have provided all the excuse I needed to keep on wishing forever.

My walk in the winter.

hen one day I blinked and the icicles had melted and the Pinkletinks were singing and it was spring again. On the ground, purple-black oak leaves were still rimmed with silver frost, and the banks along the road were patched in bright green moss.

I plan to haunt the road where I walk someday. (Fair warning to the future people.)

There was a thick crust of ice on every pothole. I pushed my toe on the edge of frozen puddles to hear the ice crack. I picked up a heavy rock and threw it at the ice to see it splash muddy water through the hole. The toe, with the slow cracking, was the more interesting of the two. Out at the opening, the sun shone pale lemon.

Ahhh, Spring...

When I got home I called Diana... "It's 40 degrees!" I said, with an exclamation point in my voice because it was such a beautiful day.

"Really?" she asked, her face muffled from sleep, "Is that good or bad?"

A tree filled with robins, happens every spring.

Soon, and in this order, daf-fodils bloomed, robins hopped on the lawn pulling worms from the ground, I turned 38, the nurseries reopened, lilacs bloomed their fragrance all over the Island, little blue butterflies fluttered down the road in front of me, Carlton's white doves twirled and wheeled over my house, dandelions took over the lawn, Memorial Day flags flew, the summer people came again, the farmers' market opened,

Saturday Morning Farmers' Market

buttercups speckled the meadows, fireflies blinked in the woods and clusters of wild daisies scattered in drifts down the road to the pond. I fertilized the roses and worked on my pages and babysat for Gwinnie when Myron, Ellie and Peggy went to Maine.

I bought a birdbath and lined the garden fence with corn-flowers and phlox because I read that butterflies loved them. I thought butterflies could be the missing link between flowers and birds and wanted as many as possible.

TISBURY
Farmers'
Market
9—Noon Sat.

In the shadow of the 160-year-old landmark Grange Hall.

Fresh flowers

All kinds of herbs

Organic pop-in-your-mouth goodness

251

Cooking everyday

I learned I didn't need most of the gadgets they were beginning to advertise as more and more people began taking up the hobby of cooking ~ I could live without a bagel slicer, electric can opener, ice tea maker, battery-powered sifter, sectioned pie slicer, electric knife sharpener or garlic peeler. I realized that (clean) broom handles made perfectly fine drying racks for pasta. I was my mother's daughter when it came to practicality.

Noodles are not only amusing, but DELICIOUS. ♥ Julia Child

All summer I was either working in the garden and slapping mosquitoes off my legs, testing recipes, painting and hand-writing new pages for the book, or walking to the pond. I was getting closer to my goal of 50 pages all the time. I had no idea what I would do after that, but Diana was coming for her birthday at the end of August, so I didn't have to think about it yet. I had a birthday surprise for her, four tickets to see Ricky Nelson the night she arrived, at the Hot Tin Roof, both shows in case her plane was late.

My grandma's piecrust & baking powder biscuits.

"The book got a name by the way ..."

As my pile of pages grew, daydreaming became almost a full-time thing, a natural part of the program. Painting gave me plenty of time to think about how I wanted my book to be. I thought certain foods and smells from the kitchen could make people feel nurtured, like chicken soup, garlic bread, or chocolate chip cookies, like at home and safe.

I decided I would call my book *Heart of the Home* because when I was growing up, our kitchen was the most important room in the house; it always smelled wonderful and that was where our mom was. It was where I learned to sew, practiced dancing with the refrigerator door handle, also where we did homework, bathed the baby, got our scraped knees kissed and bandaged, read Grandma's letters out loud, fed our dog Nipper, folded diapers, gathered around the table for dinner, and said grace. Kitchens held sacred family DNA. Everything important happened in the kitchen.

I wanted my pages to be pretty; but even more, they had to be practical. There were lots of pretty books in the world and I prayed mine would be one of them, but I didn't think that would be enough. Pretty by itself could end up in a yard sale: useful lasted forever. Useful and pretty combined was what I wanted.

To accomplish "useful," the recipes in my book had to work, which meant that even if I'd made them a hundred times, I had to make sure the measurements were right. So I made everything again. My hope, not even a hope, more like a dream, was that someday these recipes might fall into that most prized of categories: "Family Favorites."

I thought about my old mantra, "Quick, easy, elegant, and delicious," and it fit perfectly with the cookbook I wanted to make. Despite my doubts about how it would all turn out, I couldn't help but be excited. I loved what I was doing. I could barely sleep for thinking about what I might include on the next page. The pages were flat, but even so I wanted to try and "hide" surprises on them, like buried treasure, for people to discover, good quotes and jokes and words of encouragement.

Foxgloves in the garden

Obsession can be wonderful...

Each morning that summer of 1985, with the screen door propped open, the cats going in and out, and the smell of the sea on the breeze, I'd sit at the dining table and paint borders of flowers and mixing bowls with stripes. I would take breaks to meditate, weed the garden, and fill the birdbath, where I would hear convertibles drive by, radios up, music drifting through the trees, joy of Summer on the breeze.

I COULD NEVER IN A HUNDRED SUMMERS GET TIRED of THIS.

After dark I worked with the windows and doors wide open, the stars peeping through the trees and crickets serenading. And sometimes the ☆ evenings would be so balmy and starlit, I'd get wanderlust and go into town to stroll around, eat an ice cream ☆ cone, window shop, sit under the linden tree and smell the popcorn when the summer people ☆ streamed out of the movie theater and floated off into the dark in groups of twos and threes.

AFTER THAT, WORK & HOPE. BUT NEVER HOPE MORE THAN YOU WORK.

Beryl Markham

She Island fairies continued to surprise me: One cool foggy morning, I was painting hearts on a page about traditions when I heard a loud mooing sound that could only be made by a cow no matter how impossible that was. I ran to the window to see where it was coming from and found a herd of cows in my backyard! Seven of them, next to the deck, near the shack, nibbling the bushes and the flowers in the window box. This had never happened before. I wasn't sure what to do ～ they were very large, I wasn't sure if I should be afraid of cows. Would they bite?

I loved it! Felt honored the cows chose my yard.

255

What do you say to them? Shoo? Yo cow? So I ran to get the camera, and then Myron came running over to say that Pilot Hill Farm had called; their cows had escaped. We got there just in time to save my geraniums from being cows' lunch. When the cow minder from Pilot Hill arrived, the cows agreeably followed him back to where they came from. There was no biting.

Fairies in the garden again. What can I say? If you heard the birds singing on Martha's Vineyard, you'd believe in them too. I was always pinching myself. I never needed to make drama, it was all around me, from seasons to cows to ducks and bunnies, to sunsets and moonrises.

Don't think that everything was perfect at all times. Nothing is perfect ~ but who really cares that I wore my t-shirt to the market inside out? Or, that I stepped in cat throw up with my bare foot ~ who hasn't? Or that my entire head was split ends. Or that fruit flies took over the kitchen, or that a seagull did mean things to my book because I left it out on the deck, or that I waved back to someone before I realized they weren't waving at me. Then there's the tree that fell on my house during a hurricane, and the flip-flop I broke on Main Street so I had to be barefoot downtown like a nut, or that, despite my hard and fast rule of never spending money on something I couldn't wear or eat, they told me I had to buy, pay big money for, a new ugly furnace to put in the basement? It's just that when I think about my life, I don't think about those things, they aren't even interesting. Stuff happens. I had my house and my cats, and inspiration every day and the rest of it was gravy.

Barn's burnt down...now I can see the moon~.
M a s a h i d e
(A perfect example of the Pollyanna way of thinking.)

And things were going along fine. I'd amassed 41 pages in my book pile ~ only nine more for my 50-page goal, and then I supposed I would have to look for a publisher. I tried not to think about that because it was one of the things that could scare me into stopping. "WHEN YOU DOUBT YOUR POWER, YOU GIVE POWER TO YOUR DOUBT.
Honoré de Balzac

FAITH can move a mountain.

I'm not sure why I wasn't born over-flowing with self-confidence, or why

Your cheerful outlook is one of your greatest assets.

I had attached all of it to what my ex-husband thought of me, but one thing that made a huge difference in my younger life was learning to cook.

It was my first feeling of success as a person. I was so proud of myself the first time I made Julia Child's Coq au Vin ~ which is why I will love Julia Child forever, because she gave me that. Once you get a taste for feeling proud of yourself, you want more. So you try harder.

My first attempts at cooking made me think I had something to offer, and it was still true. Every time I brought my pineapple upside-down cake, or my mom's potato chip cookies to the store downtown, I was excellently received with oohs and aahs from everyone who happened to be there. It put a glow on me like almost nothing else could, pure music to my ears. I found out I could make people happy when I fed them, and when they were happy, I was happy, and when I was happy they were happy, and it just kept going back and forth like that.

257

It was something of my own to hold onto and a gift I could give away.

I wanted to help others experience that same little boost of self-confidence and the wonderful feeling of making something with their own hands. My sisters were only in their 20s when I was working on my cookbook. I hoped a collection of really good recipes would give them the same sense of accomplishment I'd felt. I had yet to meet anyone who didn't adore a person who showed up carrying a homemade banana cream pie.

It was my mother who showed me the delight that cooking could bring to others. As a child it had meant so much when she made my favorite birthday dinner. I felt special and proud when she brought it to the table. She made me feel like I mattered SO much that someone as important as she was would go to the time and trouble to make something just for me. It made me want to help moms make traditions that their children would never forget. There were only 12 years or so to stuff them with memories to last a lifetime. I wanted my book to be as encouraging to them as a letter from home. ♥

Your nurturing instincts will expand to include many people.

I ALWAYS KEPT THE GOOD ONES.

Some people assert that this was not the work of fairy enchantment, but that love alone brought about the transformation.

♥ FRENCH FOLKTALES

I wanted to thank my mother, and really all moms, for the selfless giving, the goodnight kisses, the sugared bread and butter, the skate-key tightening, the making-it-well, a million tiny things, even for spitting on a tissue to clean the ice cream off my face (even

The face of unconditional love.

though I actually hated this), for untiring gentle discipline ~ and for fixing dinner every night for ungrateful children while singing, "*How Much is that Doggie in the Window?*" I thought it might help make their days better if moms knew that, for us lucky ones, they were the fairies that ran ahead and made everything magical. My mother showed me that even the smallest of things could be special. What she did for us was nothing short of heroic.

> 13 If you've ever had a mother and if she's given you and meant to you all the things you care for most, you never get over it.
> Anne Douglas Sedgwick, *Dark Hester* (1929)

Another thing: With times the way they were in the 1980s, I was worried that moms might have gotten the mistaken idea that what they did didn't matter. What I understood from the women's movement was that we had a free choice to be anything we wanted. We could choose to stay home with the children or work out of the house, depending on our personal needs, and each of those choices deserved equal respect. But sometimes, watching Phil Donahue in the pre-Oprah days, it felt like women were being pitted against each other.

I knew how it felt to think that what I did didn't matter, and I wasn't even raising children. Whether working out of the house or working at home with the kids, moms were all doing something much harder than I'd ever done and getting no credit for it, they were heroes without medals, not even a gold star. This, I could not bear; to think that their

For as long as I can remember this has been in my mom's kitchen.

MADONNA OF THE KITCHEN

sacrifice and commitment was taken for granted really bothered me. What they did mattered more than anything.

My dad could go to work,

Know you what it is to be a child? It is to be very different from the man of today. It is to have a spirit still streaming from the waters of baptism; it is to believe in love, to believe in loveliness, to believe in belief; it is to be so little that the elves can reach to whisper in your ear...

♥ Francis Thompson

he could get raises, he could be thanked for his contribution, he got a pay-check for his labor, but that didn't happen for moms. The best they could hope for would be a crayon valentine or a squashed, limp dandelion flower offered up from the damp hand of their wide-eyed and innocent child. Which wasn't nothing. In all my days I'd never considered anything to be more important than home. In a chaotic world, it was sanctuary; it was where love grew. ♥

And I go carrying my childhood
Like a favorite flower
That perfumes my hand.
Mabel Walker Willebrandt

BLESSING

It wasn't just me, home was a common denominator among my girlfriends too, whether they had children or not, and I figured it probably carried over to all women, rich or poor, north or south, even country to country, we were much more alike than not.

I felt bad for women stuck in war-torn places or in deep poverty, women who worried sick about their kids, who did not have the luxury of the very simplest of homey things, might not even be able to flick a switch and have a light come on, who had no power to make beauty around them, might not even have any birds because they'd all been eaten. I wanted to tell them to put that dandelion in a jar near them and things would feel better (and that one of these days the world would change, is what I really wanted to say). No matter what our other interests (because we are so multi-faceted), I figured all of us enjoyed a nurturing, cozy environment, and loved seeing ourselves reflected in spotless counters, flowers on the table, and healthy children with shiny faces and combed hair. We all wanted to invite a best friend into our clean kitchens for a piece of cake and some tea. It was a luxury and a blessing to be able to do so. If I were writing the Bill of Rights, this would have been in it.

HOPE

ONE OF THE LUCKIEST THINGS THAT CAN HAPPEN TO YOU IN LIFE IS TO HAVE A HAPPY CHILDHOOD.
AGATHA CHRISTIE

To believe that what is true for you in your private heart is true for all men...
♥ Ralph Waldo Emerson

I couldn't imagine a better place to send encouragement than within the pages of a cookbook, with quotes from "distilled genius" that said things I was too afraid to say that would help remind every-one that we're all in this together. A cookbook wouldn't save the world, but it could help with dinner and maybe even bring someone a gold star.

And that was enough for me. Maybe I couldn't bring a banana cream pie to everyone, but I could provide a really good recipe for it. With a crust to die for. And that wasn't nothing.

Fill your paper with the breathings of your heart. ♥ Wm. Wordsworth

✳ ✳ ✳

By mid-August 1985 I was throwing myself into the pond daily. The humidity was so thick, bees were passed out on the lawn, bunnies laid out full length in the shade with their bellies

in the grass; I almost had to chew the air before breathing it. I opened the door early in the morning and ran into a wall of hot, wet air. Sleeping was hideous; going from room to room almost required a machete. The whine of the cicadas in the woods drowned out all other sounds. We didn't have this in California. New Englanders had a name for it: dog days. Because, I deduced, shiny with sweat and dwindling from the heat, you feel like you're wearing a very large, hot, sticky, wirehaired dog. (That probably wasn't the actual definition of dog days, but again, we had no Google, deducing was a way of life.) Diana said, "I told you! Why are you still there?"

HELP

"**H**AVE I GONE MAD?" *asked the Mad Hatter* "I'M AFRAID SO," *replied Alice.* "YOU'RE ENTIRELY BONKERS. BUT I'LL TELL YOU A SECRET. ALL THE BEST PEOPLE ARE. ♥ *Lewis Carroll*

DOG DAYS

I had given up on the garden. It was too big for one person. Everything was fine until the humidity set in. And even after I began to lose the fight in my quest for garden perfection, I continued to go there daily to weed despite the dirt that ran in sweat rivulets down my face and back. I picked off corpulent bright green tomato worms that tunneled through my tomatoes and lounged among the leaves, fat and juicy, maybe the scariest worm on earth, and I slapped relentless attacks of mosquitoes off my legs leaving them streaked with blood and mud. I flicked those little beetles into my jar of death ad nauseam. I even whipped up a little conspiracy theory. I began to think someone must have mixed weed seeds in with the fertilizer I'd used, because weeds were by far the fastest growing, healthiest things in the garden.

One scorching day, shaded by a large hot hat, dizzied by the sun, feeling a little bit deranged ~ sunburned, blistered and bitten ~ I asked myself, Why am I doing this? Have I gone mad? How important IS zucchini anyway? I threw my dirty hands into the air, broken fingernails, band aids and all, and asked myself to please explain why everyone else was at the beach frolicking in the surf while I was giving myself heat stroke and being eaten alive?

> May Sarton, *Journal of a Solitude* (1973)
>
> 7 We have descended into the garden and caught three hundred slugs. How I love the mixture of the beautiful and the squalid in gardening. It makes it so lifelike.
>
> Evelyn Underhill (1912), in Charles Williams, ed., *The Letters of Evelyn Underhill* (1943)

I turned on the sprinklers and handed the whole thing over to the voracious, unstoppable weeds saying out loud "You want it? You can have it." I figured I'd be happy with whatever vegetables survived. This wasn't a farm stand, I wasn't giving tours, and it was much too hot and sticky to weed or care.

There is something wonderful about growing your own.

And this was my final lesson in my life-course of "bigger is not better." The house had been lesson number one; the garden was how I got my diploma. This garden was Agnes's garden, I couldn't imagine how she did it without help, but next year I would plant a kitchen garden, with all the growing things I loved, but much smaller and more manageable by just me.

Garden Fresh

SUMMER TOMATOES

Put all ingred. in a glass bowl or jar, cover tightly & set in the sun 4 or 5 hrs.

Use as salad dressing, on toast for bruschetta, or fresh over hot pasta.

8 vine-ripened garden tomatoes, roughly chopped
3 cloves garlic, put through press
3 shallots, chopped
1 c. good, fruity olive oil
1/4 c. balsamic vinegar
2 Tbsp. fresh basil, slivered
2 Tbsp. parsley, chopped
1 tsp. sugar
lots of freshly ground pepper; salt to taste

THINGS GROW BETTER IN SMALL GARDENS.

A cold shower was what I needed. Afterwards, I put on a nice clean sundress, took my basket, and went to the farmers' market to buy some worm-free, farm-grown tomatoes. I chopped them and put them in a jar with olive oil, shallots, fresh basil and garlic and set the jar in in the sun on my porch so the flavors could blend. That night I made garlic bread, and poured the tomatoes over a bowl of linguine, sprinkled on some Parmesan and thought myself a very lucky girl. Then I sat down and wrote a new page for the book called, "Kitchen Gardens" to share my hard-won "expertise."

EVERYONE BRINGS A BASKET TO MARKET.

264

Last night we had three small zucchini for dinner that were grown within 50 feet of our back door. I estimate they cost somewhere in the neighborhood of $371.49 each. (And WORTH EVERY DIME.)

Andy Rooney

Roadside stands are all over the Island.

Diana came for her birthday at the end of August & made it just in time for the first of the two Ricky Nelson concerts. The Hot Tin Roof was only a half block from the airport, we went straight there and it was GREAT! So much fun. A packed house, all 300 seats were filled. We loved it so much we stayed for the second show. He played

all the best old songs, *Travelin' Man, Never Be Anyone Else But You, Young Emotions* and so many more. Ricky Nelson became our theme music for the rest of Diana's visit.

We got up early the next morning, while the dew was still on the grass, pulled skirts over bathing suits and walked down to the water carrying hand towels. There's a gulf stream that goes around the Island and Diana was very impressed with how much warmer the water was than in California where kids wore wet suits and hardly anyone grown up went into the freezing surf at all.

We had a refreshing swim, dried our faces and feet with the towels, put our socks and shoes and skirts back on, wandered the shore looking for beach glass and seashells, and walked back down the road, drip drying, as damp and salty and steamy as everything else in the woods, singing . . . . . . .Hello Mary Lou . . . good bye heart . . . sweet Mary Lou I'm so in love with you . . . back home for a blueberry corncake breakfast.

Blue heart seaglass found on beach - Score!

BLUEBERRY CORN CAKES

imple, quick & delicious. Serves two.

Start with the miracle food, a box of Jiffy Corn Muffin Mix. Empty it into a medium-sized bowl. Add half a cup of milk and one egg. Stir just until blended. Gently fold in one cup of blueberries, fresh or frozen or picked wild in the woods. Drop batter from a little measuring cup into a hot well-oiled skillet, spread batter a bit with the back of thecup and sprinkle with cinnamon. Cook slowly and well done so edges are crunchy. Serve hot with butter and heated maple syrup, ice cold freshly squeezed orange juice & a crisp piece of bacon.

uring breakfast we had a revelation. We figured out what life was all about! I made a graph, which I sketched in my diary, here it is:

HERE'S WHERE YOU'RE BORN: ← KISSES →   AND HERE'S WHERE YOU DIE:

Okay, do that with your hands.

old them up, born, then die, and see that space in the middle? That's the space for kisses because ROMANCE is the key to life. The trick seemed to be in kissing the right people (person) and filling the space with quality kisses. But we decided that if we have to err, we should err on the side of abundance.

It's all life is. Just going around kissing people.
F. Scott Fitzgerald

266

We shopped our way through town to Owen Park overlooking the harbor to watch the moon come up and hear the town band play patriotic songs along with the sound of the waves, the smell of the sea, and the halyards clanging on the small sailboats that fluttered around the harbor in the moonlight like moths.

Speaking of romance, this happens every Sunday night in the summer. I couldn't get the moon in the photo, but it's there!

We met some cute guys from France who, through sign language, invited us to go sailing the next day. Which we did, which was beautiful but largely uneventful because they spoke French and we spoke English (and Arf and Arfy) and the twain did not meet.

As part of her Island tour, I took Diana to the old cemetery in West Tisbury to visit a grave I had recently discovered, belonging to a woman by the name of Nancy Luce, better known locally as the Chicken Lady.

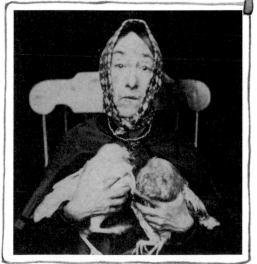

Nancy Luce, around 1864.

Nancy Luce was born in 1814, was known to be a hard worker and an excellent horsewoman, but in her middle 20s she came down with some mysterious disease which was never diagnosed. She was an only child and when her parents died, she was alone, sick and poverty-stricken. She spent her lonely disabled life in a small isolated cottage in the Tiah's Cove area of the Island. There's an old photo of her practically sitting *inside* her fireplace, wearing this same scarf, trying to keep warm.

Small towns make up for their lack of people by having everyone be more interesting. Doris Haddock

But, against all odds and despite her challenges, when she died in 1899, Nancy was the most well-known person on Martha's Vineyard. It was her determination, her gumption, and her extraordinary love for her animals (who provided her with all the sustenance she had) that made her famous. Plus, she was an original and extremely interesting.

Her cow, "Susannah Allen," lived in the house with her. Her chickens, "Ada Queetie" and "Lebootie Ticktuzy" (Nancy had a flair for names), were also beloved pets

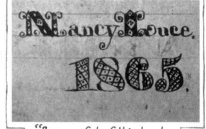

"Be careful of this book, you don't know how unable I am to do it." Nancy Luce

and inspired her to write small books of poems which she hand lettered and decorated with fancy block letters. She published the tiny volumes herself, bound in bits of old wallpaper, and sold them to tourists, who thought her love of chickens eccentric and took special trips to go out and observe her, and sometimes, sadly, to make fun of her. Nancy also sold eggs and photographs of herself to bring in extra money.

IF YOU DO IT WITH HEART ♥ THAT'S ART.

She did the best she could with what she had and never gave up fighting for her independence against serious odds. She was a rugged individualist. Lonely, cold, ill, poor and hungry, yet no one could stop her.

Ever since, to celebrate her courage, people have been leaving decorative chickens made of pottery, metal,

plastic and wood on her grave. Year-round, even in the snow, the chickens are there, circling her headstone, not too many, just sweet, a bright spot in the cemetery.

"I RAISED HER IN MY LAP;
SHE LOVED ME DREADFUL DEARLY."
ABOUT "POOR TWEEDLE DEDEL BEBBEE PINKY,"
WHEN HER PET HEN DIED.

This person is serious and true and deserves to be respected.

PROUD of HER

Diana and I went up to Lucy Vincent Beach ~ it was low tide and we could see hundreds of mussels attached to the rocks, just there for the picking ~ which we decided to do, for our dinner, gathering a couple dozen of them into a beach towel. Then it was off to the Scottish Bakehouse for a loaf of French bread.

The Scottish Bakehouse Cook Book

Back home in the kitchen I put on the Ricky Nelson tape we bought in town ~ we danced ourselves into the kitchen and made a feast. I set the oven to 350° F, we poured olive oil over two whole heads of unpeeled garlic, ground over some pepper, put some fresh rosemary around it and roasted it in the oven along with a log of creamy goat cheese. We heated the bread till it was crisp on the outside and soft and hot in the middle. We scrubbed the mussels and steamed them until they magically opened and put them in a bowl. We melted some butter, chopped tomatoes and basil (we'd scavenged from my weed garden) together with some olive oil and took the entire thing out to the deck and ate it with our hands ~ hot crusty bread, spread with

OLIVE OIL

269

creamy garlic, crisp roasted rosemary, and bubbling goat cheese, topped with garden tomatoes and basil ~ and steamed mussels direct from the sea, via our own hands, dipped in melted butter ~ all washed down with two ice cold glasses of white wine. YUM! We still talk about it.

Of course I showed Diana the book pages I'd done, and she said the most wonderfully encouraging things, because that's what best friends do.

Diana and me at the airport.

Too soon Diana was gone and I was alone again. The tourists went home, the kids went back to school, the road in front of my house was quiet, the woods were filled with singing crickets and just as the leaves began to color, with one final brushstroke, my 50 pages were done.

After all the years of doubt and wondering how to do it, and now "suddenly" here they were ~ seven years after my friend Jane suggested I write a cookbook. And I realized how simple it all really was: to do it, you have to do it. I felt like cutting up little pieces of paper and throwing them over my head like confetti. But before I could, the next question floated up in my brain like from a Magic 8 Ball putting a little damper on the celebration ~ "Now what?" Because 50 pages in the living room is just 50 pages in the living room. And the whole "I don't know how to do this" thing started all over again.

So far life had just happened to me. I had to figure out a way to happen to it.

CHAPTER TWELVE
BEST LAID PLANS

Finally the magpie, who's always cackling, said surely the lark must go often to fairyland; she ought to be able to show us the way. ♥ FRENCH FOLKTALES

Skylark... ♪

HAVE YOU ANYTHING TO SAY TO Meee?

SEPTEMBER 1985

So here was Plan A: Lots of literary types lived or summered on Martha's Vineyard ～ writers, poets, agents and editors. It's a small place. Regular people rubbed shoulders with famous ones all the time. I didn't happen to be one of them, but I wondered if perhaps someone I knew might be. So I took my pages downtown to Main Street where most of the shops were owned or run by women I knew from working at the store ～ at least well enough to say hello.

Maybe one of them would know someone who could help me.

I tried Bunch of Grapes Bookstore first; it seemed like the perfect place ～ no one could visit the Island without stopping there ～ but the guy behind the counter said that Ann, the owner of the shop, was off-Island. So I began working my way up Main Street, door-to-door, nervously showing my pages to each store owner or clerk who wasn't too busy to look.

Bunch of Grapes Bookstore, since 1964.

Everyone I spoke to was positive and wanted to be helpful, but no one could think of anyone in particular. I left my phone number everywhere, and people promised to call if someone came to mind. I drove home thinking maybe this wasn't the best strategy after all.

271

So I went to Plan B. I remembered the helpful man at the publisher I'd called in New York who advised me to do 50 pages, but when I called this time I was told, "We don't accept unsolicited manuscripts." They suggested I find an agent. So much for plan B. Agents seemed about as easy to find as publishers. None of these people were standing on the street corner with signs saying, "Pick Me."

Plan C should really have been Plan A: I called Jane in California to see if she had any ideas. She said she'd see what she could do. A couple of days later, fearless, loyal Jane called back, very excited.

"I did it!" she cried, "You're going to New York next week to meet with Random House!"

Oh my God. She had landed me an appointment with a real editor in New York City.

But, New York? By myself? It was a scary thought. It was one thing to sit in my safe little house singing, "Bibbity-Bobbity-Boo," painting all alone in my jammies at dawn with my three-haired paintbrush; it was a whole other thing to go to New York City, take my little Girl Scout project and talk to important, powerful people face to face. Suddenly I felt like a person standing in line for her first parachute jump.

IT'S HARD TO BE BRAVE WHEN YOU'RE ONLY A
VERY SMALL ANIMAL.
A. A. Milne ♥

But wasn't this what I prayed for? Shouldn't I be leaping for joy? Yes, I should! So what if the idea made me weak in the knees, I would just have to fake it. It would be an adventure! I asked myself what would Scarlett O'Hara do? So I put on my outfit of courage, which I hoped would make me look intelligent: a black wool suit with wide bell pants and

272

a belted jacket, with a white blouse, black suede platform shoes with faux mink pom-poms on the toes, and for whimsy, because there's such a thing as too much intelligence being somewhat boring (nothing I had to worry about), black and white striped socks (perfect with the mink). I tied a black velvet ribbon in my hair, put my pages into an overnight bag, said a little prayer, and left Carlton in charge of the cats while I went to the big city.

Drama is very important in life: You have to come on with a bang.
❤ *Julia Child*

I took the early boat across the water to Woods Hole, caught the bus to Providence, boarded the train to New York, wrote in my diary and watched out the window as Connecticut flew by. I arrived at Grand Central Station in the late afternoon, and walked out front to the din of speeding, honking traffic and crowds of rushing people and put my arm in the air to signal for a taxi.

I'd only been to New York once before ~ with Cliff. I'd fallen in love with the energy of the city, the museums and the history of old New York, the brownstones and the pigeons and especially Central Park, which seemed like a miracle in the middle of all the hubbub. There were ponds and meadows and trees, people roller skating, families picnicking, children running, lovers kissing on blankets in the sun, and old people on benches throwing crumbs to birds. If you looked at it the right way, it was almost small and kind of hometownish.

Just arrived in New York The Wonder City

But it was different, coming to the city alone for a meeting at the headquarters of what was arguably the most powerful publishing house in the world: Random House.

273

I hurtled up Park Avenue in the back of a cab, watching the kaleido-scope view stream by ~ open-air markets and cafés, brightly colored fashions on faceless mannequins in store windows, throngs of people all crossing the streets at the same time. I craned my neck to look up at the steel and glass skyscrapers and fell dizzily back into my seat. The most exciting city in the world, and I was in it carrying my book. Who would have imagined in a thousand years?

Up the wide, black granite steps to Random House I went. I pushed open the heavy, brass-trimmed glass door, walked across the polished marble floor as if I knew what I was doing, and took an elevator to the 26th floor to meet my first serious literary professionals ~ shaking in my shoes. I was just a regular girl from Smallville who never cared for the 26th floor; my legs weren't steady at that altitude. The elevator felt like a small, mirrored box in a very deep vertical hole held up by some puppet master in the sky. But I could do it if I had to. And I really had to.

The elevator opened to a shiny glass and chrome reception area. I walked up to the desk and quietly gave my name to the receptionist, trying to keep my voice from shaking. The young woman, polished and professional, street smart and savvy in her perfect little navy suit with her perfectly pulled-back black hair, and perfect red lipstick right out of Vogue, smiled sweetly and led me, heels clicking, to a brightly-lit conference room with a long glass table that reflected the city view from the floor-to-ceiling windows which ran the length of the back wall. There was a bouquet of calla lilies in a black vase, a black phone with lit up buttons on it, silver-framed book jackets hanging on the wall, and a chrome shelf filled with perfect rows of recently published books. The room smelled Windex.

"Ms. Jennings will be with you shortly," she said, closing the door behind her with a soft click.

274

I was careful not to get too close to the terrifying windows ~ despite the truly magnificent view of a thousand tall buildings and rooftop gardens ~ I was already shaky enough. I could never work here in a million years, I thought, just too high. Up and down in that elevator for lunch, no air, no windows that open, no birds, it would kill me. I sat with my back to the view in one of the 12 black leather swivel chairs, pulled the box with my pages out of my bag and put it on the table. I dried my hands on my pants and nervously waited for what would come next. In my mind, this was kind of it. Be nice, I said to myself. And don't forget to breathe.

It's so simple to look wise: Just think of something stupid to say, and then, don't say it. ♥ Sam Levenson

The door opened and a tall, elegantly-dressed silver-haired woman in a dark purple peplum jacket and matching straight skirt and very high black patent heels reached out and took my embarrassingly damp hand in hers; she introduced herself as Ruth. We made nice small talk about Martha's Vineyard; she and her husband had vacationed there many times.

She asked me to show her what I'd brought along. I hurried to open the box and pushed the stack of clear plastic envelopes toward her thinking, Here we go. I sat watching while she leaned forward and began slowly turning my pages.

— My first 50 pages. —

The building hummed. The air conditioning blew. The tension on my side of the table, you could cut it with a knife.

After a moment she said, "Oh, look at that," pointing a red fingernail at the page with watercolored sushi, "how cute." And, "Mmmm, Lemon Chicken." Those little noises sounded positive. I felt better. She asked about the watercolor of the house with the red door and I told her it was my house, only my door wasn't red in real life. I reminded myself not to talk too much, maybe not mention "real life."

275

She asked how long I'd been painting and I told her the story of my 30th birthday gift certificate and buying watercolors and painting my first picture of the geranium on my kitchen table (probably a little too Smallville - too much information). Then she seemed to get more serious; she asked me how strongly I felt about the title I'd chosen. Could they change it if they needed? (I didn't want to ruin my chances or be a prima donna, so I said, Yes, they could.) She wanted to know how many pages I expected to have in the final book. (I wasn't sure, whatever they wanted.) She asked how long it took me to create a page. (Sometimes one day; the longest was three).

She said I shouldn't misunderstand, she personally loved my handwriting, but how would I feel if they put it into print? (Pang in heart, but okay ~ I never really expected a publisher to like the handwriting idea). She kept going back to the pages, reading more, and seemed very interested: she loved the apple page. The toe of my shoe was going a hundred miles a minute. I saw it through the glass tabletop and made myself stop. Then she asked if I could leave my pages with them for a week or so.

I didn't expect her question, because everyone (including Jane, my dad, Cliff's dad, Myron, and Diana) had told me never EVER to leave my original pages with anyone. It was my understanding that no one left their pages; it almost seemed odd she was asking. I thought it over for a moment. Martha's Vineyard was a long way from New York ~too far. I said, "I'm sorry, I can't do that." She said she understood, not a problem, could she make copies? I breathed a sigh of relief and said, "Please do" (still vaguely worried because my pages weren't copyrighted ~ I didn't know if it mattered or not, but I feared that two "no's" in a row could be fatal).

Ruth rang for an assistant, who came and took my pages away. She turned back to me and warmly told me she loved the book, and it would be her pleasure to introduce it at their next editorial meeting.

WHAT? I could not believe what I was hearing! She wasn't saying

Coming home on the boat.

no. She said she liked it! It would be "her pleasure!" The assistant returned my pages; Ruth said she'd call me by the end of the week. Our meeting was so positive and easy that I left feeling giddy, skipping out the front door of the building with my head in the New York clouds. My book was going to be published! I couldn't wait to call Jane! I went looking for a cab singing "... I'LL MAKE A BRAND NEW START OF IT, NEW YORK, NEW YORK ..." ♪♫

Four days later, back on the Island, my phone rang, and it was Ruth from Random House.

Confucius Say: Before you leave Bloomingdale's today, you will spend a fortune, cookie.

Couldn't go to NY and not visit Bloomingdales!

I was so excited when she said her name my hands started shaking. When she said how much everyone loved the idea of the book, my heart leaped. They loved it! But then she said, "But, I'm sorry, I don't think this is the news you're hoping for," and my shoulders fell. I leaned on the wall, head down, to hear the rest of what was turning out to be a rejection.

She was so, SO sorry, but my book wasn't a good fit for them. She felt that perhaps the copies they'd made of my pages hadn't done the book justice. She said everyone loved the drawings but were a little put off by the handwriting; maybe the copies were too light, because they'd been hard to read.

I was just realizing, this decision hadn't been hers alone, it was made by a committee. She wasn't just showing them my pages, she'd been looking for approval. Duh.

She said they also had a problem categorizing it. It wasn't New England cooking, it wasn't California cooking, it wasn't French, Italian, Mexican or gourmet . . . the recipes were all over the place. It didn't really fit anywhere. And, another problem, they weren't sure who the audience would be for the book. Maybe it could only be regional, because, she reasoned, why would people in Indiana want a New England author? She told me not to give up; Random House was only one publisher, and sometimes people had to approach 10 different publishers before they found the right fit. She wished me all the luck in the world. I said "Thank you," and we said good-bye.

I fell on the bed, crushed. *Ten different publishers, how could someone live through that?* The cats jumped up next to me and I pulled a pillow over my face. Categorize it? It was supposed to be in a category? I never heard of that. Was Fannie Farmer in a category? I didn't know what to do next. Bag lady here I come.

I had to stop thinking about what I did wrong and go find something else to think about. I'd been so excited about Random House and New York that I'd told everyone ~ my parents, Cliff, his parents, all my friends, probably the guy at the post office too. I had to call everyone back and tell them it wasn't happening.

When I told Jane how bad I felt that I'd blown this huge opportunity, she said, "Don't you dare give up. I'll keep looking and you should too."

No day is so bad it can't be fixed with a nap.
Carrie Snow

I set the pages on the dining table, turned the oven to 350°, made corn pudding, ate a bowl of it, hot with maple syrup, took half to Ellie, buried my hands in the fur behind Peggy's ears, and then walked through the wild and blowy woods to the sea and sang *I'm the Greatest Star* to the birds. The season was changing and the first chill was in the air. I came back to my house filled with good smells from baking, closed my eyes, took a deep breath, counted

backward starting from 10, and shut down the voices in my head for a while. Then I turned Frank up loud, "*If they ask me I could write a book . . .*" which totally cheered me up as Frank always did.

I left the door open so I could hear the music, grabbed my clippers and went out to play in the garden ∼ the best place to count my very many blessings. And then I thought, if I can't get through one door, I'll try the next, or I'll go through a window. Something good is going to happen. Red-Letter days are not provided by others ∼ even Random House didn't have that power.

I HAVE NOT FAILED. I HAVE SUCCESSFULLY DISCOVERED TWELVE HUNDRED IDEAS THAT DON'T WORK. ♥ *Thomas Edison*

✻   ✻   ✻

Mr. Little and Mr. Brown

A VERY LITTLE KEY WILL OPEN A VERY HEAVY DOOR. ♥ *Charles Dickens*

Later I discovered that the Island fairies were watching over me the whole time. It turns out they just wanted me to practice on Random House, because here's what happened next.

Sandy Haeger called; she was the manager of David Golart's clothing store on Main Street. When I worked at the gourmet food store Sandy came in for coffee every day. She was one of the people I originally showed my pages to when I was going door-to-door downtown.

279

"Did you find anyone to publish your book?" she asked.

"No, not yet."

She said Good because she had remembered a customer of hers by the name of Stan Hart who had worked for Little, Brown and Company at one time. "You've heard of them," she said, "They're a famous old Boston publishing house." She had called Stan, told him about my book, gave him my phone number and suggested he stop by and take a look. And he said he would.

A couple of days later, Stan came by my house to see my pages, and then another miracle happened. This perfect stranger who did not have to do this, called his friend, the president of Little, Brown, and told him about my book.

The next thing I knew, an editor from Little, Brown called me and introduced herself as Mary. She said she heard that I had an "interesting" book and asked if I would like to bring it to their offices in Boston.

"Of course," I said, "I'd love to!" We made a date for the following Tuesday. This time I only told Diana and Ellie. I tried not to get too excited because I was already pretty sure nothing would happen since my book wasn't in a category. Even so, my fingers had a cramp in them from being crossed all the time.

Boston was only an hour-and-a-half drive from Woods Hole, much easier to get to than New York. The other good thing, because of Random House, I had a little experience. I knew what questions they might ask; I wasn't going into the complete unknown. This time I would try harder to get them to keep my title. I loved "Heart of the Home." It said just what I wanted it to say.

> Your talents are in fine shape
> utilize them to their fullest.

I arrived in Boston on a beautiful early October morning, in plenty of time ~ but got lost looking for 34 Beacon Street. I could find my way anywhere in California, but driving in Boston was a constant mystery to me. The old part of the city, where I was trying to go, was an unplanned maze of narrow streets, originally cow paths that had become permanent. I'm not kidding. Cow paths. The meandering of cows. I sat forever in traffic behind a stopped truck before I realized it was triple parked and the driver wasn't even in it. I threw the car in reverse, backed up and got around it thinking (as my mother used to say), The nerve of some people's children. I hurried up and down one-way streets, but could not seem to get over to Beacon Street. (No GPS ~ how did we survive?)

A little frazzled and now 20 minutes late, I finally pulled in front of the next big hotel I saw, handed my keys to the doorman,

Beacon Street in the 1940s.

got a valet parking ticket, took my purse and my box of 50 pages, and grabbed a cab to Beacon Street.

The driver dropped me on windy Beacon Hill on the edge of Boston Common. I paid and ran across the street to the old Cabot Mansion, a four-story brick townhouse that was converted into offices for Little, Brown in 1909. The receptionist offered me a seat in the large front room and called upstairs to announce my arrival.

Looking around, I thought I must be in the original parlor of the house. It was a real house, elegant and old, polished parquet floors and lovely ornamental woodwork, a wall of bookcases, a large fire-place with a carved mantle, a dark blue Persian rug, and an over-sized round mahogany coffee table stacked high with piles of books.

I put my box of pages on the sofa next to me, took off my green corduroy coat and sat down, wiping my damp hands on the skirt of my brown-flowered dress with the two inches of eyelet showing from my Laura Ashley underskirt. Then, too nervous to sit, I stood up to pace (in my brown Mary Jane's with the teardrop holes over the toes, and because I was a sock person even with dresses, beige socks with thin brown stripes). (I like to know what people are wearing at certain moments of their lives, hope you do too!)

There is another reason for dressing well, namely that dogs respect it & will not attack you in good clothes.
♥ Ralph Waldo Emerson

I wandered around the room reading titles on old volumes that filled the glass-front bookcases, all published by Little, Brown. I was thrilled to see a whole row of Louisa May Alcott's books, including a leather-bound copy of *Little Women* with the title flourished in gold-leaf script ～ not to mention *Fannie Farmer's Boston Cooking School Cook Book*, and also, my old friend, *Bartlett's Familiar Quotations*. Little, Brown had published them all. I asked the woman at the reception desk how long Little, Brown had been in business, and she told me it was started by Mr. Little and Mr. Brown in 1837, "when Dickens was alive," she added. What cute names, I thought. Little and Brown. Like a children's story about a mouse: so very little and so very brown.

A young dark-haired woman came into the room and introduced herself as Mary, the woman I'd spoken to on the phone. I apologized for being late, lamely fretting to her about the one-way streets. She was very nice; I followed her into the tiniest elevator I'd ever seen ～ barely big enough for the two of us, more like a dumbwaiter. We made small talk, nose to nose, as we creakily rose via what felt like ropes and pulleys, to the perfectly reasonable height of the third floor. Mary (wearing a black-and-rose flowered Laura Ashley midi dress with a wide lace collar and black flats) showed me through the dimly lit hallway into her narrow, wood-paneled office with one open window way in the back that looked at the brick building next door. There were disorganized piles of books everywhere, including three tottering stacks on the floor. The book smell took me back to my childhood and the Reseda Public Library. I thought about all the thousands of books that must have come through this building. Mary sat down at her desk, and I sat in a little armchair on the other side, watching as she began to turn my pages under a pool of light from her desk lamp.

"HEART of the HOME?" She looked up from under her lashes, the title page open in front of her.

Have a vision. Be demanding.

"Yes," I said, deciding to explain a little more this time, "because the kitchen is where everything happens in families. I thought it would be a good name for a cookbook."

She looked back down, nodding, seeming to agree. I sat with my hands folded in my lap and watched while she slowly turned the pages, reading each one. I can not tell you how quiet it was in that office, just the tick of a clock and me, barely breathing. After a few pages, she looked up at me with a smile, "Your drawings are wonderful." My heart jumped with reawakened hope. Really?

I have to say, it's a lovely thing when your friends and family tell you your drawings are wonderful, but it's a whole other thing when a perfect stranger behind a publisher's desk says it. The first is a delicious stew, fragrant with tomatoes, red wine and herbs. The second is essence of violets, new mown grass, and fairy wings.

HEART
OF THE
HOME

If in your house
this book you see
Please hurry!
Bring it back to me. ♥

She was quiet for a moment, turning another page, then said, "I've never seen a cookbook like this. This is your handwriting?" I nodded, fingers crossed, praying she meant that in a good way.

BREAKFAST

"You have to eat oatmeal or you'll dry up. Anybody knows that."
Eloise ♥ Kay Thompson ♥

She came to the page about Breakfast, and a quote about how you will dry up if you don't eat oatmeal, "Charming," she said, under her breath.

I didn't know what to say. Since she wasn't really talking to me, I didn't say anything. I was thrilled to hear it but still, I reminded myself, the lady at Random House had said nice things too.

I sat there, barely breathing, while she scanned all 50 pages. She said, "Mmmm, my mom used to make German pancake." Which I took as a good sign, that she mentioned her mom. When she finished, she said, "Very nice," and asked if I could leave the pages so that she could present them at a meeting the next day.

I was much better prepared this time, first off, I knew the decision wasn't hers alone and ~ because she said, "Charming" and because I loved the book smell of that old house, and because of Louisa May Alcott in the bookcases downstairs, and because of "little and brown," and mostly, this time, because I was taking no chances ~ I said yes, I would leave my pages. I wouldn't be that far away from them, and anyway, if Louisa May Alcott trusted Little, Brown, I felt sure I could too.

Since this book had sort of become my baby, leaving it wasn't as easy as it sounded, but I courageously walked out of the building alone. I stood on the porch under the fluttering flags, looking at the historic Common, the oldest city park in America. It was October-crisp, the wind swirled dry leaves into the corners of the porch. Cars and Yellow Cabs honked their horns and whizzed up Beacon Street. I blinked and it was a sea of Model

T's with horns that went ah-ooo-ga. I blinked again, the road was dirt and filled with horses and carriages. I looked over the blowing trees at the blue sky and the clouds, clutched my hands to my chest, and said a one-word prayer: *Please*.

Boston Common, c. 1909, it still looks the same only now it's in color.

Mary had suggested I come back on Thursday at around 2 p.m. to pick up my pages. Instead of going back to the Island and worrying what might happen with Little, Brown, I had planned, no matter how this meeting with Mary turned out, to keep a promise I'd made to my grandma. She wanted me to hunt for our New England ancestors, walk where they walked, and take some pictures for her. I got my car, spread the map on the seat next to me, and started north, staying off the highways, taking the back roads to my first stop, historic Salem, Massachusetts.

♥ ♥ ♥ ♥ ♥

THERE WAS NOTHING SO FINE IN ALL THE WORLD AS STEPPING OUT INTO THE FRESH MORNING WORLD. UP HILL & DOWN DALE THROUGH WOOD & FIELD, BY STREAM & MEADOWS, SHE WENT. ♥ *The Italian Fairy Book*

The next morning I woke from a good night's sleep to the smell of French Toast, in a cozy room over the kitchen of a local B&B. I put a cardigan and a wool vest over my turtle-neck, jeans and boots, ate a good breakfast and headed out in the early-morning mist to Burying Point Cemetery in Salem, the second oldest graveyard in the country, beginning around 1637, where I thought I might find the grave of my "witch" ancestor, Elizabeth Howe. A sliver of moon was still in the pale blue sky along with airy clouds, flying along, constantly changing shapes ～ a chilly day, perfect for wandering through a historic old graveyard.

285

I slipped through a crooked iron gate and wandered around the gently slopping yard in the long blue shadows and dappled light reading headstones sunk deep in thick grass. I had the whole place to myself just as I'd hoped.

WHEN THE TREES BOW DOWN THEIR HEADS, THE WIND IS PASSING BY. Christina Rossetti ♥

My boots crunched over leaves as I walked the rows, reading the grave markers. Each stone was a handmade work of art in granite or slate, intricately carved with urns, moons, angels, sculls and bones, flowers and weeping trees. They were engraved with years of births and deaths with names like Ebenezer, Mehetible, and Hephzibah, and lots of normal Abigails, Johns, and Elizabeths.

The epitaphs were bits of history: There was a man who'd come over on the Mayflower, one who'd been Governor of Massachusetts, and another who was a Revolutionary War hero ~ and regular people: a furniture maker, a constable and a wig maker . . . there was someone killed by a moving house, a person who died of the flu at age 97, a man struck by lightening, and I found the grave of Judge John Hathorne, the man who sentenced the "witches" to die.

But no Elizabeth Howe.

Delicate red woodbine, lichen and ivy crawled up grave stones ~ acorns and brown pine needles lodged in the cracks. Except for the wind blowing through the trees, the yard was quiet and earthy with composting leaves.

286

I imagined those long-gone souls alive, in their time, riding horses at full gallop through bright color-spangled woods on sharp fall mornings like this one, brilliant with life and filled with dreams. I was sorry for the many children in the tiniest graves, who never had the chance to make dreams of their own.

That time is past, & all its aching joys are no more, & all its dizzy raptures. ♥ Wm. Wordsworth

🎵 "Don't wish it away, don't look at it like it's forever..." ♥ Elton John

I decided to have coffee and wait for the library to open and go see what else I could find out about my relative and the other "witches." They had to be somewhere.

The librarian was around 60, had worked at the library for the last 25 years and was a fount of interesting information. She gave me lots of details about the people buried in the cemetery.

But the bad news was that apparently the twenty people, mostly women but some men (one man was 80 years old and his crime was not that he was a witch, but that he refused to admit he was a witch, but of course admitting you were a witch wasn't good either), that were sentenced to death were buried in unmarked graves near where they were hung, or "pressed" to death (with stones). I wasn't going to find my relative. She'd been buried in a crevice along with four other women hung on Gallows Hill that same day in 1692. No one knew where it was for sure.

287

WHEN WE WOULD RIDE, WE TAKE WINDLE-STRAWS, OR BEANSTALKS, AND PUT THEM BETWIXT OUR FEET, AND SAY THRICE: HORSE AND HATTOCK, HORSE AND GO, HORSE AND PELLATTIS, HO! HO! AND IMMEDIATELY WE WOULD FLY AWAY WHEREVER WE WOULD.

The confession of Isobel Gowdie (1662)

I thought about that hanging judge, buried in a nice cozy little grave in a beautiful leafy place that he'd helped to make infamous, but the innocent and abused didn't even rate a headstone. Unfair. I suddenly wished to march on Washington.

Lucky for Washington I didn't have to, because a few years after this, in 1992, to honor the 300th Anniversary of the trials, the people of Salem built an awe-inspiring memorial to the victims of the Salem Witch Trials of 1692. And of course, I took another trip back to see it.

There was an engraved "bench" for each of the victims.

The new memorial was a little higher on the hill overlooking the rest of the graveyard, almost as a kind of testament to the people of the town. It was as if my "witch" ancestor, Elizabeth Howe, a 56-year-old wife of a blind man and mother of six girls, and the other unfortunate victims of fear, ignorance, intolerance, and superstition, were still watching over their neighbors and families (who let this thing happen). Including Judge Hathorne himself, reminding them, and now, all of us, "Don't forget what happened here. Watch carefully so it never happens again. Next time, it could be you."

ELIZABETH HOWE
HANGED
JULY 19, 1692

I brought her some flowers.

FEAR (in a no symbol circle)

We can easily forgive a child who is afraid of the dark; the real tragedy of life is when men are afraid of the light. ♥ P L A T O

The Memorial was as simple and plain as the people of those times. Unpolished charcoal granite stones were elegantly engraved with the names and fates of each of the 20 victims. I left flowers on the memorial for Elizabeth and took pictures for my grandma, and stepped back over the stones that had been placed at the entry to the Memorial, engraved with last words of the victims such as

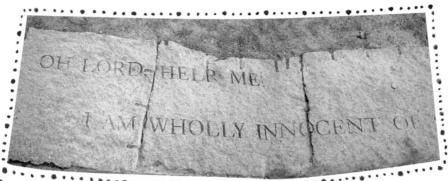

OH LORD, HELP ME.

I AM WHOLLY INNOCENT OF...

Whoooo went the wind around me, shhh went the leaves. And the church clock rang the hour.

*   *   *

Later that fall afternoon (back in 1985), while waiting for the people at Little, Brown to make a decision that could change my life, I left Salem and drove north along a narrow country road, past lakes, barns and farm-houses, winding through shimmering yellow trees bright as sunflowers, with leaves flying up behind my green Volvo, into New Hampshire to the tiny village of Canterbury, consisting of a general store, a town hall and a graveyard where I hoped to find another long lost relative.

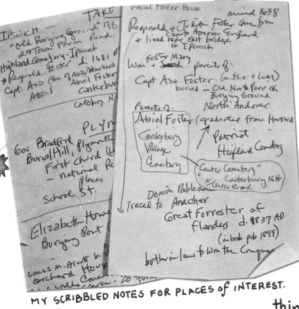

MY SCRIBBLED NOTES FOR PLACES OF INTEREST.

Center Cemetery, Canterbury,
New Hampshire

After wandering and reading names on headstones for about an hour, thinking maybe I wasn't going to find him either, I chanced upon the marker I was looking for, the one belonging to our Patriot ancestor, Abiel Foster. I almost couldn't believe I found it.

Abiel was the illustrious relation that my grandma especially wanted me to search for, the one who graduated from Harvard College in 1756 (a year after John Adams), became a pastor, a delegate to the Continental Congress

1735-1806

and a member of the first U.S. House of Representatives. Most importantly to my grandma and me, he was the father of eight children. His wife, Hanna, was there, so was his brother, Asa. I took more photos to send to my grandma.

I had a tear in my eye thinking about the courage and sacrifice made by these patriots for our country. The debt we owed to them, the army of regular people, ministers, farmers and shopkeepers who put country even before love of family.

And our future before theirs in their own time. The older I've gotten, the more I've realized what a miracle our country is and understand the reasons Abraham Lincoln called it "the last best hope of earth."

Canterbury Town Hall

What we did and still do mattered and matters. We might never be perfect, but it should never be taken lightly, that awesome ability we have to inspire for good. I think I like that better than any other thing about us and hope we will always take great advantage of it.

God shed His grace on thee. ♥ KATHARINE LEE BATES

While I was poking around in graveyards, I was also stopping at every antique store and bookstore along the way. I bought a Beatrix Potter cereal bowl with a tiny little chip in it I could use for the cats' water dish, an old cookbook I'd had but lost (only 50 cents!), and a Johnson Brothers mug, made in England, showing Mount Rushmore. That mug almost gleamed at me from a shelf across the room. I ran to it, saw it was

"Mine."

365 WAYS TO COOK HAMBURGER

$6.50 and almost threw my body over it so no one else would get it first.

I stopped at roadside restaurants in old houses with pumpkins on the porches, littered with leaves that blew through the door with me. American flags fluttered at rooftops, and I wrote in my diary (I was never really alone) in front of fireplaces while eating waffles (with "real" maple syrup).

But no matter what I was doing, the meeting at Little, Brown was never out of my mind. There was nothing I could do but hope and wait. It could go either way, the decision was not in my hands. I had done all I knew how.

Pray to God but continue to row toward shore.
♥ RUSSIAN PROVERB

291

Summer's loss seems little, dear, on days like these. ERNEST DOWSON

BEAUTIFUL NEW ENGLAND

That night, when everyone was asleep, she started out in a little wooden cart drawn by a large sheep & went to consult her fairy godmother.
French Folktales

The Season of Good Luck

Chapter Thirteen

HEART of the HOME

*N*ow & then, in this workaday world,
things do happen in the delightful
storybook fashion, & what a comfort that is.
Louisa May Alcott

I found my way back to Boston on Thursday morning, this time to an underground parking lot near the Little, Brown offices. Once again, Mary met me downstairs. In the elevator she told me the meeting had gone well. I was afraid to ask what she meant or in what way it had gone well; I feared she might say, Yes, everyone liked it, but it's not for us, it's not in a category, so I didn't ask. She went on to say that Arthur Thornhill, the president of Little, Brown, suggested she bring me in to say hello. Which I thought was a little odd, that he wanted to meet me, but nice.

*D*own the dim hallway we went, into a large office with a beautiful black marble fireplace and walls lined with hundreds of old books. Arthur Thornhill Jr. had been at Little, Brown since 1948. His dad was chairman before him. Little, Brown had been a family affair for almost a hundred years.

*M*r. Thornhill was a grandfatherly sort of man, at least to me, wearing an elegant pinstriped suit and a red tie. He shook my hand warmly and said, "From what I've seen, and what I hear from Mary, you are writing an enchanting cookbook." I must have blinked 60 times in a row trying to take that in, my normal disbelief doing a very good job of deflecting most of it. I'd never heard the word "enchanting" used in a sentence by a living person in my whole life. This was fairy-tale vocabulary he had used for my book.

ENCHANTING

He motioned me to follow him to the wall beside his desk and said, "I know you'll enjoy seeing this." He tapped his glasses on a tiny, framed, handwritten note, yellowed with age, hanging on the wall. I had to get up close and stand on my toes to read the signature . . . Louisa May Alcott (cATCH OF BREATH...).

The note said something like "Please give my father $12. Thank you, Louisa May Alcott." It was written in ink, but Mr. Thornhill pointed out that the original number wasn't $12; it was $10. The zero had been roughly scratched out and changed, in pencil, to a two ~ $12. It was funny and sweet and, of course, I took a quick trip to the moon just looking at something so personal and historical, written in her own handwriting by someone I admired so much. The history and this wonderful old house ~ if my book could be with them, I thought, I would be in heaven for life.

I was still in a daze when Mr. Thornhill shook my hand and said, "I look forward to seeing you again." I didn't know what any of it meant, or if it was anything more than extreme politeness. Mary made small talk as we headed back to her office; she gave me back my box with my pages saying, "I'll be in touch." I guessed they hadn't made a decision. All I could do was smile and say, "Thank you."

Back home I found a note Mary had tucked inside the box. It said their meeting was "good" and we'd talk "soonest." I loved her P.S.

Did it mean they were going to publish my book? I paced the floor. No one had said that. What if the costs came out wrong? I looked for clues. Why else would Mr. Thornhill ask to meet me? Did that happen with everyone? I had no idea. Probably he just wanted to get a look at me, see if I was author material.

10/3/05

Susan

Our meeting was good! Let's talk soonest (I still have to figure costs).

P.S. I tried the apple crisp recipe -- it's fabulous.

I weighed every nuance of the meeting, "Enchanting" rang in my ears; if it was true they wanted my book, it would be a miracle. Could it be? Is that what it means? Mary had under- lined good on her note so it must! Yes, I thought, it has to!!!!

Unless, they felt sorry for me. Maybe that was it. Maybe they just couldn't tell me to my face. I certainly couldn't have done it. I looked up the meaning of "enchanting" in my dictionary just to make sure.

This emotional roller coaster went on for a couple of days. I was afraid to hope, afraid of the crash that would follow.

It was around 10am, I was making a grilled cheese sandwich when the phone rang. It was Mary, and she said, nonchalantly, as if she thought I already knew, that the Little, Brown legal department was putting together a contract for us ~ and that they hoped to have Heart of the Home ready for publication in a little over a year, in time for the 1986 Christmas season.

I thought my ears were deceiving me ~ it sounded like she said they were going to publish my book. And she called it Heart of the Home. Was it true? How could that BE?

But it was true.

I said, "Oh my goodness! Thank you. Oh my God, thank you so MUCH." My brain was scrambled; I was leaping around the kitchen in my kitty jammies (birthday present from my mother) as quietly as I could, not having the words to say too much more.

Mary was so calm and I feared I might accidentally ruin everything with incoherent babbling.

T hung up the phone and just stood there staring out the window at the bird feeders, thrilled and scared to death at the same time. Here I was, alone in the woods, on the other side of the world from home, on an island out in the ocean, with almost no voice at all, and suddenly, I was being handed this gift. Why? I didn't know. I tried not to think, I was afraid it might disappear. Or, I might wake up. It was all a big, happy, accident.

I burst into tears and walked around in circles not knowing what to do first. So I called my mother and said, "MOM, you're not going to believe this, they're going to publish my book!" She said, "Oh Sue!" Then Jane, who laughed, "Didn't I *TELL* you?" Then Diana, who said, "I knew it! I hope you told them it was me who discovered you!" Then Shelly and my dad and my grandma and Sarah and Cliff and everyone I knew including Betty (Cliff's mom), because I knew she'd be thrilled. Each time I told someone it became a little truer.

G ood thing I lived in the middle of nowhere, because after that, every so often, I would whoop and holler and scare the cats to death, but I couldn't help it, *Heart of the Home* was going to be a real thing. The impossible had happened anyway.

I sound my barbaric yawp over the rooftops of the world. ♥ *Walt Whitman*

A week went by before I heard from Mary again, during which time, that little doubting voice once again began to nibble at the edges of my confidence. Did she really say that? I still couldn't believe it. But with the next call from Mary, all that went away forever.

She said they hoped I would allow them to add a few words to the title: it would be *Heart of the Home, Notes from a Vineyard Kitchen.* She said everyone loved the handwriting and to just keep doing it that way.

They would show me how to do the copyright page and the index, and give me a template for the cover, but otherwise, the pages should look just as I'd been doing them, the paper I was using was perfect, she said. In addition to the 50 pages I'd already done, she asked for another 110 by the end of the following May. That was all! She didn't mention a word about a "category" and needless to say, I didn't bring it up. I thought how amazing it must be to have a job where you could give people this much happiness.

TRA-LA

If there was such a thing as destiny, maybe this had always been there, waiting for the clock to tick the necessary minute, so the phone could ring on time, and the door could magically open. I glanced over at the geranium I'd painted eight years before in a galaxy far, far away. God had thrown me a lifeline. And after all the starting and stopping and self-doubt, when I thought back to how it happened, it almost seemed planned. I said thank you to the room, to the house, to Agnes, to God and all the powers that be. Then I ran next door to tell Ellie who exclaimed, "Jolly good show!"

Suddenly she spread her brown wings for flight, & soared into the air. She passed the grove like a shadow, & like a shadow, she sailed across the garden. ♥ *Oscar Wilde*

Little wings sprouted from my ankles. I lifted about three inches off the floor and never really touched down again. (Ever.) I was going to be published by the same publisher that had published *Little Women!* It was more than I ever dared to dream, it almost made Louisa and me related.

And they were sending me an advance ～ my own paycheck for my own art! I decided to inform my brain that this was all for real; brain said, "Sorry, does not compute." I would need another six months for it to sink in, and all these years later, you can probably tell, a part of me still can't believe it.

Thursday Dec. 5, 1985. 1:15pm - Got the Contract from Little, Brown & I cried. It all seems so unbelievable and I don't know if its truly true, but it is. Thankyou God.

IT COULD HAVE TURNED OUT DIFFERENTLY, I SUPPOSE.

BUT IT DIDN'T.

Mansfield Park

They sent two contracts, one for me to keep and the other to sign and send back. Fourteen pages each, on heavy paper, bound with blue covers, my name and "Heart of the Home: Notes from a Country Kitchen" (later fixed to say: "Vineyard" Kitchen).

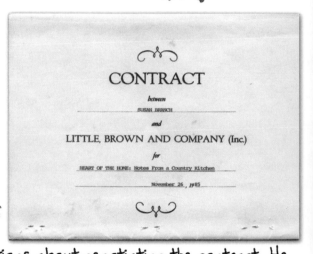

CONTRACT

between

SUSAN BRANCH

and

LITTLE, BROWN AND COMPANY (Inc)

for

HEART OF THE HOME: Notes From a Country Kitchen

November 26, 1985

Cliff had suggestions about negotiating the contract. He wanted me to get a lawyer and ask for more than they offered. I told him I appreciated his advice. I was sure it was the smart thing to do ～ but in real life, I told him, I should probably be paying *them* to publish my book. I thought I should take whatever they offered and be grateful. It seemed to me there was always a chance they could change their minds.

There is a gigantic difference between earning a great deal of money & being rich.
♥ Marlene Dietrich

So I handled this contract just like I did when I bought Holly Oak. No lawyers, no due diligence. I was ignorant, but I was lucky and Little, Brown was wonderful to me. (I think the world has changed. Don't do what I did ~ when you get your book contract, don't take chances, have a lawyer look at it. Dot your i's and cross your t's like a good boy or girl. Business people expect you to do that. It's normal. This was a long time ago. I was an idiot. I hope you see that.)

I DON'T WANT TO BE RICH
I JUST WANT TO BE WONDERFUL.
♥ Marilyn Monroe

While I was talking to Cliff on the phone, the snow began to fall outside my kitchen window, light flakes floating down, dancing around in the breeze. I watched a bright red boy cardinal put a seed in the girl cardinal's mouth. He made that kissing noise they make that sounded like sweet-sweet-sweet.

I went right to work on the new pages.

My mom and my sister Shelly came for Christmas. I worked on pages for the book early in the morning while they were still asleep. We made chocolate pancakes for breakfast, went for walks in the woods, and Christmas shopped in Edgartown. We listened to the church bells, had lobsters at the Black Dog looking out the window at the snow swirling across the harbor. We got a tree and decorated it together, while playing old Christmas Carols, Frank and Dean, Gene Autry and Louis Armstrong, like we did when we were kids.

It got dark very early, we pulled the curtains, lit the lamps, made tea and meatloaf sandwiches with iceberg lettuce, bundled up

Me, Mom & Shelly at the Black Dog.

and drove around the Island looking at Christmas lights and singing *Christmas in the car*. We stopped for Keoki Coffee's with whipped cream at the Square Rigger. We invited Ellie and Myron and Peggy to Christmas dinner. During a snowstorm we built a fire, and made my grandma's stuffing and my mom's layered Jell-O, and mashed potatoes *with* lumps and my mom's delicious gravy and every other family thing we loved. We filled the house with the fragrance of sage, pumpkin, apples, and cinnamon.

helly was eating olives off the ends of her fingers; my mom was basting the turkey and laughing, reminding me of the time I found the neck inside my first turkey, and how scared I'd been of it. "What did you think it WAS?" they asked, laughing hysterically and I said, "I didn't know!! But I wasn't taking any chances!"

WE MADE COOKIES!

e had fun decorating cookies and I made a pumpkin pie with my grandma's easy piecrust recipe that is beyond delicious. She said that a flaky crust was the magic, without it there was no pie. I had to agree, a tender-crisp homemade piecrust, twisted and twirled at the rim, made the world a better place.

My Grandma's Piecrust
425°

Double this recipe for a two-crust or lattice-topped pie. Leftover dough scraps should be cut in strips, twisted, sprinkled with cinnamon-sugar, and baked on a cookie sheet, then handed out to children or saved for Twine.

1⅓ c. unbleached flour
½ tsp. salt

½ c. Crisco
4 to 7 Tbsp. ice water

Fill a large drinking glass with water and ice and set aside. In a large bowl, stir the flour and salt together with a fork. Cut the Crisco into the flour with a pastry blender until nothing in the mixture is larger than a pea. Sprinkle in just enough water, a tablespoon at a time, mixing lightly with a fork till the dough sticks together. To test for correct moistness for baking: press together a small ball of dough ~ if it crumbles, you need a little

Blend till it looks like this.

more water. Form the pastry into a firm ball, then flatten it to about a half inch thick. Wrap it in plastic wrap and put in the fridge for a half hour (or overnight).

On a lightly floured board, roll the dough starting from the center and working out, into a circle 2" wider than your pie pan. Fold the dough in half and put it into the pie pan. Drape it evenly, and trim the edges with scissors, leaving about an inch overhang. Fold the edge under and flute it between your thumb and finger. Repairs, should your dough crack, can be made with pastry and ice water.

More...

It doesn't have to be perfect.

Prick the crust carefully, all over, with a fork, even up the sides. This will help keep it from shrinking (although it will anyway, so don't worry, it's the sign of a good home-made pie, at least to a point).

Bake for 10 to 12 minutes at 425° until it's golden brown.

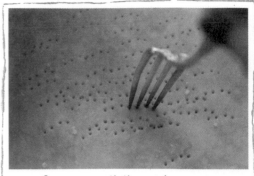
Go crazy with the pricking.

Voilá! You are a genius. Gold star for you! ⭐

Good for blueberry, apple, banana cream, lemon meringue, custard and chocolate pie too. Good pie is a wondrous thing ～ if you'd like to see someone melt before your very eyes, surprise them with a pie. As my dad said to the grasshopper, " **Be an Elf** "

I set the table with Agnes's mother's button-up baby shoes perched on top of my new Louisa May Alcott book, the new/old dishes I'd found in a yard sale, and the three-foot square antique linen napkins (like the ones I'd seen in England all those years ago) that were so big they made us feel like children when we draped them on our laps. We lit the candles and made a fire and held hands and said my grandma's grace and it was perfect (all except for the unfortunate choice of shoulder pads).

We walked Ellie and Myron home through the snow, and the last thing I heard as we each took a kitty and crawled into our beds was the sound of the snowplow rumbling by out front.

```
Sue Branch
Midget Island
Merry Christmas, USA


Dear Sue—
```
Cliff kept in touch.

Winter
1986

After Christmas, when they'd gone and all was quiet once more, the kitties and I hunkered down for the winter.

Because now I had a real deadline. I had a purpose. It had taken me more than a year to do the first 50 pages for my book; I now had six months to write, paint and test recipes for the other 110.

You might think that when you have been touched by fairy dust, all your troubles fly away, but unfortunately, that's not how it works;

you stay the same old person you always were. If you were lonely before, you still are. Only now, you're lonely with a job you adore, which admittedly is about a thousand times better.

I worked feverishly to meet my deadline. Other than my walk, I went nowhere but the grocery store and the P.O. The quiet and isolation of winter allowed so much space for inspiration I couldn't move my brush fast enough. I had a kind of tunnel vision: with my face so close to a page, it was like seeing the world through a straw. Even when I went to make my tea, I seemed to have no peripheral vision. I was like headlights in the fog as I painted a basket filled with vegetables, a quote about the seasons, a Fourth of July picnic, and a gratitude page about friends, where I thanked Jane, Stan, Sandy, and Cliff, thinking he would be the mystery man with my same last name.

Seeing the world through a straw.

I would wake up thinking about my newest page, gasp when I remembered the perfect quote, throw off the covers and leap up to write it down before I forgot. I wouldn't bother to dress, just change from jammie bottoms to sweat pants and put on a bunch of sweaters; I fed the kitties, made a fire, and ran to my watercolors.

Big winter jackets and boots covered everything when I went to the market to get food to test recipes. The clock ticked off the hours, the fire crackled, the sun went from window to window as it traveled across the frozen sky; and suddenly it would be midnight, and I'd fall, like a dead thing, into bed. The next morning I'd get up and do the exact same thing. No one could see me. I loved every minute of it, in a tormented, driven sort of way. I did things I'd normally never do in mixed company. I went on a strict five-thousand-calorie-a-day diet, which meant that mini powdered-sugar and crumb donuts were staples.

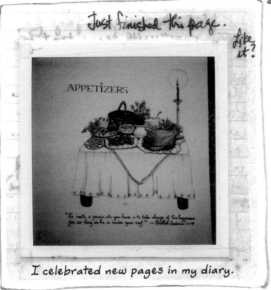

Just finished this page.

Like it?

APPETIZERS

I celebrated new pages in my diary.

In the spirit of full disclosure of my "creative process:" As the winter wore on, I became more and more consumed with my work. I hated to stop, even for a moment. I only allowed sleep because I got so many good ideas while I was doing it. I was new at this, wanted it to be right, and worried that I might not make my deadline. And besides, I loved it. So I turned into a maniac.

On some hill of despair, the bonfire
you kindle can light the great sky—
though it's true, of course, to make it burn
you have to throw yourself in.
♥ *Galway Kinnell*

Standing in the soft glow of refrigerator light, I ate standing up, whatever was handiest and required the least effort — cottage cheese directly from the carton, Fritos dipped into the sour cream container, a leg or thigh torn from a chicken carcass, celery dug into a peanut butter jar. Afterward I washed the grease off

Not Normal ↓

my hands, ran a wet paw across my mouth, dried off with a dishtowel, and went back to work. I was happy as a cow and did not slow down, working late into the night almost every day. I was glad no one could see me, it wasn't very Heart of the Home-ish of me, but I couldn't help it.

OUT OF THE WAY! WOMAN WORKING!

I finally realized I'd hit bottom one day when all the hand-to-mouth-type food was gone — the cereal box was empty, the can of nuts was on its side, the mini donuts eaten, the empty bread bag, ice cream box, tater-tot bag, and peanut butter jar were in the trash — and all I had left was half a can of Hershey's Syrup. I had spoken to no one, had gone nowhere, and had very, very bad personal hygiene. When I was at my most disgusting, deranged, and exhausted, berating myself on my way to fall into bed, the phone rang. It was Diana.

RRRING

"Heeeeey," she said with a giggle.

"Oh God, Diana, I'm so glad it's you. I couldn't even talk to anyone else in my condition."

"Why? What's your condition?"

"I'm a MESS. I haven't had a shower in three days. How's that for starters? It's freezing here.

Man Kitty telling me it's bedtime.

I'm in my living room with a hat on. All I do is work. I don't even know what day it is. I don't get dressed, I sleep in the same clothes I work in, my hair is permanently glued to my head. Any cuteness I ever had is   totally gone. I look like a mountain."

She thought this was funny; the hat about killed her.

It was good hearing her perspective, it was starting to look a little humorous, so I went on, "Everything I've eaten for the past week is on my sweater. You should see the kitchen; it's a dump. Teacups, toast crumbs, chicken bones, dried cat-food bowls. I probably smell worse than the dump." I was saying things you could only tell a best friend.

She snorted, laughing and said, "Please! Stop! My God, Sue, don't you know you're working? Do I have to tell you? You think Picasso smelled good when he worked?"

Picasso. Perfect comparison. There was no one more "Picasso" than me. I was so surprised I burst out laughing. My first out-loud laugh in days felt wonderful. "I'm not so sure Picasso smelled good when he wasn't working!"

I am like a blind pig when I work.
Ernest Hemingway

Hemingway and me, and what we had in common.

306

*D*iana's laughter broke the spell. I flew around my house for a while, in conversation, on the wings of my best friend. After we hung up I filled the bathtub with hot water, poured in lavender bath bubbles, slipped completely under the water, my head too, then up for air, and there I stayed until the water cooled. I dried off, put on clean flannel jammies, blew out the candles, and took my piggy self to bed with my kitties who loved me no matter what I did. I was just glad they couldn't talk or write tell-all books.

PLEDGE for a BEST FRIEND

When you are sad,
I will dry your tears.
When you are scared,
I will comfort your fears.
When you are worried, I will give you hope.
When you are confused, I will help you cope.
And when you are lost & can't see the light,
I shall be your beacon, shining bright.
This is my oath, I pledge 'til the end.
Why, you may ask. Because you're my friend.

♥AUTHOR UNKNOWN

THERE IS A WISDOM OF THE HEAD, & THERE IS A WISDOM of THE HEART. ♥ *Charles Dickens*

*D*uring this time, I decided I absolutely had to have three more hours in the day. Getting up at 8 a.m. meant I hardly had time to do laundry much less grocery shop and pay bills. I had to find a way to gain balance. So I thought about it and realized after eight o'clock at night, I didn't do much but sit around and veg.

I decided I didn't need nighttime TV, I didn't need Johnny Carson, and since there was no one around to argue me out of it, I started going to bed at eight or nine p.m. and getting up at four or five a.m., thereby magically gaining three more productive hours in my day. Another plus: Nighttime had too much loneliness in it ~ in this new way of living I had a whole lot less of it.

REMEMBER, YOU'RE ALL ALONE IN THE KITCHEN & NO ONE CAN SEE YOU.♥J.Child

DEAR DIARY

Feb. something or other — 20th? Tuesday! 1986
Well, I've been working solid for several
days — have done some very nice work —
this book will be beautiful!

But tonight I am discouraged. My life
is so routine & so desperately lacking
in human contact.

Well! So that's the whole story. ♥

Feb. 22, 1986 Geo. Washington's Birthday —
Happy Birthday President Washington, SIR.
The book is coming along so nicely —
Today I did Popovers with a basket &
just turned out beautiful — took me all
DAY!!

*My diaries were never pretty, but they gave me
someone to talk to.*

WORK
DO BOOK
DO IT RIGHT   Mark Twain
GET IT DONE
Food supplies energy
EXERCISE
WALK
RIDE BIKE
LIFT WEIGHTS

Walk — be energized —
God filled
BREATHE
Expend God energy
into book
CREATE FUTURE
DISCIPLINE
FEEL LOVE
MEDITATION
FEEL ENERGY —
LIGHT
EXPAND
GARDEN
GROW GOD ENERGY IN GARDEN VEGGIES, EAT FOR STRENGTH
VEGETABLES
&
FLOWERS
EARTH
BREATH
♥
ME ... Baths, Facials,
Massage, READ,
Arrange Flowers, Write
Care for home, Sleep

*I painted this to remind myself
of BALANCE.*

POPOVERS

400° Makes 12

These will pop up and over the top of the muffin
pan ~ Serve them with marmalade and jam. ♥

3 eggs
1½ c. milk
1 Tbsp. melted butter
1 tsp. salt
1½ c. unbleached flour

Butter 12 cups in muffin pans. Beat all ingredients
together until smooth. Fill muffin pans ⅔ full.
Bake at 400° for 45 minutes. Take them out and
slit the tops ~ return to the oven for 5-10 minutes.
Serve them in a large basket wrapped in a pretty cloth.

discovered the morning, and
fell in love with dawn. I
didn't need an alarm and I woke
up happy and often times, singing.
In the dark before sunrise I
felt like I had the whole Island
to myself ~ the snow-hushed
morning, the hum of the furnace,
the crackling fire, the sound of
my paintbrush ringing against

the water dish. In the quiet I would reread my starred quotes to choose the perfect one, or turn on the oven and test a recipe for baking powder biscuits and pop four or five of them into my mouth, one after the other, hot and buttered, spread with homemade apricot jam, and later, I would clump through the snow to take the rest to Ellie for tea.

Silence is the language of God; all else is poor translation. ♥ R u m i

IF YOUR HAVE A MIND AT PEACE
A HEART THAT CANNOT HARDEN
GO FIND A DOOR THAT OPENS WIDE
UPON A LOVELY GARDEN

Apricot Jam
Makes four ½ pt. jars

Jam, made with dried fruit instead of fresh, is a fun winter project. ☆Easy & satisfying.

1 lb. dried apricots   2 c. sugar
8 oz. can crushed pineapple w/ juice   1 tsp. cinnamon

Put apricots in lg. saucepan; barely cover w/ water & cook until soft. Reserving the water, remove & finely chop apricots & return to pan. Stir in pineapple & juice; bring to boil. Stir in sugar. Boil rapidly, stirring often, until thick. Toward end of cooking, stir in cinnamon. Bring to jellying point on candy thermometer. Pour into hot sterilized jars & seal. ♥ Makes a great homemade gift.

April was all golden daffodil days with evenings of frosty pink twilight. Dappled light shimmered around the room every afternoon and danced up the walls. One morning, I walked out through the woods to the opening and noticed that the barely-budding leaves made the trees along the shore look like ethereal lollypops of palest greens, pinks and yellows. It was still very cool in the breeze, so I lay flat on my back, whale like, in my hat and jacket in the cold sand at the end of the spit, and closed my eyes in the warm sunshine. Nature

Spring

serenaded me: the waves rolled on shore; I could hear the tiny peeps and screeches of osprey and hawk. I sat up shielding my eyes from the light, watching the shorebirds play tag with the waves, thinking it's never the same out here, every day is a new discovery, every day, another little miracle. I watched a seagull fly way up high and drop a clam on a rock below, then fall like a stone to eat the meat from the broken shell.

Springtime in the woods.

On the night of my birthday I went outside to call the kitties and stood barefoot on the cold deck looking up at the moon and stars. The wind rippled the hem of my nightgown, I pulled my shawl tighter, scooped up Man Kitty, cradling him on his back like a baby and together we watched the wood smoke whirl up to the stars that twinkled above the chimney like fireflies. I felt lucky to even know what a firefly was.

Me, in my spot.

Tomorrow was her birthday, & she was thinking how fast the years went by, how old she was getting, & how little she seemed to have accomplished. Almost 25 & nothing to show for it. ♥ Louisa May Alcott

Every night brimmed with stars.
Gladys Taber

I was 39 and thinking next year I'd be 40; I never thought I'd be 40 and living alone. Actually, I never thought I'd be 40. Forty was so old, 28 years past 12. Then I remembered that Julia Child's first book came out when she was 51 and Beatrix Potter got married for the first time at 47, and Laura Ingalls Wilder wrote *Little House* at age 65, and I felt much better. I was a baby! The old adage was true: *It's not over 'til it's over.*

Until I was 32, all I did was eat.
Julia Child

Having read the stories of their lives I saw that the stars had to align for their dreams to come true. Everyone had to grow into themselves before they could offer anything. On top of that, neither Julia Child, nor Beatrix Potter, nor Louisa May Alcott, nor Jane Austen nor Margaret Mitchell had children, and all left behind the gifts they'd made of their lives. Like my Jane said, "People do it all the time."

A society grows great when old men plant trees whose shade they know they shall never sit in.
♥ GREEK PROVERB

Cliff called and yakked at me about his new Maserati while I watercolored a three-layer-carrot cake. While he talked I went over the penciled recipe in pen and ink.

"I hope you're telling everyone you burned up a stove," he said with a laugh. "Better put that in your cookbook. Give them fair warning."

"Nooooo." I said, "I'm not telling them that. I think they should get to know me first."

"You're putting in the chicken breasts with cheese recipe, aren't you?"

"Yesssss," I said, "don't worry, you will be well represented."

"I just don't want you to forget how to make them."

What was that supposed to mean? He was always saying things like that. Every so often I wondered what I would do if he wanted to get back together. He could be so sweet, and that's when I only remembered the good things.

Captain Hook: Look who's still a fairy.
TinkerBell: Look who's still a pirate.
                J. M. Barrie

As I finished the pages, I'd pack them up, eight or 10 at a time, then Little, Brown would send a cab to my house to pick up the box of artwork and take it to the airport and put it on a flight to Boston where a courier retrieved it and took it to Little, Brown for editing. The pages, with corrections made, came back to me the same luxurious way. This is how I discovered that the rest of the world didn't say "cube" of butter like my Iowa mom did, they said "stick." Also, I didn't know how to spell refrigerator. I thought, because of "fridge," it had a "d" in it. But it didn't. I had to use correction liquid to fix it in five different places. Writing over the corrected bumps with a sharp, steel tipped Rapidograph pen was like writing over dried oatmeal.

HAVE NO FEAR of PERFECTION ~ YOU'LL NEVER REACH IT.
                ♥ Salvador Dali

The seasons & Holly Oak.

This was my first stab at designing the cover for *Heart of the Home*, but Little, Brown wanted bigger words and stronger art so they asked me to try again. Now this one is framed & hanging on the wall of my sewing room.

I finished the table of contents, the cover and spine and a poem next to the title page that began, "Go little book . . ." Mary sent me the layout for the index, and called with suggestions and comments.

May

Lilacs bloomed along the roadsides, violets speckled the lawns, baby birds fluffed out like dandelion puffs and the ferry whistle echoed over the town like a long pull from the deep end of an accordion. I walked out the dirt road at first light, when the spring day was just beginning, and everything smelled fresh and new.

I thought sometimes the book might never be finished, but the clock kept ticking and I kept going, and one day, right on schedule, it was done. Done. How wonderful but also, how strange. One tick of the clock, like any other, and the thing I'd thought about, worried over, and worked on forever was done. The very next tick of the clock was almost confusing, being so empty and all.

I piled the stacks of plastic-sleeved pages into boxes and drove them to Boston for a meeting with several senior people at Little, Brown. I did have to pull off the road for one small anxiety attack, wait in a supermarket parking lot for it to go away, got back on the freeway, then off again at the next exit, to wait some more. I thought it might be something having to do with fear. I really never knew. But by that time, I was relatively sure I wouldn't die. And I was finally able to go on.

Mary and I sat at a conference table with five or six people behind us, looking over our shoulders as we turned the pages. It was the first time they'd seen the finished book with all the pages together, and I was happy and relieved to hear murmurs of approval. I learned we'd be receiving color proofs from the printer and that they expected Heart of the Home to be in stores by the end of October. After the meeting, they surprised me with a gift ～ a copy of Little Women published in 1933 with illustrations by Jessie Wilcox Smith. I was touched; they couldn't have given me anything I would have loved more.

314

I walked out of Little, Brown on a cloud, like a person that just lost 15 pounds, and twirled under the spring-blooming trees in the Common and went to "celebrate" on Newbury Street. I bought a cotton dress, two hats and two adorable lampshades at Laura Ashley and treated myself to tea around the corner at the Ritz-Carlton where I sat and wrote in my diary and ate a chocolate éclair. Because all of a sudden I was free as a bird. I didn't have to BE anywhere or DO anything. I felt like the luckiest person in the world.

~1980s Laura Ashley hat & dress; we loved her.~

I walked back through the front door of Holly Oak and everything seemed different, almost hollow, quieter than it had ever been. I'd been immersed in the book for so long, I had to learn how to live again. Drumming woodpeckers echoed in the woods on my daily walks to the sea. I went on a diet and ate only roughage to remove tater-tot poundage from my behind. I opened the doors and let spring air whoosh through the rooms, and cleaned the house, top to bottom. I shined all my pots and pans, oiled my wooden spoons, hung quilts on the line to air, filled the bird feeders, swept the porch, and put a pot of yellow and blue pansies on the kitchen counter. And waited for the book to be printed.

While I was writing the book, Carlton had been outside adding a bedroom onto the house ~ that's what I had decided to do with some of the money from the advance for the book ~ get an actual bedroom, with an actual closet in it. He finished just as I did.

315

MY NEW BEDROOM

Stained glass window courtesy of Brimfield.

Look at that tiny TV!

♥ Through the new door in the corner to the bedroom. A Red Letter Day. ♥

Louvered closet doors on each side of the dresser.

I chose yellow wallpaper scattered with flowers, and decided to put in the same carpeting I had in the living room, and when it was done, I washed my bedroom curtains, starched and ironed them, and rehung them in my airy new bedroom with the high ceiling, and got ready for Jane to come visit in August.

Carlton made the armoire. Closed door goes to living room.

June 23, 1986
The lady at the supermarket said hello to me today! A red letter day! She said it like it was the most normal thing in the world!

My House is a very very very fine house with three Cats in the Yard...

CHAPTER FOURTEEN

There Are Fairies at the Bottom of her Garden

GOD IS ALIVE,
MAGIC IS AFOOT.
Buffy St. Marie

Unhindered she went thither & found everything as the night wind had promised.
Brothers Grimm

At the end of June, Myron and Ellie were going to England on the *Queen Elizabeth II* to visit Ellie's family. They'd be gone for a month; I was thrilled because while they were away Peggy was coming to live with me and the kitties, and I'd be going over to their house to feed Gwinnie. The day before they left, I grabbed the box of Chilmark Chocolates I got for them to take on the ship and crossed through the clover and the blueberry bushes to have a goodbye tea with Ellie and pick up Peggy.

Ellie, wearing a dark-blue check homespun apron with a little red rosebud pinned to it, filled the kettle with water while I set out the teacups. We talked about her trip, six days on the high seas, and how excited she was to see her sisters and the little village where they grew up in Yorkshire.

317

This time when Ellie poured the tea she didn't strain it; she said she was going to tell my fortune in the tea leaves. She'd learned to read tea leaves from her mom when she was little; her sisters could do it, too, but Ellie was the one that "had the gift."

I was intrigued; I didn't know she did this. I loved all that sort of thing. The fortune in the fortune cookie was my favorite part of the Chinese restaurant.

We let the leaves settle to the bottom of our cups (real English china cups and saucers with flowers on them, mine had apple blossoms). When we'd sipped almost down to the dregs, Ellie said, "Now, hold the cup by the handle in your left hand, swirl the rest of the tea and the leaves three times counterclockwise so that the leaves stick to the side of the cup."

I WAS SWIRLING, THINGS WERE STICKING...

"Gently turn the cup upside down into your saucer," which I did, ever so gently.

"Take a deep breath and close your eyes and just be for a moment. Now, open your eyes, tap the bottom of the cup softly three times, and push the cup and saucer toward me."

I did what she said, sliding the cup and saucer over to her. She turned the cup over, gazed into it for a moment, looked at me over her gold-rimmed glasses, and pointed into the cup, "See here?"

I leaned in to see little clumps of leaves clinging to the sides of the cup. "Doesn't that look like a tree?" she asked. "And, here, that's a bee if ever I saw one." She said the leaves formed symbols ~ anything from a hat to a cat to a rose or a man.

"Each symbol has a meaning. A tree means family roots; a bee stands for hard work. The reading of the symbols is the creative part, but I do have to say," she looked into my eyes, "I'm hardly ever wrong." I felt a little chill. I was ready.

There was a sprinkle of tiny leaves, almost flakes, that went all around the side of my cup in one line. "This means long life," said Ellie. Yay, thought I.

"And see the butterfly? That means your wishes have wings."

"And this, this bell shape? It stands for mental clarity."

That was where she almost lost me.

(The fact that Ellie was doing this made me want to believe. The woman had connections. I loved the idea of wishes having wings. But mental clarity? Even she knew that couldn't be true. Then I thought, perhaps I didn't understand the actual meaning of mental clarity.)

On the bottom of my cup she pointed out the letter "H," a crown, a ladder and a long beard. Her wooden chair creaked as she moved in closer to the cup. Gwinnie jumped up on the table, narrowed her green eyes, lay down next to the sugar bowl, and began to purr loudly, like Pyewacket in the movie Bell, Book and Candle.

Ellie ignored her, concentrating on the cup, "Hmmmm, okay, look right there, you're going to meet a tall man with a beard. He will have the letter 'H' in his name. You'll fall in love with him, but you need to know, this isn't just any man," she said, piercing me with her blue eyes, "He's special. First off, he's quite handsome, as handsome as a prince, and see this circle with the little one inside? It means he'll be your guardian angel. He's coming to take care of you."

319

Her eyes were wide open, clear as English bluebells in the snow.

I was thinking about what she said. I liked tall, but I wasn't that excited about the beard, and I wasn't sure I needed to be taken care of. "Can he cook?" I asked.

She laughed, pointed and said, "Ohhhh yes, I was just going to say, this looks like a wee frying pan to me!"

I kissed her cheek goodbye, wishing some of her magic would rub off on me. She gave me a dish of her homemade "Yorkshire" butter to take home, made the way her Scottish mother had taught her, by shaking heavy cream in a jar until it turned to butter. I shook my head in wonder at her. Butter-making, tea-leaf-reading people, you have to love them. ♥

Come. Sit. Stay.

MY STEPDOG

Myron was locking the barn when I left. I hugged him and wished him a wonderful trip. He bent down and rubbed Peggy behind the ear; she followed me home quite happily on her leash.

Ellie and Myron were going to England on an ocean liner, my every dream come true, but having Peggy come home with me was the next best thing.

Mary from Little, Brown called to say she was sending the colorpages for my approval. She wanted me to match the printed pages to the originals and let them know where colors were washed out, what should be toned down or punched up. She also sent me aprons, printed with the cover of the book, for me to give away at book signing events. Everything that happened was exciting. But the way it all happened made it seem so normal.   *   *   *

Me and my new apron.

Jane was coming to visit in the middle of August. I cleaned the house, filled pots and baskets with pink geraniums and herbs, and put sunflowers on the picnic table. I made the shack ready by hanging lavender bunches from the rafters, arranging apples and grapes in a bowl, filling an old jar with roses and mint sprigs, and adding more candles and a bottle of water. I knew Jane would love the summer nights out there with the hooting owls, cooing doves and foghorns.

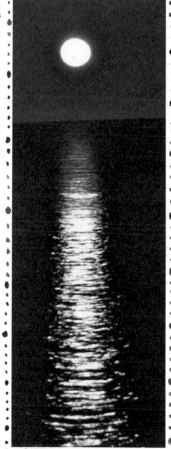

I brought her breakfast in bed and let her read in there for as long as she wanted and then I took her on my most de-luxe Island tour (I was getting pretty good at it by then) ~ to Morning Glory Farm for zinnias and muffins, to the Farmers' Market for tomatoes and local honey, to the Agricultural Fair for the dog show, and for a twilight walk on East Chop for moonrise and the "grand old ladies" which is what Islanders call the huge summer "cottages" with the wide porches, that front the sea.

We shopped all the cute shops on Main Street, ate ice cream on a bench in the shade of the old linden tree and then drove out to Mill Pond to see the swans. At Lou's Worry, a comfy dive bar in Edgartown, I made her tell me the whole story, again, of how she met Elvis Presley when she was 14.

321

Elvis and Jane

She let me put her treasured photo here for you. That looks pretty flirtatious if you ask me!

One afternoon we followed a dirt road deep into the woods of west Tisbury. I wanted to show Jane Christiantown, established in 1659 by the local Native American Wampanoag tribe for those who had converted to Christianity. We walked around the tiny chapel and the ancient graveyard with the small rough-hewn stone markers, some of them just rocks, but none of them with names. It doesn't feel haunted, it feels sacred and historical. You can almost smell the campfires and hear the horses whinny. The Wampanoags are the same tribe that helped the Mayflower Pilgrims with the first Thanksgiving in Plymouth; there were 90 of them along with 51 Pilgrims. One hundred and forty-one for dinner in 1621.

We crunched around there for a while and I told Jane a little bit of something I'd learned, that Benjamin Franklin's grandfather (Peter Foulger, the father of Ben's mother), lived on the Island and taught English to the Wampanoags and that the first Native American to graduate from Harvard College (in 1665) came from Martha's Vineyard.

So much history. Benjamin Franklin's grandfather! Right here! It's like connecting the dots.

By this time Ellie and Myron had returned from their trip, and I wanted Jane to meet them, so I invited them over for dinner at the picnic table out back on the deck. I made pink champagne cocktails in honor of their crossing (like in An Affair to Remember), covered the table with a white tablecloth, put out the little pillows I'd made for the benches so people would have soft places to sit, lit candles

Cunard R.M.S. Queen Mary

and served coq au vin, mashed potatoes and roasted carrots, and for "afters" (what Ellie called dessert) blueberry angel food cake, with our own blueberries.

Our background music was the English singer Vera Lynn, who sang the best songs during the war ("We'll Meet Again" and "The White Cliffs of Dover"). We listened while Ellie and Myron told us all about their wonderful trip.

It had been a sentimental journey because during World War II, Myron had been transported to England on the Queen Mary when it had been converted to a troopship, repainted blue-gray to match the color of the sea and nicknamed "the Grey Ghost" ~ and then, after the war, Ellie came to America on the very same ship along with thousands of other war brides and their children. Jane and I had tears in our eyes listening to her talk about the "bonny" stars over the ship at night while they were at sea, now that the war was over, and they knew they were safe, and they knew their husbands were finally safe, and she was on this huge adventure, and leaving home.

PINK CHAMPAGNE COCKTAILS

Chill the champagne glasses. I've read that the tall deep glasses are best for lots of bubbles, but I love the old-fashioned bowl-shaped ones made of the thinnest glass that make the prettiest ringing noise, & find the bubble situation to be just fine. To make the cocktails you need: good quality pink (or regular is just as good) champagne, sugar cubes, & angostura bitters. Put a sugar cube in each glass; add enough bitters to soak the sugar cube thoroughly. Fill glass with champagne. (Don't try this with granulated sugar; it must be a sugar cube.)

As they sailed up the Hudson they were welcomed by a boat with a full orchestra on top serenading them with lovely old songs.

If you were the only girl in the world & I was the only boy... Vera Lynn sang, Myron looked at Ellie and put his hand over hers and Jane and I melted. *Awwww, we said to ourselves.*

Lucky in Love

Ellie talked about what it felt like to see the Statue of Liberty for the first time. It was wonderful to see it through her eyes. I already knew it was hard to move far from home but I wondered what it was like for her to leave her entire country behind. She said, her blue eyes sparkling in the candlelight, that it wasn't easy, but she was lucky because she had Myron. I could have listened to them talk about their memories forever. I asked her to describe what she wore on the ship and what they ate, did they have to dress for dinner, was there any music, and did everyone sing along, etc. etc. etc.

You can see Agnes's bird feeder in the tree on the right.

Jane's favorite part of her tour was Illumination Night at the Methodist Campground, a tradition famous on the Island since 1869. We packed a picnic and spread a blanket on the lawn next to the open-air Tabernacle and watched the kids running and playing in the cool evening as the sky turned purple and dusk fell. We joined the hundreds of people on benches inside the Tabernacle where American flags flew from the rafters and the town band played "It's a Grand Old Flag," "Someone's in the Kitchen with Dinah," and "Bing-O Was His Name."

There was a screen with the words and a bouncing ball and the whole crowd sang along and even did rounds.

At 9 p.m. the street-lights went off. That's when the tiny 19th century cottages that crowded around the Tabernacle ~ brightly painted in bubble-gum pink, aqua, creamy yellow, and pale green, each of them filled with charm and history, and dripping with intricately carved gingerbread trim and jigsaw curlicues, lit up like Christmas.

For over a hundred years, the owners of these little houses have given Islanders and visitors the gift of Grand Illumi-nation every August ~ by festooning their cottages with thousands of hand-painted Chinese and Japanese lanterns in all colors, shapes, and sizes. When darkness fell and the lanterns were illuminated (originally with candles, but by then mostly with electricity), everyone strolled around the promenade under the stars, up and down the narrow lanes (built for horses and buggies) lined with luminarias, glowing with the colors of the lanterns suspended from porches, roofs and trees, stopping to admire and applaud the special charm of each cottage.

325

magic!

The homeowners sat in pastel-painted wicker rocking chairs on their candlelit porches with their dogs and glasses of wine, basking in compliments and thank-yous, answering questions and watching us watch them.

FIREWORKS

Two days later, we packed another picnic and took it to Ocean Park in Oak Bluffs for fireworks over the water and music at the bandstand . . . everything on the Island happens in August.

On her last night I took Jane to dinner at my favorite restaurant. It was a picture-perfect early fall evening, clear skies, with the tiniest nip in the air and first stars twinkling in the pinky blue sky over the harbor. Half a block from the water, *The Ocean Club* was in a two-story white building with tall ceilings and huge double-hung windows wide open to catch the sea breeze. We went

326

JANE

through the screen door into a room crowded with diners, and festive with conversation, music, and the clink of silverware on dinner plates. We were told we'd have to wait too long for a table, so instead we grabbed a couple of stools at the clam bar. To go with the white wine we'd brought from home, we ordered clams casino, pesto on pasta with grilled shrimp, and oyster stew with bacon.

Two guys came in and sat down on the stools next to us. I knew one of them ~ Jim ~ he owned the clothing store next to the gourmet food shop where I used to work ~ so I said hello.

Over the restaurant clatter, he introduced his friend Joe, who was sitting next to me ~ a tall, pink-cheeked, handsome guy with sandy hair peeking out from under a black beret, eyes the color of the sea after a storm, and a short neat beard. In the normal way of things when you're practically rubbing shoulders with the people next to you, we started chatting.

He mentioned that he ran the Black Dog, and somewhere along the way I referred to Ellie and Myron's recent trip to England and Joe told us about a transatlantic crossing he took on an ocean liner with his mother when he was 12, which got us all talking about Fred Astaire. The whole time he was offering us bites of food from his plate. Such a nice guy. He reminded me of a cardinal, feeding us like that.

THE OCEAN CLUB

OOOOH...

AHHHH...

On the way home, Jane said she thought Joe was interested in me, but I didn't see it, and said no way. First off, he was too young, five years younger than me. "He's a baby," I told Jane, "a tall cute baby, but still, a baby." Although, I mused, in a scientific way as an interested bystander, it's not very often you meet a guy in a beret, who smells like Old Spice, has sailed to England, AND knows who Fred Astaire is. But I was through with love. And he was a baby. So I put him out of my mind.

You would think by then I would have listened to Jane, wouldn't you?

Girlfriends Forever
HAPPY NEW BOOK
from Jane

The next day it was time for yet another goodbye . . . to my darling friend Jane ~ who believed in me long before I ever did and was such an inspiration. I could never say "Thank you" enough. I promised I would send her the first book the minute it came off the press. I put her on the boat, and waved and waved until she was gone.

Soon after Jane left, Cliff called. Nothing important, "I just wanted to hear your voice." He reminded me he'd always been my biggest fan and even apologized very sweetly for being a jerk (jerk was my word, he said "brat"). He told me he was proud of me and only wished me the best. I wondered to myself if there was something wrong with him, he was being so nice, but basked in his shower of gold stars, and told him not to worry, I knew he was doing the best he could. I said, "Everything's turning out the way it's supposed to."

328

We talked about Jane's visit and how fun it was. He seemed a little sad and weary; he'd just broken up with another girl. I was surprised when he said she was too young, he was 36 by then and it had actually gotten to him that she'd never heard of The Doors.

And, incredibly, she thought the Dali Lama was, in fact, a llama. ♥ MARK LAWRENCE

I knew I still loved him then, but differently because I felt bad for him in a whole new way. I didn't have a single drop of joy for his sadness. I knew what he was feeling was only temporary, too fleeting to worry about because he'd never be alone for very long. While we talked, I wandered around the house doing chores. In the kitchen, I cleaned out the junk drawer, washed my Beatrix Potter people and twirled Man Cat around on a dishtowel. I told Cliff he should get a cat, no one can be unhappy or sad if they have a cat.

There are no ordinary cats. ♥ Colette

BUT GAD, SIR, I AM ONE of THE MOST FANATICAL CAT LOVERS IN THE BUSINESS. ♥ Raymond Chandler

Cliff ignored the cat idea and went on, lamenting about women in general, how all they wanted was to get married, and never left a guy alone. He asked me for advice for "next time."

A KITTY RED-LETTER DAY

Caught renegade fly & ate it
Played with string until she took it away
Drank her paint water
Lounged on her art work
Got let in & out about 12 times
Partied on catmint
Chewed grass
Drank sink water
Had tummy rub
Performed manicure on tree
Walked to pond
Ate bug
Ignored her when she called
Had catnap. MEOW

I said, "You really want advice? You won't like it. But here goes: Look around. See all the men who are happy in their relationships? Those are the ones who just do what the woman wants. If you could

329

do that, you would be happy, not to mention, that it would probably save you hundreds of thousands of dollars."

He snorted.

"No, really, I'm serious. You could make it your mantra. For example, when a woman wants a coffee table or thinks you should go on a walk with her, eat more fruit or drink more water ~ when she says you should take her out to lunch more often, keep your eyes on the road when you're driving, don't tail gate, or use a chain saw to make a bandage out of your shirt, why don't you just do what she asks? It's not that hard, and everyone will be a lot happier."

Aristophanes
c. 450–385 B.C.

13 There is no animal more invincible than a woman, nor fire either, nor any wildcat so ruthless.⁷ *Ib. l. 1014*
14 These impossible women! How they do get around us!
The poet was right: can't live with them, or without them!⁸ *Ib. l. 1038*

¹See Shakespeare, 220:32.
²Translated by B. B. Rogers (Loeb Classical Library).
³See Horace, 106:18.

And the beat goes on.

I could hear his eyes rolling in his head right through the receiver.

Women were Cliff's cross to bear. He couldn't live with us and he couldn't live without us. As the oldest of eight, and born to serve, I was just there to help.

I HAVE ALWAYS BEEN BOSSY. ♥ Shirley Temple

AUTHORHOOD

After that, the fairy tapped the Princess with her fan, & the smothering coarse apron flew away. ♥ Charles Dickens

And then one wonderful day, I looked out front to see a big brown UPS truck come plowing through the leaves in my driveway and stop at my front door. The uniformed driver jumped out with a box containing 20 brand-new copies of *Heart of the Home; Notes from a Vineyard Kitchen.*

I was overwhelmed. I'd been on pins and needles waiting for the book, not knowing what to expect, so my eyes filled with tears when I opened the box and saw

it for the first time, with my art and my name on it. Between the covers were my pages, looking exactly the way I painted them, all neatly bound. And it smelled exactly like a real book! I hugged it and danced around the room, and propped it up on every counter to nonchalantly glance over and pretend to see it for the first time. I signed copies for Ellie, Carlton, Sandy and Stan . . . and sent books home to my parents and my grandma, my brothers and sisters, Jane, Diana, and everyone I loved.

From then on, I never left the house without my book ∼ not to show it off, I just wanted it with me. It was like my baby. It wasn't even in the stores yet, but it waited in the car while I grocery shopped, was there for me when I came out of the post office. I thought maybe I should get it a car seat. I wrote about it in my diary, pointing out that my little finger was touching the edge of "my baby book" at that very moment. Because it still did not seem possible.

♪ . . . if all of your dreams survive, destiny will arrive . . . ♪
♥ Olivia Newton John

Keep all your dreams alive . . .
for someday . . .

Little, Brown arranged my first book signing at the Bunch of Grapes Bookstore on Main Street. I made lots of finger food for it and all the recipes came from my book ∼ platters of spicy, sticky, chicken-wing drummettes, a basket with crusty French bread stuffed and baked with hot cream cheese and clams, a bowl of cherry tomatoes filled with homemade pesto, and a tray of 60 mini chocolate éclairs on white paper doilies, filled with whipped cream and covered in chocolate.

It was a chilly late-fall evening in November. I wore a long, navy-blue-and-red plaid flannel shirtwaist dress that buttoned all the way up the front with a matching belt, my Laura Ashley eyelet lace underskirt sticking out from the bottom, and short brown work boots. I was nervous and tried not to show it but I had never been to a book signing before, much less one for me and didn't know what to expect. What if no one came?

Ann Nelson, the owner of the bookstore, put me at ease. In her positive forthright manner she laughed and said, "Don't worry about a thing, it's easy. I'll take care of you. It'll be fun!" She sat me down at a table with stacks of Heart of the Home

piled around me, handed me a pen, opened one of the books to the title page, and said, "Sign it here ～ that's where all the authors do it." "Author" ～ such a strange new word to hear in relationship to myself (it got even stranger when I had to put it on my tax return).

A Bunch of Grapes Bookstore signing was a family affair; Ann's mom and dad, Peg and Al, were there helping; Peg made her famous Port Cheese.

The event had been advertised in the Gazette (coincidentally, right next to the story on how Billy had seen a blackbird) and maybe 20 or 30 people came (I was too nervous to count). Carlton and Tammis were there, and Miranda and a couple of the other girls from the gourmet food store, and of course Ellie and Myron; Sandy Haeger brought her little daughter Posie, and Stan Hart came too. Everyone was wonderful, turning the pages of the book, commenting on the watercolors, talking about the recipes ∼ saying such nice things. I felt like a bride on her wedding day.

I signed books and visited with people for two hours. One guy I didn't recognize stationed himself next to the chocolate éclairs and began popping them into his mouth like jelly beans. I laughed when I heard Ann whisper to her dad, "Go get that guy away from the éclairs." And that's when I knew for sure that Ann and I would be friends.

Little, Brown arranged several off-Island book signings ∼ to some of them, no one came at all. I felt a little silly sitting there alone, I never knew what to do with my face ∼ but you have to start somewhere. I began to bring along my knitting, just in case . . . I was happy there were book signings. The bookstore people were always nice; they'd come visit with me and I'd sign books for them.

I gave my first talk in front of an audience at the Fall Book and Authors' Seminar in Falmouth over on the Cape. By the time it was my turn to stand at the podium and speak to the sea of expectant faces, I was gripped by fear, my hands dripped, and for all practical purposes, I lost consciousness. I don't know how I got up there. I didn't know I should have prepared

something to say. That doesn't mean I fell down like an uncon-
scious person would normally do. I actually spoke for 20 minutes
but didn't remember a word of it. Whatever I said must have
been okay, because on the boat back to the island I wrote in
my diary:

DEAR DIARY

"That was so scary ~ I was a wall of adrenalin all day. I have
NO idea what I said! I should have done that oral book report
in school   and learned how to talk in front of people!. I can't
believe   public speaking would be something I would do in
         real life! But the ladies smiled and laughed all the
         way through it, their faces were beautiful,
         they were like friends ~ they applauded! They
         made it so easy, asked me nice questions while
         I signed their books. It was a perfectly
exquisite day! I LOVE BEING AN AUTHOR. I ADORE IT!!!"

I was interviewed on a Cape Cod television program
called Books of the World with a local legend, Marion
Vuilleumier. I still have the tape of it. The program was only
broadcast to the Cape and Islands (thank goodness). In it, I
am 39 going on 10 when I talk about how tall the buildings are
in New York, and say something like "Oooooooo." (Kill me, kill me
now.) And I had no idea where on that camera I was supposed
to look. I'm sure I would be better at it if I got used to it, or if
I had to, but really, TV and me go together like pork chop gravy
and chocolate cake (actually that was one of my grandfather
Willard's favorite things to eat. I come by my weirdness
organically).

But what I really loved were the interviews
Little, Brown arranged with radio programs, cooking
shows, and talk shows, all over the country. Almost all of them
were done over the phone, which meant I couldn't see the audience,
and they couldn't see me. So I wasn't nervous. And, for an added

dividend, I could do them in my pajamas. The interviewers would call me with their big booming radio voices; I knew exactly who they were the moment I picked up the phone. They were always funny and enthusiastic. I did one interview while riding my exercise bike, another while fixing dinner and feeding the cats. It was all so homey.

I was supposed to go to  WGBH in Boston to do NPR's *All Things Considered*, but we had a huge nor'easter, and I almost slipped off the porch trying to get to the car to get to the boat. Then I found out the boats weren't running. So I stayed home and was interviewed over the phone by a true doll of a guy named Noah Adams who was funny, teasing me about calories and éclairs. And there was a bonus to that radio program: A high school friend who'd moved to North Carolina heard it and called me to say hello!

The little wings on my ankles kept me floating on air through it all.

> Laziness may appear attractive, but work gives satisfaction.
> Anne Frank

MY DAD MADE IT ↓

The first printing of *Heart of the Home* was 20,000 copies. It was published on October 29, 1986, and sold out before Christmas. When Mary called from Little, Brown to tell me they were all gone, and that *Heart of the Home* was going for a second printing. I wasn't sure if I should be happy that it sold out or sad that there weren't anymore, but I chose happy. My original pages came back to me, just as I painted them, still in their clear plastic envelopes. I wrapped them in tissue paper, put them in a box, and packed them away in the attic next to the Christmas decorations.

SMALLVILLE

After all the excitement, things settled down and I went back to real life in Smallville.

Everything that had happened so far paled (slightly) to what happened next. It was a freezing December afternoon, I'd been feeling a little isolated, but it was a regular day, so I went about my normal business, running errands, going to the grocery store and to the post office to get my mail. At the P.O., I parked my green Volvo in front of a grey snow bank and left the engine (and the heater) running, steam billowing from the tail pipe. I picked my way over the dirty parking lot ice, trying not to slip and kill myself, and through the glass doors of the post office. I got the mail and threw away the catalogs and flyers. When I came out, little snowflakes were drifting down.

Such a beautiful day.

Back in the car, I started going through the mail. Mixed in with bills and letters from home was a blue envelope with a return address I didn't recognize, bearing just my name and Martha's Vineyard on it, no real address. I sat there in the parking lot with the heater going, the snow coming down, windshield wipers thumping back and forth, and opened the envelope with the unfamiliar handwriting.

You're going to LOVE this...

"Dear Susan," it began, "I want you to know this is my very first fan letter . . ." Gulp, fan letter? I had to read it again to be sure. She went on to say how much she liked my book. Tears welled in my eyes. It "made her laugh and made her cry." She said it was "her." The last part was a blur, I could barely see. This was something I never expected. I didn't even consider the possibility there might be "fan mail."

My hand with the letter lay in a heap in my lap while I stared out at the white sky, overwhelmed because my world had changed. I wasn't isolated; I wasn't alone. I was connected in a way I couldn't have imagined. I clutched the letter to me. If it was bigger I would have hugged it.

MORE THAN KISSES, LETTERS MINGLE SOULS.

It was the cherry on top of the pie on top of the cake on top of the world. More than anything that letter changed my life. My book had reached out, left the Island in fact, and brought me back a new friend. I sat there in the snowstorm and sobbed.

There would never be an answer to my question as to why all of this had happened. All I could do was bow my head and say, "Thank you," 10,000 times or so. Then I went home and wrote back to that return address and said thank you one more time.

Mary called from Little, Brown, taking me by surprise once again when she said, "So what will you call your next book? You do want to write another one don't you?" Next book? Something else I'd never considered. I was momentarily stupefied by the question ~ but I came back to consciousness in time to say, YES! I'd love to! I got out my paints and brushes and wrote the first words on a page:

A little house ~ a house of my own ~ out of the wind's & the rain's way ♥ *Padraic Colum*

337

In the end he'll lead you
through a garden to a
tall tree full of birds. & he'll
tell you to take whatever
bird you wish. Beware child,
take only the littlest & greyest
one singing away
on the highest branch.

French Folktales

CHAPTER FIFTEEN

FINDING THE GOOD IN GOODBYE

Go not to the Elves for counsel, for they will say both no & yes. ♥ J. R. R. Tolkien

A few days before Christmas, Cliff called and said, "What are you doing this weekend? If you're not busy, I thought I'd come get you."

"What? What do you mean, come get me? You're coming here?"

"Yeah. I thought I'd fly in and pick you up. It's a surprise. You can meet me at the airport . . . I have something to show you."

"In a plane? You're asking me to go in a plane? Have I mentioned I don't like to fly?"

"Yeah, I think I heard that somewhere. But this is different. I'm bringing you your own plane. I chartered a Learjet. I'll hold your hands, you can tell the pilots what to do. It's only an hour ride, maybe less. I know you're going to love this! It won't be bad, I promise."

"It's already bad," wiping my suddenly damp hands on my sweat pants. "What's so important? You're not even coming over to see where I live?"

"I would, but there's a window of opportunity and I won't have time . . . It's a house I'm thinking of buying. I have everything set up."

"You are saying this house is an hour plane-ride from here? On the East Coast? Why? Why would you buy a house *HERE?*" Suddenly I felt unsafe, a butterfly with vulnerable powder on her wings, just hanging out there where anyone can get hold of them.

"That's part of the surprise. Wait till you hear."

He was all excited. He had rented this house in Vermont and was thinking of buying it and wanted me to see it first and get my opinion, because he'd received an offer for his business that he wasn't going to be able to refuse, which would put him in New York much of the time from then on.

All terrible news.

But I was curious. I was doing nothing, most of the excitement surrounding the book was over, this would be an adventure; Christmas in Vermont ~ like my favorite movies, *Holiday Inn* and *White Christmas*. I loved looking at houses. It might be fun. I decided I should go.

Diana at home in prime phone position.

Diana had a fit. She was worried he'd "been dumped" and now he wanted me back. I told her she, of all people, should know better. It was just real estate; something Cliff and I had done a thousand times before.

"Right," she said, "in Vermont. I can't believe you would fly for him. You wouldn't fly for me; that's the main reason I'm worried. You are willing to kill yourself. In your way of thinking, that's what flying is, you are willing to die."

I laughed and told her I was not willing to die. It wasn't like a commercial flight. I would have complete control over the pilots. But she wasn't buying it.

Resigned, she said, "This doesn't sound like real estate to me. It sounds like a date, and it sounds like playing with fire. I knew it. I've been waiting for this. Vermont! There is no place on earth you can hide from him when he makes up his mind. I hope you have a wonderful time."

I said, "Don't be like that. I haven't been around anyone normal since Jane left in August. Christmas in Vermont, don't you think that sounds won-der-ful?" I sang it. Her disgust came dripping through the phone so I kept talking. "And it's not a date, because number one, Why would it be? All that is over. He's not even interested in me; I'm too old for him. And, B, I'm done with men, which he knows and YOU know, and C . . . uh, I forget what C is."

"C is for Crazy. You just called him normal. I heard you."

"Well, you should know, he's changed. He really has. He's not like he used to be. C is for Changed."

"Oh my God, listen to you. You are a danger to yourself and others. I'm a nurse you know, I could have you committed. C. For committed."

One-upmanship, may I say, is never attractive.

I forgot to mention I just happened to have the perfect outfit in my closet for this exact event. I got it at

The wonderful artsy Banana Republic Catalog, c. 1986, filled with fun stories to go with the clothes.

Banana Republic: a straight, calf-length, brown leather skirt over brown boots and a matching short leather jacket with a cream shirt to tuck in under it. Opportunities to wear flyer-girl outfits like this did not come every day.

I'll go with you to your human world, O man, but fairyland is where I'm from.
French Folktales

A thrill ran up my spine when the little jet came screaming out of the sky, hit the runway, and tore past me in a blur. My ride. I watched it taxi back around the airport and came to a stop about 50 feet in front of me (eek, my heart was racing). The door went up, the stairs came down and Cliff poked his head out, his face so completely out of place that it almost didn't seem real. He walked toward me, tall, all smiles, cute in khakis with a buttery leather jacket over a Huey Lewis T-shirt. He looked me up and down and said, "Nice. You look like Amelia Earhart."

Exactly what I was going for. We were starting off on just the right foot.

I thought he was going to kiss my cheek, but instead he reached around and pulled me to him for a kiss on the lips. I put my hand on his chest, pushed back, laughing and shaking my head.

"What?" he asked in mock innocence, his eyes twinkling with adorable masculine self-confidence. He'd called himself "brat king" since he was about eight, and never was it truer.

♪ ALTHOUGH I CAN'T DISMISS THE MEMORY of HIS KISS... ♫
I GUESS HE'S NOT for ME... Words & music by
George Gershwin & Ira Gershwin

I was heartened to see that the two pilots were wearing uniforms and looked sober. One of them gave us each a glass of wine with perfectly steady hands. The other one's eyes sparkled when he told me about his children. So that was good. Neither seemed in any way deranged. They passed inspection with flying colors.

The cabin was all cream-colored leather splendor and white plush carpeting that went up the walls. Running along the ceiling were curved pinpoint pink lights like on the inside of a limo.

While I was trying to figure out how to work the fancy gold seatbelt, Cliff popped a pair of headphones on my head and said, "Listen to the words ~ it's our song." Holding hands, we zipped down the runway, jets squeeling, the State Forest flying past the windows in a blur, and straight up into the ice blue sky while Jackson Browne sang "Fountain of Sorrow" and white wine guzzled down my throat.

We zoomed across New England and before I knew it we were flying over snowy woods and mountains and pristine white villages into the winter wonderland of Vermont, where we landed at a small airport near Waitsfield and picked up a rental car.

We drove through a covered bridge, into a small snow-covered village, and curved up a hill just out of town, before Cliff pulled into a driveway.

The house was almost 200 years old, a rambling New England farmhouse sunk deep in the snow, the kind I love, with a wide graceful wooden porch that had a pale-blue painted ceiling (so you could look up and it would be like seeing the sky), big rooms with high ceilings, several fireplaces, a large, square, old-fashioned kitchen with a pantry that was really a whole other room, lined with white painted shelves neatly stacked with jars of beans and rice, cans of chili and soup, vinegars and oils, tins of tea, baskets of onions and potatoes, and bottles of Perrier.

The owners lived in Boston, and just used the house on weekends, so it was furnished with comfy chairs and couches, bookcases filled with books and lots of reading lamps. Someone had left us snacks and set a fire with logs. I tried to picture Cliff's Maserati inside the big red barn next to the house ~ if this was what he really wanted. Had he grown out of mitered windows? Maybe I'd finally rubbed off on him. Anyway, the house was wonderful. Anyone would love living there.

343

I knew I could never tell Diana this next part ～ it would have been too much for her to bear ～ because waiting in the snowy driveway to take us for a ride was a beautiful, chestnut horse and sleigh, all decorated with red Christmas bows, bells, and streamers ～there were even ribbons tied in the horse's mane ～ plus a little old driver (so lively and quick) wearing a red wool plaid jacket.

"False advertising," a voice whispered in my head. "Shut up," I replied.

Covered in layers of furry lap robes and drinking steaming Irish coffee from a thermos provided by the driver, we jingle-belled across the thirty-acre property ～ trotting next to horse fences and across meadows, putting tracks on a pristine blanket of snow. Warmed by the whiskey, chilled by the air, our cheeks turned pink and we sank deeper under the blankets. The horse snorted clouds of condensation, red ribbons streamed, snow blew up behind us and tumbled from tree branches. I felt like Barbara Stanwyck in *Christmas in*

344

Connecticut. Cliff was so proud of himself, if he'd been wearing anything with buttons, they would have popped. I got to use my new favorite word: *Enchanting*

*T*hat night, over a candlelit 🕯 dinner at the local inn at a table in front of a cozy fire, Cliff was excited to tell me that the offer he'd negotiated for the sale of his company was loaded with perks: They wanted him to stay on as CEO, with a salary and stock options; they'd pay for the house in Vermont, plus a penthouse apartment in New York. And then with a straight face, as cool as asking what day it was, Cliff said, "You should sell that little cracker box on midget island and come live here with me. I miss you, miss us."

I blinked. What did he say?

"If you want," he went on, not noticing my stricken face, "we can buy that old farmhouse and make it like new. Remodel the whole thing, get rid of that ugly porch, put in some cool stainless sinks and a SubZero fridge ~ design a professional kitchen for you. Granite counters. Anything you want. Even add on a big art studio. You'll probably want to write another book, right? That'd be okay. The location couldn't be better, so close to the airport. It's a good investment. I'm ready to make it work. We were a great partnership."

A thousand disjointed thoughts raced through my mind. I was not expecting this. *Partnership? We? Here?* Him living here, me living with him? Him telling me it's okay if I write another book? And, yes, thank God, it's close to the airport cause then I could fly more. And of course, let's get *RID* of the porch. Porches, bleh. A SubZero? *SELL* my cracker box, my darling little cottage in the woods? He couldn't mean this. There had to be something more.

"What's wrong?" I asked. "Are you dying or something? You can tell me. I can handle it."

"No," he glanced around the restaurant at the other diners, gauging their hearing distance, and leaned in closer, "I'm not dying but I'm glad to know you can handle it." He was laughing, but then got serious again, "I just think it's time for me to settle down and you have always been the one, always."

"Really." It wasn't a question, it was total disbelief. "Are you saying you love me?" I was bent forward, chin almost level with the table top, leaning in, and almost whispering. He didn't say a thing about love, but wouldn't that be part of something like this?

"Of course I love you," he hissed (he couldn't whisper, whispering was for girls), "that's exactly what I'm saying. Would I be offering to give up my whole life if I didn't love you? You're not listening to me!"

"Are you kidding?" I sat back and laughed and then leaned in again, "Do you not hear yourself? Give up your whole life? Oh, my God. I'm sorry, I can't do any of that, Cliff. You know you don't really mean it. Really, honey, after all this time? As much as I wish I could in some ways," I laughed, "But not now, I can't go back. You don't mean this. You're just between victims and it's making you desperate."

Son, I'd like to spare you many troubles. Forget this fairy of yours!
♥ F r e n c h   F a i r y t a l e s

"Haven't you forgiven me yet?" he asked, not able to keep the smile out of his voice at my word "victims." "You know all that was just wild oats, right?"

Five years of wild oats? "Listen," I said, "neither of us knew what we were doing back then. I still don't. But it's taken me all these years to dig myself out of the hole I fell into after we broke up. Of course, I've forgiven you, I don't blame you." I stopped. "Well, maybe a little . . . ha-ha, just kidding." He wasn't laughing. "In fact," I went on, "when I look at it the right way, you're almost my guardian angel."

346

"Guardian angel? How?" His face was disbelieving. He knew his angel credentials walked on thin ice.

"In so many ways.

"One, I wouldn't be living on Martha's Vineyard or have my house if you hadn't taken me to the Island to meet your grandmother. That's one reason I know everything was meant to be. Too much serendipity.

"If you didn't do what you did with Kimmi, I would never have been brave enough to leave on my own. I had to be pushed and, as a guardian angel, it was your unfortunate job to be the pusher.

For the trouble with the real folk of Faerie is that they do not always look like what they are. J.R.R. Tolkien

"And let's not forget, you provided me with almost 10 years at the homemaking college of my dreams. You're my alma mater. You let me practice cooking on you. You told me my art had value. I might never have written a book if it weren't for you. If I'd stayed, I don't know where I'd be now. It was hard, but in the end, it turned out exactly the way it was supposed to."

"Well, then you owe me," he said. "We would have been back together a long time ago if you hadn't moved so far away. We could do this, you know, we could put it all back together. I know you still love me. You're not getting any younger, by the way." This time he noticed my expression and said, "I don't mean that in a bad way, but is that what you want? A spinster old-maid life on midget island? You'll never meet anybody there. You're 40 years old. You have a better chance of being kidnapped by terrorists."

He was bringing out the big guns. Spinster. Where did he get that word? He used to be such a good salesman.

347

"That terrorist thing isn't true, that was never true. And, I'm not 40, by the way, I'm 39. I don't want to live my life alone, it's not the way I planned it, but apparently, at least so far, this is the way the cookie has crumbled.

"And P.S., the way to a woman's heart is not by calling her an old maid; you should keep that in mind for your future life. Anyway, you were never the real problem. I stopped being in love with you a long time ago. It's the dream that wouldn't die, the one I had of us together. We're just victims of my childhood imagination. Remember what you said to me once: 'I love you but I'm not in love with you?' That's how I am now. You were my guy, you were the one, I pinned it all on you; you were my person forever. But that was a long time ago. It doesn't even seem real anymore."

I almost couldn't believe this was me talking. I always wondered what I would do if it ever came to this and now I was finding out. Despite the fact that I had moved 3,000 miles to get away from him, there had always been a tiny glimmer in the back of my mind that whispered of a second chance, that my leaving him would bring him to his senses; now he was here, much too late, and it was me who had come to her senses.

"What would be different?" I asked him. "I'm so much worse than I used to be, you have no idea. You thought I was spoiled then. You should see me now."

"I never said you were spoiled. I never said that."

"Only a hundred times, you can't rewrite history. Don't forget, I have the di . . ."

"Those diaries!" he interrupted, slumping in his chair and rolling his eyes. "How can I forget, you tell me all the time. I never get to win any arguments because of those things. I should have stopped you when I could."

OH, THE POWER. There are just a few moments in life as good as that one. Like twirling in a full skirt with crinolines under it. ♥

348

"And I have to tell you," I continued, laughing, ignoring that last thing he said, "I LOVE the porch on that house you're looking at. I would never in a thousand years take it off; that porch would be our first fight. You see what I mean? You don't want a train-riding, Frank-Sinatra-loving, Fred-Astaire-watching, Volvo-driving, tea-drinking, Christmas-obsessed, best-girlfriend-having, walk-taking, diary-keeping, tradition-loving, three-kitty-kissing, quilt-adoring, tag-sale-going, 39-almost-40-year-old, *illogical* wife, do you? No!

"You don't even *like* those things ~ but that's who I am. I want to go to England on an ocean liner someday. You would die if you had to spend a week trapped on a boat. You like football, motor-cycles, fast cars, jets, rock and roll, and blondes. You should have all those things, but you keep your cars longer than your women. What we had in common was youth and you. But I don't need to be rescued anymore. Unfortunately. I wish I did in a way. But that's gone. Just like the Easter Bunny and Santa Claus. Not without regret."

Fun while it lasted

(Wow, I thought for a moment. Listen to me, I know who I am and I was just true to myself. My eyes welled with tears. I looked across the table; he thought I was crying because of him and put his hand over mine to comfort me. But that wasn't it. I was crying for happy.)

...And in her eyes you see nothing, no sign
of love behind the tears, cried for no one,
a love that should have lasted years... ♪
♥ The Beatles

It had come down to respect. He deserved to have the Jet-Johnny, porchless, coffee-tableless, stalactite life of his dreams, no matter how strange it seemed to me. He was still a dynamic, attractive maniac of a guy, funny and sweet and hugely generous, but it wasn't enough anymore. We were too different. I felt com-fortable when he was 3,000 miles away, but definitely not when he was in my own backyard. Shoo. Go home. Call me later. We'll talk. As Diana always said, When you see trouble coming, cross the street.

He didn't give up easily, but at the end of the weekend he kissed me good-bye and put me back on the plane alone ~ not good-bye forever, because we would always be friends. I'm a collector; nothing gets away. My past, as he used to tell me, was as important as my future. I wanted it all, the whole delicious enchilada.

I desire no future that will break the ties with the past. ♥ George Eliot

So, two days before Christmas, I flew back over the lights of New England on the last plane flight of my life, to the Island, floating in the dark sea, my heart magnet, pulling me home. ♥

Being true to myself meant I had made my choice. For better or worse, for richer, for poorer. I knew where I belonged. It was like my footprints were already there and I had no choice but to step into them. Even if I was meant to be alone. There were worse fates. I already had everything else.

And still, after all this time, the Sun has never said to the Earth, "You owe me." Look what happens with love like that. It lights up the sky. ♥ Hafez

I would have changed some things in the past if I could, but I had forgiven myself and was no longer sorry. There was no perfect life. I just felt grateful for everything the way it was.

I LOVE. I HAVE LOVED. I WILL LOVE.

✳   ✳   ✳

HOLLY OAK COTTAGE

The wind blew, the tea kettle sighed, the bedroom door creaked, the phone sat silent. Billy had a bad dream, he cried in his sleep and his back leg shook. I stood at the window holding Man Kitty who'd buried his head under my shawl, and watched the snow fall through the oaks, frosting the red berries poking through the holly.

HOME for CHRISTMAS

Was Thoreau ever lonely? Certainly. Where do you think writing like his came from? Camaraderie?
♥ Jessamyn West

351

January
1987

TREE AND HOUSE AND HILL AND LAKE
ARE FROSTED LIKE A WEDDING CAKE.
Robert Louis Stevenson

And now let us welcome the
New Year, full of things
that have never been.
♥ *Rainer Maria Rilke*

☺ You will have a bright future.

352

CHAPTER SIXTEEN

Going It Alone

I've locked my heart, I'll keep my feelings there,
I've stocked my heart with icy, frigid air,
And I mean to care for no one,
because I'm through with love.
♥ Marilyn Monroe

At five o'clock on a cold, dark morning, I poured a cup of tea, stirred in a spoon-ful of honey, added some half and half, and wrapped myself in my green plaid scarf. The cats were still asleep, cuddled in the rumple of the unmade bed. All was quiet, except for the ticking of Agnes's clock, the crackling of the fire, and the foghorn blowing in the distance.

B e a u t y i s as beauty does ♥

If you flew up to the stars and looked down over the dark island, that one little beam of light you saw bouncing off the snow? That would be me, in my little house, with a blank piece of paper in front of me, pristine as the meadow after the first snow, waiting for my pen and watercolors. I thought I'd call my new book Vineyard Seasons, and this time I'd write about summer, winter, spring and fall, and tell about the fairies that live on Martha's Vineyard.

Being alone wasn't all bad. At least my heart was safe from the ravages of unpredictable love. I blessed the day I found this house in the woods filled with welcome-home gifts I didn't even know I needed. I came a long way to find it.

I put on my list all the busy, useful independent spinsters I know, for liberty is a better husband than love to many of us. ♥ Louisa May Alcott

But I believe in LOVE. ♥

It dumped snow all that January. The wind howled and blew off the roof in swirls. One wild, raw afternoon, after too many days inside hunkered down over the art table, I decided to get out of the house. I wrapped up in my scarf, hat, black and white check full flannel skirt, and man's leather jacket, swept the snow off the windshield of my Volvo, and took myself and my magazines and a couple of letters from home down to the Black Dog to do my favorite thing, sit in front of the open fire, listen to logs crumble to ash, eat, read and people watch from my post as incognito person, while the storm raged and waves crashed on shore just outside the windows.

PERFECTION

The darker the storm
The cozier the fire.

354

I ordered lunch and pushed the soles of my boots toward the crackling fire, and draped a napkin over my lap. I laid a dinner knife across my new *Country Living* magazine to keep the pages flat so that I could use my hands to eat, while reading a most interesting article about making curtains from vintage table-cloths from the 1950s. With hot bread buttered, and in the glow of perfect contentment, I was just about to dip my spoon into a steaming bowl of clam chowder when someone I vaguely recognized, a tall, handsome guy with a beard, and wearing a black beret, came out of the kitchen, and started walking toward me.

No, no, no, I thought, *don't come here, don't come he . . .*

"*Oh, hi!*"

I remembered his name: it was Joe, that cute, young guy I'd met a few months before at the Ocean Club with Jane. The one who went to England on an ocean liner when he was 12. I thought, *Oh yeah, he's the manager here.*

He asked to sit down but was already scraping the chair back across the wooden floor, so what could I say? I said, "Nice to see you again, sure, sit down," glancing at my magazine, feeling interrupted from the delights lurking within. I looked over to hear what he wanted, thinking, *I hope he makes this quick.*   ✳   ✳   ✳

IT'S ASTONISHING HOW SHORT A TIME IT TAKES FOR VERY WONDERFUL THINGS TO HAPPEN. ♥ *Frances Burnett*

Boy Howdy

And that's my story and this is the end, because here I am, 56 years past 12, still securely anchored to the Island by more heart magnets than one, still walking through the woods to the pond every day, surrounded by all the kindred spirits a girl could ever hope for; still writing and painting books and trying to work everything out ~ living in constant wonderment at the scheme and serendipity of life.

What I thought had been a fairy tale had turned into a nightmare, and then the nightmare turned into a fairy tale. I haven't figured out how that happened, but as my mom would say, "Mine is not to question why. . ." I also haven't figured out how to save the world, but I'll never give up. Believing that there is hope for the world is in every brushstroke I make.

THERE IS NO SUCH THING AS A HOPELESS DREAMER. IT'S AN OXYMORON.

Now in a cottage built of lilacs and laughter
I know the meaning of the words "ever-after". . ."
♥ Frank Sinatra

A Boy After My Own Heart

I did manage to find a little corner of the planet for myself, and I don't live there alone. The clock ticked forward to the correct and proper place and right on time, I discovered I was supposed to find true love after all. Because that handsome, beret-wearing, "six-foot-two Leo who can cook," "tall man with a beard" who loves trains, Christmas, cooking, books,

Joe B. Hall & Lucky me.

kitties, old music, ocean liners, and me (not necessarily in that order) did not make it quick. He took his own sweet time, because (as you know) guardian angels are nothing if not persistent. ♥

I don't know how I got so lucky, but he says he likes me just the way I am. He built a picket fence around my garden, with a gate and everything. I've hung my hat on it for the last 29 years. Ellie saw it all in her tea leaves, just exactly right. He is my guardian angel. ♥

Don't ever think that a ravaged heart is all done with life, because miracles can happen.

♪ The wind is blowing, the snow is snowing, but I

Never let anyone tell you magic doesn't exist or that fairies aren't real. It isn't cynicism that will change the world. Do your best to believe in yourself, and even if you don't, keep trying to and never give up. If all else fails, use your imagination and pretend.

Because this ˄relatively modern fairy tale comes with the only ending I ever wanted:

And they lived happily ever after. ♥ ♥

The End

Sigh, deep breath, close eyes, hug book to chest, ahhhh. ♥

I WILL NOT BE HAUNTING ALONE.

can "weather the storm... I've got my love to keep me warm..." ♪ Ella Fitzgerald

I didn't want to give away the ending, so I saved the dedication for last.

For Joe Hall the Love of MY LIFE & THE GIFT THAT KEEPS ON GIVING. ♥

My editor, pathfinder, in-house lobster cooker, pillow-talker extraordinaire, best friend and the Heart of my Home. And best of all is that if I wrote a book about him, I could call it the Fairy Tale Boy (if he would let me. Which he wouldn't).

♥　♡　♥

Grow up, fall in love, get a little house, plant some roses, get a kitty, live happily ever after. What could be more simple? Every movie had it in it. ♥

EPILOGUE

Find a girl, settle down, if you want you can marry... ♥ Cat Stevens

Because inquiring minds will want to know, I'm happy to report that with the understanding guidance, patience and forbearance of the women in his life, Cliff has matured into quite a fabulous old guy. These days he lives on top of a hill in a house that he built for his family of the past 18 years, with his smart and funny wife, Lynette, his stepson Tyler; their dog, Ollie; and cat, Lucy.

I think he wants you to know that he is now the proud owner of a coffee table (I do too have one!). And a new Maserati. He still listens to rock and roll, though he's not so sure it's going to change the world after all, but that doesn't mean he's given up. He follows politics closely and in his spare time, he looks at real estate. Most weekends he's in the garden. Lynette has thanked me for the early training. I've apologized to her for leaving so much undone. Sometimes it takes a village.

Cliff recently wrote a wonderful memoir called *American Made; A Boomer's Reflection.* It's not exactly a he-said/she-said, but I'm in it and I have to say that he was a lot easier on me than I was on him. Lately he's been sending me YouTube links to Kacey Musgraves's music. He was a doll to give me his blessing to tell this story, and I thank him from the bottom of my heart. For everything.

And Diana? She's a mom and a grandma who runs away to Hawaii as often as possible because a couple of years ago she retired from 38 years of heroic service as a neonatal nurse for newborns in crisis. Last winter, when Joe (of whom she very definitely approves) and I were hunkered down in the "deepest Vineyard snowstorm in history," I answered the phone and without even a hello she almost sang, "Just want you to know, it's 85 degrees here today." When we're together, we sing in the car and still feel 22 when we do it.

My California girlfriends: Sarah, Liz, Lorrie, Nancy, Jeanie, Janet, Marguerite, Kip, Elaine, Terrie, and Beverly ~ my mom and dad, and my brothers and sisters are all good, still crazy after all these years, making memories, and steeped in blessings.

I am forever in debt to Jane Bay, Sandy Haeger, and Stan Hart, to Little, Brown ~ and to Julia Child. They changed my life. And to Carlton Sprague, thank you. Wasn't that fun?

TICK TICK TICK

In Memoriam

My dear grandma, Florence Orr Smith, whose father called her "Spitfire," a very wise woman and light of my life, is in heaven and is my guardian angel, in death as she was in life. Cliff's parents are also both gone now, and I miss them. Also Myron and Ellie. Myron was my first friend on the Island, his kindness and Ellie's magical spirit will live forever in my heart. I feel her near me every time the sky turns to dots and dashes, because you know, she was enchanted, she had the gift. And of course, Agnes, whom I never met, and will never forget.

TIME HAS PASSED THROUGH ME & BECOME A SONG.
♥Holly Near

Man Kitty, Girl Kitty, and Bill are in kitty heaven with Pooh. They saw the whole thing and never said a word, just cuddled in for the duration. What an extraordinary gift they were to me. They were only five when Joe met them, and he loved them too. When they died, we wrapped them in lace curtains and buried them out back next to the barn under a flowering dogwood, and planted white bleeding hearts over them. I still find myself looking out the window in the kitchen door to see if any of them want to come in. Some habits never go away. (And yes, of course we still have kitties, Girl Kitty II and Jack keep us laughing now.)

And, in closing . . . I want to mention, because if I read about an especially beautiful old tree I would probably want to go see it, so I thought you should know. The lovely hundred-year-old landmark linden tree that used to grace Vineyard Haven is no more. It was cut down in 1996 due to structural instability. There is a new one coming along, but it's not quite the same yet. We need to give it a few years because everything worth having takes a little time.

Carlton made a table with the wood from the old linden for the Vineyard Haven Public Library. You can visit it there.

Okay, it's time to clean the house, wash my Beatrix Potter people, cook something wonderful, sweep the porch and get ready for Spring.

I guess I should stop writing now.
I seem to be done. XOXO *Bye for now.*

With Love from the
Heart of the Home & me...
Susan Branch

Kellee Sheri

Thank You

To Kellee Rasor, Sheri Honeycutt, and Alfredo Jimenez, the smart, creative people who keep the home fires burning at Susan Branch Studios. And to our Studio kitties, Sami and Sasha who make everything more fun.

To You from Me

Alfredo

Sami & Sasha

The Full Course:

The Appetizer

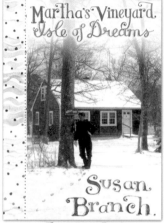

The Main Dish

and Dessert ♥

Want more? We have it! Read the third book in this trilogy and see how Joe and I fell in love. Come along on our first date, and then join us as we realize our dream of going to England on an ocean liner and driving the country roads to visit the houses and gardens of our literary and artistic heroes, to Beatrix Potter's Hilltop Farm, and Jane Austen's home in Hampshire, and many more. It's a totally hand-written "you-are-there" kind of diary called

A Fine Romance
FALLING in LOVE with the ENGLISH COUNTRYSIDE

Please come to my website and say hello ~ you'll find lots more recipes and decorating tips, book and movie lists, homemaking, and stories about linens, dishes, quilts, Martha's Vineyard and England, and lots of wonderful conversation with kindred spirits ~ and you can also sign up for my free Newsletter. www.susanbranch.com

To celebrate the 30th Anniversary of my first book, *Heart of the Home*, I am revising the cookbook and adding new pages and recipes. This new edition will be available July 2016.

This is our vacation which we are spending on different parts of Martha's Vineyard. With best wishes.
Oct. 16. 1904 — Mrs. A. W. Parker

5976. THE BATHING BEACH, VINEYARD HAVEN, MASS.

DETROIT PHOTOGRAPHIC CO., PUBLISHERS,

Musica

Oh for a book and a shady nook,

either in door or out.

JOHN WILSON